CULTURE AND SOCIETY

CULTURE

Twenty-Four Essays

George Peter Murdock

Foreword by Alexander Spoehr

AND SOCIETY

University of Pittsburgh Press

Acknowledgment

The author wishes to thank those publishers and journals who kindly gave their permission to reprint the essays in this book.

Foreword

ANTHROPOLOGY has reached a healthy maturity among the academic disciplines. Yet it was not so long ago that anthropology in the United States was struggling for wider recognition among the educational and research institutions of the land. That the discipline has developed as it has and that it continues to exhibit a vigorous potential for future growth is due primarily to the dedicated efforts and accomplishments of those whom we respect as the leaders of our field. Among these, George Peter Murdock occupies a distinguished position.

The collection of twenty-four papers comprising this volume reflects the varied and productive interests which have engaged the attention of the author during his professional career. Spanning a period of thirty-four years, these papers attest to the intellectual development of an active and inquiring mind, and in many ways also provide an historical perspective on contemporary anthropology. The papers are grouped according to six subject categories, each of which has its special interest. Together they reflect that clarification of concepts and of theoretical points of view applied to substantive data which characterizes the progress of anthropology during the last decades. Although the papers which follow speak for themselves, a few comments are appropriate.

The first group of essays deals with the relation of anthropology to its sister sciences—in particular, to sociology and psychology. Murdock received his scholarly introduction to social science through an eminent sociologist, Albert G. Keller. Later joining the faculty of the newly formed Department of Anthropology at Yale, he thereafter participated in the University's Institute of Human Relations, and through close association with his colleagues became explicitly involved with the interrelations of anthropology, sociology, and psychology. Out of this experience grew his view of anthropology as a behavioral science—a view which he sets forth in both historical and theoretical dimensions in this book. He notes differences in how each discipline has come to regard its common subject—man—and those relations among them which can contribute to an integrated science of human behavior. Noteworthy is the fact that he has pursued this concern with the behavioral sciences as a totality beyond the examination of their written product to the coordination of their working relationships, most recently as Chairman of the Division of Behavioral Sciences of the National Research Council.

As a colleague, I would also offer a postscript. Anthropologists continue to be involved in how the behavioral sciences are to join their efforts toward a larger goal. In the last few years there has emerged a common denominator which is coming to characterize these disciplines. There was a time when the business called "field work" was the hallmark of the anthropologist. He spent, and still does, much of his time planning his next excursion to foreign places to add through empirical experience his bit to the comparative study of man. What has happened is that he is no longer alone in this preoccupation. Sociologists, psychologists, political sci-

entists, psychiatrists, and even economists are now actively prose-
cuting field work—that intensive, firsthand involvement with the
raw data of human behavior among peoples of differing cultures—
in many parts of the world. Although it is easy to place too much
importance on this trend, it argues well for a clearer discourse in
the future on the common problems of the behavioral sciences.

The nature of culture and of the factors responsible for culture
change are recurrent themes in anthropology. They are also tough
nuts to crack, despite all that has been said about them. In Murdock's two sets of papers on these subjects, he again brings to bear
an understanding of sociology and psychology, as well as of anthropology, while at the same time pointing out the limitations of
each, in considerable part a product of their historical development.
On the subject of culture change, his remarks on cultural relativity
are significant in a contemporary world concerned with development and the processes of what is often today called modernization.
In setting forth his opposition to the position on cultural relativity
expressed by Herskovits, Murdock states that cultural relativity
must be viewed in the context of culture change and that "What we
need is . . . knowledge about the choices for change which
peoples do and do not make when presented with an opportunity,
the criteria according to which such decisions are made, and the
modes of implementing them effectively." It is in this area of choice
that pragmatic action and value systems merge. Fortunately, contemporary research is increasingly directed toward the examination
of this area.

Murdock is perhaps most widely known for his contributions to
the study of social structure, and for the distinctive approach and
method he has developed in cross–cultural comparison. As one
who has spent some years on the subject, I cannot help but feel
that a principal point of progress has been the clarification of analytical concepts covering the social and cultural forms and processes
with which we deal. In other words, we have a much more precise
understanding of what we are talking about than was the case forty
years ago. When Murdock entered the academic field, scholars

were still writing about "mother-right" and "father-right." In the ensuing years, field research and conceptual analysis has been raised to a much more penetrating level. Murdock has made a major and distinctive contribution to this progress, and has remained at the center of a vigorous, continuing discussion which will undoubtedly carry on the momentum already achieved. In particular, he has combined a receptivity to and appreciation of new achievements in the field of social structure with the capacity to recognize promising unexamined problem areas, and to point out the latter succinctly. His awareness of the significance of cognatic forms of social organization is exemplified by an outstanding paper in this volume. A second example is his long-held belief that structural studies should not be limited to synchronic analysis, but should incorporate a diachronic dimension to provide a necessary understanding of the dynamics of change, a view set forth in his paper on changing emphases in the study of social structure.

Murdock's pioneering contribution to cross–cultural studies is so well known as to make comment unnecessary. These introductory remarks close with an appreciation of the personal interest which he has shown throughout his career in the work of his colleagues, a personal interest given concrete expression by his founding the journal *Ethnology* for the scholarly benefit of the profession. To this interest he has added a lively enjoyment of the human scene within his purview, whether it be perceptive friendship with a Tenino shaman or the implications of waging baseball on Truk.

In presenting this volume, the University of Pittsburgh pays tribute to a devoted scholar and eminent member of the anthropological profession.

Alexander Spoehr

Contents

TABLES

ANTHROPOLOGY AND ITS
SISTER SCIENCES

I

•

This paper, originally published in the *Scientific Monthly* (69: 377-381, 1949), reflects the impact on my thinking of my participation in the Institute of Human Relations at Yale University prior to World War II. Constant interaction with such men as John Dollard, Leonard Doob, C. S. Ford, Clark Hull, Bronislaw Malinowksi, Mark May, Neal Miller, Robert Sears, John Whiting, and Earl Zinn created an intellectual environment of mutual stimulation and osmosis unparalleled at any other period of my life. As a result, I came to regard myself first and foremost a behavioral scientist, though one with a specialty in anthropology. In this respect I have felt a special sense of kinship with other anthropologists, notably John Gillin, A. I. Hallowell, and Clyde Kluckhohn, who shared in part the same experience.

The Science of Human Learning, Society, Culture, and Personality

THE past decade [the 1940's] has witnessed a revolutionary development in the psychological and social sciences. A number of disciplines that had previously pursued independent courses in the analysis of particular facets of man's individual and social behavior have been discovered to dovetail into one another so neatly that they are well on the road to being fused into a single integrated science. The first major steps in achieving this integration were made at the Institute of Human Relations at Yale University, but the movement has spread to other institutions and is being pressed forward with especial vigor by the Department of Social Relations at Harvard University.

This development has been widely misunderstood as a mere pooling of separate scientific skills and techniques on cooperative research programs. The significant fact, however, is that the integration has taken place at the level of theory. At least four previously distinct systems of theory have been found to interdigitate so that each supports the others and is in turn illuminated by them. These four are the theory of learning and behavior developed by experimental psychologists, the theory of social relationships and social structure developed by sociologists and social anthropologists, the theory of culture and cultural change developed by anthropologists with significant assistance from sociologists, and the theory of personality and its formation developed by psychoanalysts and psychiatrists.

There is as yet no general agreement as to an appropriate name for the emerging unified science. Such terms as "human relations" and "social relations" slight the psychological components and, to some, suggest application rather than theory. The "science of human behavior" carries too strong a connotation of behaviorism and too weak an implication of important social and cultural factors. The general term "social science" seems to exclude psychology. In default of an apter expression, we shall, with tongue in cheek, use "lesocupethy"—coined from LEarning, SOciety, CUlture, and PErsonality THeorY. Perhaps it will irritate some reader into proposing a more satisfactory name.

The position of "lesocupethy" in the hierarchy of the sciences poses no difficulties. It is rooted in biology as the latter is rooted in chemistry. But as biology is differentiated from chemistry by complications introduced by living matter, so is "lesocupethy" distinguished from biology by complications resulting from the interaction of learning and society.

In themselves, learning and society represent two of a considerable number of major types of adjustment which have been independently developed several times in the course of organic evolution. Other examples include parasitism, symbiosis (e.g., plants which depend for pollination upon bees, which in turn depend upon the nectar of the plants for food), and aerial locomotion (independently achieved by insects, pterodactyls, birds, and bats).

The most basic type of behavior mechanism with which nature has equipped its living species is instinct. The organism is provided by heredity with a structural organization whereby it automatically responds to stimuli by specific forms of behavior which through natural selection have become established as adaptive in the life conditions typically encountered. Being essentially rigid, however, instincts cannot help the organism if conditions diverge from the typical. To meet this situation and prevent wholesale extinction of species under fluctuating conditions, organic evolution has developed inherited mechanisms of learning in all but the simplest species. These supplement instincts by enabling the individual organism to modify its behavior adaptively within a greater or lesser range of varying conditions. A notably flexible mechanism of learning is hereditary in all mammalian species. Experimental psychologists who have made intensive studies of animal learning agree that the basic mechanism in man differs in no significant respect from that in other higher mammals. The fundamental principles of acquired behavior are thus mammalian rather than specifically human, and can be illuminated by experiments with rats and dogs just as experiments with fruit flies have advanced the knowledge of human genetics.

Social life is another major type of adaptation which organic evolution has repeatedly produced. Gregarious species are exceedingly numerous, but the most startling superficial resemblances to man are found among the social insects—bees, wasps, ants, termites. In most instances natural selection has created social aggregations by equipping a species with hereditary mechanisms which have the effect of attracting individuals instinctively to one another. Sex is one example. Another is the sweet juices exuded by certain social insects for the delectation of their fellows. Brought into association in some such way, the members of a society enjoy advantages not available to isolated individuals—for example, mutual protection, insurance, enhanced power, and the benefits of a division of labor.

Although neither learning nor society is peculiar to man, in conjunction they have produced something unique in nature—a new level of complexity in natural phenomena which demands for its understanding a distinctive body of scientific theory. The inherited mechanism of learning and the hereditary bases of social life will ultimately yield their secrets to biological science, but the products of their interaction will require the special sciences that compose "lesocupethy," at least until the millennium when all biology has been reduced to chemistry and all chemistry to physics.

Except in man, what the individual of any species learns in his lifetime dies with him. Every individual in every generation starts from scratch. All or most of what he learns he acquires for himself. He derives little or no benefit from the experience of others, even if his species is one of those characterized by social life. In man, however, most of the behavior acquired by any individual, in whatever part of the world or period of history he may live, has previously been learned and found adaptive by other and older members of his own society, and he in turn transmits this behavior, together with any adaptive modifications acquired through his own life experience, to other and younger members of his social group. The interaction of learning and society thus produces in every human group a body of socially transmitted adaptive behavior which appears superindividual because it is shared, because it is perpetuated beyond the individual life span, and because in quantity and quality it so vastly exceeds the capacity of any single person to achieve by his own unaided effort. The term "culture" is applied to such systems of acquired and transmitted behavior. Since cultures change with the varying and cumulative experience of individuals in social groups, it becomes possible to say of man, as of no other species with the hereditary capacity to learn, that societies as well as individuals learn. Social learning is synonymous with cultural evolution.

In social species other than man, the forms of social organization are primarily determined by the biologically inherited mechanisms which produce association. They are therefore the same in all societies of the species, except for minor modifications dependent upon ecological or demographic factors. Among fur seals, for example, one does not find some groups with matriarchal and polyandrous families, nor among honeybees some hives with kings and male workers. In man, however, extreme differences in social organization are common, even in tribes of the same subrace, language, and geographical area. Among the Siouan tribes of the Western Plains, for example, the Omaha are patrilineal and the Mandan matrilineal, and among the Malayan tribes of Sumatra the Batak are patrilineal and the Minangkabau matrilineal. The conclusion is therefore inescapable that in man—alone among the social animals—society itself is largely learned, i.e., is the product of cultural rather than of biological evolution. To be sure, biologically conditioned social bonds are not wholly absent. Thus lactation helps to link mother and child, and sex to bind husband and wife, in the organization of the human family. No biological or innate basis is discernible, however, for the overwhelming proportion of the social ties which produce the complex organizational structures characteristic of human groups.

Since human society is never a spontaneous expression of biological potentialities but must always be learned as a part of culture, it follows that man must be molded to his society much as a colt is broken to harness. He must, in short, be "socialized." In all societies this is largely accomplished during infancy and childhood, when the culture of the group is implanted by inculcation, and the unsocial or antisocial impulses with which the child is born are disciplined and redirected to fit him for the social roles he must fill as an adult. Conflicts are thus inevitably set up in the developing child between his biologically inherited impulses and the demands of his society as these are imposed upon him by his parents and later by others. The manner in which these conflicts are resolved by the individual, reflecting the concrete circumstances under which the social disciplines are impressed upon him, largely determines his "personality."

It should by now be abundantly clear that learning, society, culture, and personality are far indeed from being separable entities, even though until recently they have mainly been studied in isolation by psychology, sociology, anthropology, and psychoanalysis, respectively. Their interrelationships are so intimate that leaders in all four fields are coming more and more to recognize that they form the subject matter of a single integrated science. So significant are the interrelationships that they deserve somewhat fuller exposition.

Since society, culture, and personality are all learned, students of any of these phenomena must constantly bear in mind the fundamental principles of learning as these have been worked out by such behavioristic psychologists as Hull. Unless they do so, their conclusions will suffer in clarity if not in validity.

Knowledge of the structure of society is equally fundamental to the students of learning, culture, and personality. It forms an essential part of all normal situations in which human beings learn. Unless he reckons with it, the behavioristic psychologist can never explain adult human learning, however accurately he may account for the acquisition of habits by rats and other nonsocial animals. Culture only exists in, and is borne by, organized human groups, and the anthropologist who ignores the latter can tell us little of significance about the former. Since personality is largely the product of group pressures, the psychoanalyst should reckon with all important aspects of a society's structure. In our own society, for example, if he deals only with the family situation, and overlooks such significant structures as those of status and prestige, his interpretations will fall far short of completeness.

Culture is deeply relevant to the study of learning, society, and personality. Most of what any human individual learns is already part of the culture of his group, and the cultural habits that he already possesses in large measure predetermine his behavior in any new learning situation. The psychologist can ignore culture when he studies the behavior of rats or dogs, but if he does so when his subject is man, his explanations may be wide of the mark. Since social interaction always takes place within a framework of social structure, which is regularly a part of culture, sociological generalizations made without reference to culture are likely to be meaningless. Culture is crucial to the analysis of personality, not only because traits of the latter are often socially shared but also because the disciplines through the imposition of which personality is formed are largely prescribed by the culture.

Personality is no less significant than is culture for an understanding of human learning, since the reaction of any individual in a learning situation is likely to reflect significantly his resolution of the conflicts arising during his socialization and the unconscious anxieties and hostilities generated thereby. Society, too, reflects personality factors. Thus, as the sociologist Sumner showed long ago, human societies are characterized by "antagonistic cooperation" because of the conflict between individual impulse and social pressures, and they exhibit the phenomenon of "ethnocentrism" because the hostilities generated but suppressed by in-group disciplines are displaced toward other groups in such forms as race prejudice, religious intolerance, and national rivalries. Personality also affects culture. It appears, for example, to be a significant factor in the development of what is called "national character." Moreover, as Kardiner and Linton have shown, certain aspects of culture, such as religious beliefs, tend to be reflections or projections of attitudes commonly engendered during the socialization process.

During the early attempts at the Institute of Human Relations, in 1935-42, to assemble the theories of learning, society, culture, and personality into a single integrated discipline, two very important discoveries were made. The first was that the four theoretical systems, although developed in relative isolation, fitted together almost as well as the adjacent pieces of a jigsaw puzzle. The gaps and inconsistencies were unexpectedly few. Other systems of theory fitted much less well—some because of dubious validity, others because of their more limited scope or more pragmatic character. Economic theory, for example, appeared to be related primarily to the conditions prevailing in a restricted group of complex societies during a limited period of history, and thus to be culture-bound rather than universal. It had, for this reason, afforded little help to anthropologists in understanding the economic behavior of primitive peoples.

The second major discovery was that each of the four systems shed new light on the others and often converted ambiguity into clarity. Thus, learning theory demonstrated that personality is really learned, despite Freud's persistent invocation of "instinct," and it corroborated Malinowski in his insistence that culture is always functional and does not persist through sheer inertia. Personality theory showed that the concept of "drive" as well as of "stimulus" is necessary in order to comprehend the motivation of learning, and it illuminated the view of Sumner that the elements of culture are emotionally charged rather than neutral or devoid of affect. The theory of social structure revealed that Freudian psychology rests on sociocultural as well as on biological or physiological assumptions, being concerned with the products of learning under conditions presented by family organization and the imposition of social sanctions. Culture theory demonstrated that psychological principles are never competent to explain any social phenomenon unless account is taken, not only of behavior mechanisms, but also of the historically determined conditions under which these mechanisms operate, particularly the so-called cultural base and the prevailing structure of social relationships.

The manner in which the four originally independent systems of theory have been found to dovetail gives confidence in the essential validity of each, and the new insights that each has brought to the others confirm the impression of their essential unity. Recent work by anthropologists like Gillin and Hallowell, sociologists like Merton and Parsons, psychologists like Mowrer and Sears, and numerous others reveals that the integrated discipline which we have dubbed "lesocupethy" is approaching maturity. It is perhaps best exemplified to date in the volume *Social Learning and Imitation,* by Miller and Dollard. I have myself recently shown, in *Social Structure,* that there are some problems of social science—e.g., the incidence of incest taboos—that are capable of solution only when findings from all four of the constituent disciplines are applied conjointly.

The juxtaposition of the several behavioral sciences has also revealed areas in which intensive research is urgently needed. One such is related to the fact that much of human behavior is ideational, depending upon the use of linguistic and other symbols. What the Gestalt psychologists have called "insight," and others "intelligence," is known to be of enormous importance in learning. When exhibited by human beings this is believed to involve a transfer of trial-and-error behavior from the motor organs to an ideational process utilizing implicit linguistic symbols, the individual resorting to a motor response only after he has "thought out" a promising solution to the problem facing him. That this symbolic process can use other than verbal tools is demonstrated by the fact that the anthropoid apes as well as man exhibit insight or intelligence. At present it can only be assumed that the same principles of learning are involved in ideational as in motor behavior. This conclusion must, however, be established or revised by experimental methods, for until this is done the exact bearing of learning theory upon personality and culture, in both of which symbolic behavior plays a highly significant role, will remain uncertain. In any such research the participation of experts in linguistics and semantics will be as essential as that of psychologists.

The disciplines that compose "lesocupethy" have in common the fact that they all deal exclusively with acquired behavior. It is readily admitted that biological factors bear directly upon human behavior in diverse ways. Learning is obviously affected by the physiological condition of the individual. Society, as already noted, has biological underpinnings in such phenomena as sex and lactation. Culture is possibly influenced in some small measure by racial heredity, and, as Gillin has pointed out, definite limits are set to its variability by man's innate endowment. Constitutional factors certainly play a prominent role in psychotic aberrations and very likely also in normal personality. The interpretation of all these and other comparable influences, however, is a task of the special biological sciences. "Lesocupethy" is concerned only with what is left when these are factored out. That this is a major assignment there can no longer be any doubt.

Incidentally, there is not yet sufficient recogniton of the fact that vastly more is scientifically known about the acquired than about the innate factors in man's social behavior. Precise knowledge of the latter must in many cases await the full development of human genetics, which in the very nature of the case cannot be achieved until several generations have elapsed. By that time the integrated science of acquired behavior should have developed a hundredfold.

In all fields of science there are segments of verified knowledge which have not yet been integrated with the basic theoretical system of the discipline. In the social and psychological sciences there are comparable segments—most notably perhaps in sociology, economics, linguistics, and social psychology—which "lesocupethy" has not as yet assimilated. Thus far, however, there is in this field little evidence of major alternative theories, verified but unreconciled, concerning the same body of phenomena, comparable to the wave and corpuscular theories of light. Can it be that man's social behavior is actually less complex, not more complex, than the subject matter of physical science? And is it not perhaps possible that we may have more of the essential answers to the basic scientific problems even earlier in the former field than in the latter?

The union of disciplines which we have called "lesocupethy" is a pure science. Its objective is the maximal theoretical understanding of the peculiar ways of men. It does not directly seek the solution of any practical problem. Naturally it has much in common with such applied sciences as psychotherapy, social work, education, industrial relations, and colonial administration, just as the physical and biological sciences are applied in war, engineering, industry, agriculture, and medicine. Admittedly the applied sciences continually add substantial increments of knowledge to the pure sciences upon which they depend. Nevertheless, history has shown, and both industry and government now recognize, that the support of research in pure science frequently yields richer dividends through the application of newly discovered basic principles than are obtainable by a direct attack upon specific practical objectives. It is therefore not inconceivable that the cultivation of "lesocupethy" as a pure science may lead more quickly to a solution of international conflict, economic insecurity, industrial strife, family disorganization, and individual mental disorders than research oriented directly toward the solution of these pressing problems.

But whether or not such high aims are realized, the emergent integration of the basic theoretical systems of the social and psychological sciences undoubtedly represents one of the great turning points in the history of science. In significance it may prove the equal of the contributions of Darwin and Mendel in biology. In kind, however, it perhaps resembles more closely the extraordinary integrating achievement of Einstein in the field of physical science.

2

This paper was originally published as a chapter in *For a Science of Social Man,* edited by John Gillin (New York, 1954, pp. 14-31)—a pioneering volume in which a number of American anthropologists, psychologists, and sociologists examined one another's disciplines in a collective effort to ascertain the extent to which an integrated science of human social behavior had begun to emerge.

2

Sociology and Anthropology

CIENCE is a part of culture. To be sure, it belongs with those aspects, like technology, economy, and warfare, whose changes depend heavily upon success or failure in coping with realities in the external environment rather than with aspects like language, art, and religion, in whose dynamics a substantially greater role is played by internal imperatives and "historical accident." Yet even science exhibits trends, fashions, and differential social support. Its course of development thus conforms at least as closely to the ordinary dynamics of cultural change as to the abstract ideal of a coordinated rational attack upon the unknown.

This is probably particularly true of sciences in their fledgling phase, which sociology and anthropology have barely begun to outgrow. A consideration of the relationships of these two disciplines today and of their probable interdependence tomorrow must therefore take account of their historical development and of the devious ways in which they have interacted in the past.

At the risk of but slight oversimplification, the development of sociology and anthropology can be likened to the life histories of two individuals whose ways have crossed on numerous occasions. The date and exact circumstances of the birth of both are obscure, but not so their parentage. Sociology was clearly born of a union between social reform and philosophy; anthropology of one between antiquarianism and natural history. And the careers of both have given ample evidence of the influence of their heredity.

We also know exactly when and how both infants were weaned and thereby established as independent personages. For sociology this event was presided over by Auguste Comte (1798-1857), who was also the child's baptismal godparent. The positive philosophy of Comte was appropriately tempered with a strong ingredient of social meliorism from Saint-Simon (1760-1825). For anthropology the officiant was Adolf Bastian (1826-1905), a colossus whose wide-ranging travels and bulky tomes brought such acclaim that he was able to establish autonomy for the child in whose blood ran both the interest in archeological and folkloristic antiquities and the urge for the systematic collection of artifacts and customs from all corners of the globe.

The socialization of the two children was hardly underway when both came under the influence of a prestigeful but dominating foster parent known to history as Charles Darwin (1809-1882). Identifying strongly with him, they overlearned his doctrine of organic evolution, and for half a century, i.e., until the period of adolescent revolt set in, they reflected his influence in a series of unilinear theories of social and cultural evolution. Some of the giants of this period, like Bachofen, Frazer, Lubbock, McLennan, Morgan, and Tylor, are usually classed as anthropologists; others, like Durkheim, Lippert, Spencer, and Sumner, are more commonly ranked as sociologists. From the perspective of the present, however, they all look remarkably alike, not only in their common use of ethnographic data and a comparative method but also in the majority of the conclusions they reached. From Darwin until after the turn of the century, sociology and cultural anthropology were nearly indistinguishable.

Though the theories of unilineal cultural evolution so widely accepted in the nineteenth century are now almost universally discredited, three of the sociologists of the period have left important and enduring impressions on anthropology, as well as on their own discipline. The first of these is Herbert Spencer (1820-1903). Though it is currently fashionable to discount his *Principles of Sociology*, this work contributed substantially to the definition of the subject matter of anthropology and provided the first outline of what has come to be known as the universal culture pattern, in addition to adding permanent though modest increments to our knowledge of particular aspects of culture, such as religion. Perhaps even more important in the long run has been the influence of his *Descriptive Sociology*. This work, so little known among sociologists that the author has encountered few who have even heard of it, inaugurated a commendable effort to organize and classify systematically the cultural data on all the peoples of the world for the advancement of cross-cultural research, and thus clearly foreshadowed the development of the present Human Relations Area Files.

The second of the significant early sociologists is Emile Durkheim (1858-1917). Though he accepted the unilinear evolutionary theories current in his day, he did not emphasize them. He also drew heavily upon ethnographic materials, but instead of amassing quantities of cases torn from their cultural context he immersed himself in the literature on one group of primitive peoples, the Australian aborigines, and sought explanations of such cultural phenomena as religion in terms of their functions in social interaction. He thus paved the way to the development of functionalism, which ultimately infused new vigor in anthropology after both evolutionism and historicism had revealed their essential sterility. Malinowski, Radcliffe-Brown, and Redfield, and through them their many students, were strongly influenced by Durkheim in diverse ways, and the structural approach now dominant in British social anthropology is specifically his intellectual grandchild.

Unfortunately Durkheim, in his effort to stress the autonomy of cultural science, erroneously rejected psychology as irrelevant. Consequently, though the integration of sociology and anthropology has indubitably been advanced through his influence, the rapprochement of both with psychology has been inhibited. Those anthropologists who have followed his lead, for example, have remained aloof from the promising developments in behavior theory and in "culture and personality." Many have tended to short-circuit genuine scientific problems by reifying social structure, much as other anthropologists have reified culture. Either approach would deny psychology a place in a science of social or cultural behavior.

The third influential sociologist of the early period, William Graham Sumner (1840-1910), foreshadowed functionalism in another way. He insisted on what is now a commonplace of anthropological thought but was novel in his day, namely, that culture is adaptive, satisfying individual and societal needs and altering over time in response to the changing conditions of life. He was the first to promulgate explicitly the doctrine of cultural relativity, shocking his contemporaries by asserting that even slavery, cannibalism, and infanticide are adaptive and socially justifiable in the societies that normally practice them. In his *Folkways* Sumner also demonstrated that the elements of culture are very much more than neutral "traits" or shared habits, being commonly invested by the members of a society with affect, moral values, and an awareness of sanctions. These views are thoroughly congruent with the participation of psychology in cultural science. Though Sumner's direct influence on anthropology has been slighter than that of Durkheim, his indirect impact has been enormous, and he probably stands closer than any other social scientist of the late nineteenth century to the theoretical position of most contemporary behavioral scientists.

The years just preceding and following 1900 brought the first serious doubts as to the validity of the unilinear evolutionary theories which had bound sociology and anthropology in a premature united front. The accumulation of ethnographic evidence began to reveal the extreme importance of cultural diffusion, undermining a basic assumption of evolutionism, and sociologists like Howard and Westermarck suggested alternative explanations for customs which had previously been accepted as survivals of earlier stages of social development. The basis of their unity shattered, the two disciplines parted company, and for several decades followed courses reflecting their separate pre-Darwinian origins.

Sociologists, with a few notable exceptions like Keller and Thomas, lost interest in ethnography and abandoned comparative studies. Many reverted to the well-trodden paths of philosophy—some, like Ward, Park and Burgess, and Sorokin to build ambitious theoretical systems; others, like Giddings, Cooley, and MacIver, to speculate in the armchair on a lesser scale, too often with the comforting but enervating assumption that the study of human behavior, as a *Geisteswissenschaft*, can never hope to make successful use of the methods of science. Another large group returned to a frank interest in practical social problems—delinquency, dependency, divorce, racial discrimination, population, etc. Not being averse to observation or obsessed with the greater virtue of theorizing, they did amass a modest body of verified knowledge. But since they naturally had little interest in data from societies other than their own, they would have converted sociology into a culture-bound discipline, like economics and political science, had it not been for the system-builders, who fought valiantly for a science of universal validity, comparable to anthropology and psychology. Ultimately, of course, the fact-mindedness of the one group and the theoretical preoccupation of the other were to fuse and produce a mature discipline which could make common cause with the sister sciences of man.

In the meantime anthropology, too, was exhibiting signs of regression. In part its practitioners stressed the original natural-history objective and strove energetically, through intensive field work, to record in detail the customs of the simpler peoples while there was yet time to recover them. In part they followed the equally time-honored antiquarian lure, unearthing the remains of the more spectacular prehistoric civilizations, following hobbies in primitive art and folklore, and tracing the origin and geographical spread of interesting traits. Concern with the study of man as a science gave way to a widespread insistence that the only legitimate objective of anthropology is the reconstruction of history for the periods and regions lacking written records. Theories of prehistory involving the intercontinental diffusion of great culture complexes were elaborated by Smith in Great Britain, Graebner in Germany, and Schmidt in Austria. American anthropologists were in general more cautious, preferring to build the edifice of prehistory more slowly, brick by brick. The formulation and testing of scientific hypotheses, especially by comparative methods, was considered, if not entirely taboo, at least premature and thus to be deferred to some millennium when the ethnographic evidence would be complete.

The most striking characteristic of American anthropology during the first quarter of the twentieth century, which was dominated by Franz Boas, was its negative attitude toward most theories which had gained a measure of acceptance in the human sciences. It combatted, nearly always with eventual success, not only unilinear evolutionism, but also geographic and economic determinism, the organismic analogy, the group mind, racism, instinctivism, eugenics, and theories of primitive mentality. In short, it swept the decks clean, retaining little except the basic concept of culture itself. In so doing, it rendered a genuine service to the human sciences, as is apparent today from our longer perspective, for nearly all that went overboard is now recognized as rubbish which needed to be swept away before genuine scientific advance was possible.

During this period sociology and anthropology almost completely lost contact. The ambitious philosophers and earnest meliorists who dominated the former could hardly be expected to be impressed with the importance of the purely historical study of grubby and vanishing peoples in remote places. The fact-minded and field-minded anthropologists in their turn viewed with scarcely veiled contempt the "armchair theorists" and "do-gooders" in the other camp. This had the unfortunate effect of closing their eyes to the important gains, however few these may have been, that were actually being achieved in sociology. The field of culture theory itself, presumably the special preserve of the anthropologist, provides a spectacular example. Substantial contributions to the dynamics of culture change made by the sociologists Keller and Ogburn passed unnoticed in anthropology, which continued to limp along for another quarter century with crude concepts of invention and diffusion, derived from the nineteenth-century sociologist Tarde and only inconsiderably improved, before it achieved a comparable level of theoretical sophistication.

By the 1920's Boasian anthropology had exorcised all its devils and, being committed to a negative bias, was threatened with the sterility that ultimately overtakes all "schools." It was rescued by a revival of interest in scientific problems, which stemmed from several sources. Wissler, who had been trained in psychology, promoted the study of acculturation. Sapir and M. Mead, by different paths, became interested in depth psychology and pioneered the field of "culture and personality" which was to lead to rapprochement with psychology. Still more electrifying was the impact of "functionalism" as promulgated in different ways by Malinowski and Radcliffe-Brown though derived ultimately, as previously noted, from the sociologist Durkheim. Fortunately functionalism was never accepted as a dogma in American anthropology but rather acted as a ferment, leading to an integration of synchronic with diachronic interests, methods, and objectives and to an eclectic, dynamic, and basically scientific approach well exemplified, for instance, in the work of Linton and Eggan.

It is an ironic fact that most of what modern anthropology has absorbed from the functionalists it could have learned decades earlier from American sociology had it chosen to listen. Essentially the lesson from functionalism has been that cultures and subcultures are organically related to the structured social groups and subgroups that carry them, which has been axiomatic in sociology at least since the days of Sumner. Utterly incredible as it must seem to the psychologist and sociologist, it is nevertheless almost literally true that no work by an American anthropologist recognized this fact until the appearance of Linton's *Study of Man* in 1936. The prevailing point of view was expressed as late as 1937 by Lowie in his *History of Ethnological Theory,* where he expressly rejects the position of Malinowski and insists (pp. 235-236) that "a culture is invariably an artificial unit segregated for purposes of expediency" and that there is "only one natural unit for the ethnologist—the culture of all humanity at all periods and in all places"! The present writer cannot conceive of a more telling object lesson for the need of interlearning among the sciences concerned with human behavior.

Happily, evidence is increasing that anthropology and sociology, as well as psychology, have overcome the traumas of their birth and weaning, corrected their childhood dependency on biology, and resolved their adolescent conflicts, so that they are prepared to interact with one another on an adult level. It is clear that sociology and anthropology are becoming reconciled after their long separation and already share, to a marked extent, the same body of basic scientific theory. Their further rapprochement with one another and with psychology, however, will be hindered rather than promoted by failure to recognize certain fundamental differences between them, stemming largely from their historically divergent developments. In attempting to clarify these differences, the writer must not be understood as wishing to justify or perpetuate them, or to stake out jurisdictional claims for either discipline, or to make points in favor of one at the expense of the other. He happens to be a practitioner of the one who had his professional training in the other, and he acknowledges a loyalty to both. His aim is solely to set forth their major differences, as he sees them, in the belief that this may point the way to the areas in which each can learn most from the other in the future.

Anthropology owes one of its major differences from sociology to its natural-history antecedents. The natural sciences, such as botany, zoology, and geology, recognize a professional obligation, over and above the investigation of theoretical problems, to record systematically the forms of plants and animals and natural formations in all the parts of the earth which they visit. Anthropology shares this sense of obligation. Field work is the *sine qua non* of professional standing, and the ethnographer, whatever special problems he may go to the field to investigate, is expected to bring back and publish, not only an answer to his special problem, but also a descriptive account, as complete as he can make it, of the entire culture of the people studied. The result has been the accumulation of a vast body of professionally gathered descriptive materials on the approximately 3,000 peoples of the primitive world.

Among the other human disciplines only geography shares this natural-science sense of obligation for full descriptive reporting. The psychological sciences, by contrast, have produced only a handful of complete case studies of individuals, their presumed special subject of investigation. In sociology, "sociography" enjoys nothing like the standing of ethnography in anthropology, and the body of accumulated descriptive studies produced by professional sociologists is inconsiderable, consisting mainly of a few regional descriptions, a few accounts of urban groups or areas, and a few community studes, of which a substantial proportion have actually been produced by anthropologists like Arensberg, Davis, Gardner, Miner, Powdermaker, Warner, and West.

Much sociological research starts with a scientific problem, for which the researcher gathers the material he needs by questionnaire, schedule, interview, or other techniques; he then publishes so much of the data as shed light on the problem, but no more. Most other sociological research utilizes data gathered by official agencies, notably census reports and vital statistics for the Registration

Area. Sociologists display laudable ingenuity in inducing other people, like the War Department or the Census Bureau, to assemble the information they require, but remarkably little motivation to gather and report descriptive data through their own efforts.

An ironic consequence of this difference is that there is scarcely a single aspect of modern American culture, not alone for the country as a whole but even for any single community within it, which is as adequately described in the literature as is the comparable aspect in scores or hundreds of primitive societies. That this is not due to population size or cultural complexity is demonstrated by numerous adequate descriptions of complex African societies with populations numbering hundreds of thousands or often millions, as well as by the rich sociographic literature on several Eastern European countries.

The fields of research of sociology and anthropology are, of course, differentiated, the one working mainly in complex Western civilizations, the other chiefly among simpler preliterate societies. This is, however, merely a practical division of labor, and is in itself of little consequence. Practitioners of both disciplines have amply demonstrated that each can operate effectively in the other's field. There is no "anthropological method" or "sociological method" as such, characterized by special virtues. Nevertheless, the division of labor between the two disciplines has given rise to a fundamental difference in the kinds of data primarily sought and in the techniques for securing them—a difference which, because largely unrecognized, has been the chief source of friction between the two disciplines.

Anyone who studies a society with a culture differing markedly from his own—whether he be an anthropologist, a missionary, a colonial administrator, or a sociologist—must first gain a comprehension of the patterned norms of that culture before he can even begin to understand the behavior of the people. And if he writes up his findings for members of his own society, as he usually does, his first task is to make those norms explicit. The inevitable result has been that anthropologists have devoted their primary attention to patterned behavior, i.e., to those norms which are verbalized as the ideals to which behavior should conform, are taught to each oncoming generation, and are enforced by the formal and informal punishment of deviations. Any member of the society knows a large proportion of these norms, whether or not they govern his own behavior, for the norms incumbent upon persons in other statuses constitute an aspect of his expectations in his social interaction with them. To gain an accurate account of patterned behavior, therefore, an ethnographer needs only a few competent informants, selected judiciously but not necessarily in accordance with any standard sampling technique.

The situation is quite otherwise when a scientist is studying his own society and is writing up his results for other members of the same society. He and his readers, as participants, already know the major norms of the culture, and it would be trite to detail them. What neither he nor they do know, however, is the incidence of unpatterned behavior—both variations within the limits of prescribed patterns and deviations from such patterns. And these, rather than the norms themselves, are what he reports. American "voting habits," to an anthropologist from a different culture, would mean, first of all, such patterned practices as being transported to a polling place in a car provided by a political party's headquarters, checking with the registrars, and X-ing a ballot or pulling a lever on a voting machine; to an American sociologist, on the contrary, the term refers exclusively to such nonpatterned behavior as how many people turn out to vote and how many vote Republican and how many Democratic. An accurate record of the incidence of unpatterned behavior is obviously impossible, short of a full count, except through the use of the most refined sampling techniques.

It should now be clear why sociological community studies, like those of the Lynds on Middletown, though commonly compared with ethnographic reports by anthropologists, are in fact poles apart. They include data of a basically different type, with surprisingly little overlap. It should also be apparent why we know so little about American culture. We know so little precisely because, as participants, we know so much to begin with, and are thus almost inevitably motivated to concentrate on the enormous mass of behavior about which we know little or nothing, namely, unpatterned behavior.

To students of man, of course, all behavior is important, patterned or otherwise. It is a serious defect of anthropology that it has traditionally concerned itself so exclusively with the former. Sociology has made a major contribution in calling attention to the importance of the latter. That anthropology is learning this lesson is revealed by the increasing attention being paid in recent ethnographic literature to variations in behavior within the prescribed patterns and to deviant behavior. If the anthropologist in the future provides the sociologist with more data of a type which he can compare with his own, perhaps the latter will reciprocate by telling the anthropologist some of the things he would like to know about American culture.

Doubtless because of its almost exclusive concern with patterned behavior, cultural anthropology possesses a much more unified body of theory than does sociology. This revolves about the concept of culture and embraces, among its major divisions, (1) culture dynamics, or the body of theory concerning the processes by which culture changes over time, (2) social structure, or the body of theory concerning the patterning of interpersonal relationships in social groups and status categories, and (3) culture and personality, or the body of theory concerning the transmission of culture and formation of personality norms through the socialization process. In addition, of course, there are special segments of theory concerned with particular aspects of culture such as language, technology, art, religion, and government. To a remarkable extent this system of cultural theory is shared by all anthropologists. There are, of course, still differences of emphasis, and even some basic cleavages, but they are notably fewer and less critical than they were a quarter century ago.

Impressive as it is in its essential unity, this body of theory is by no means the exclusive creation of anthropologists. Culture and personality derves mainly from psychology, and social structure to a considerable extent from sociology. Even the central concept of culture itself owes as much to the sociologist Sumner as to any anthropologist who has ever lived, and lesser contributions of significance from sociologists are legion.

Sociological theory—at least to the extent that it is not derived from or shared with psychology or anthropology—is a much less monolithic structure. It gives the impression, if one judges by the periodical literature rather than the tomes of the system-builders, of being composed of a very large number of fragmentary and isolated propositions, each tested and at least tentatively validated, which are mainly of a relatively low order of generality and often hardly more than empirical generalizations.

Several possible explanations come to mind. One is that the very wide range of behavior encompassed presents a problem of much greater complexity than has faced the anthropologist in his concentration on patterned behavior. A second flows from the fact that no conclusion from a piece of research conducted in one society, however promising the hypothesis and convincing the proof, can be accepted as an increment to the general science of human behavior until it has been cross-culturally validated. Until then it can be assumed at best to be established for the one society only, and there is no way of knowing to what extent the seeming confirmation is due to the common nature of man or the universal conditions of social life and to what extent it may merely reflect conditions peculiar to the particular society or its unique historical assemblage of culture traits. Wherever factors of the latter general type preponderate, of course, verified propositions that are unrelated and even occasionally unreconcilable are to be expected. Since exceedingly few of the propositions established by sociological research have as yet been cross-culturally validated, their seeming heterogeneity may simply be a result of the fact that they represent an as yet unassorted mixture of intra-cultural or particularistic generalizations with cross-cultural or universally valid generalizations.

A third possible explanation of the heterogeneity of sociological as contrasted with anthropological theory may reside in the differential determination of research problems in the two fields. In sociology research attention is commonly directed to areas of social problems, i.e., to situations defined as unfortunate, particularly where commonsense efforts at correction have failed and more precise knowledge is clearly called for. The melioristic tradition in sociology makes such areas congenial to many, but probably even more important is the availability of large research funds for their investigation. Industries wish to reduce labor turnover and increase production; the armed forces wish to improve morale and select effectively for specialized training; the media of mass communication wish to sell products or influence attitudes more effectively; public opinion deplores crime, high divorce rates, poor housing, and racial discrimination; and organizational, foundation, and government funds are made available for research that may lead to their reduction. The demand for trained sociologists from such sources is imperative, and those who respond need not work on a shoestring.

Among anthropologists, by contrast, the problems for investigation are much less frequently set by others. Funds for field research are restricted by geographical area, if at all, and the worker is relatively free to select his own scientific problem. If he goes to the Bongo-Bongo, neither the foundation that backs him nor anyone else is so concerned with the high divorce rate or poor housing of the tribe as to direct his research to a particular subject. He is at liberty to concentrate on whatever he pleases, and he commonly picks a topic, like kinship, which is no social problem at all. With this freedom, the determining factor in his choice is likely to be the theoretical structure of his discipline; he chooses a specific research project which will revise that structure or advance one of its frontiers. In consequence, anthropological research tends constantly to expand the discipline's central core of theory rather than to proliferate a heterogeneous body of uncoordinated special theories.

The sociologist's difficulty is not only that his research tasks are so commonly set by others, rather than by himself, but also that he is thereby compelled to start with a situation which needs explaining instead of an abstract question which needs an answer. This is, of course, essentially the old problem of pure versus applied science—a dichotomy which the writer considers in many respects misleading and thus prefers to restate. The crucial distinction seems to be that a scientist who starts with a theoretical question, a "pure-science" hypothesis, can select a situation adapted to testing it, one in which he can exert maximal control over the variables, whether in the laboratory or in the field, whereas the scientist who begins with a situation cannot expect comparable control of the variables, must be prepared for extensive exploratory work to isolate them, and is under compulsion to assess the influence of every important variable, not merely that of a particular one manipulated to test a single initial hypothesis. Since the variables in any situation are likely to be numerous and diverse, not only the sociologist but any scientist whose research begins with situations will almost inevitably emerge with a number of validated hypotheses, and these will often be discrete, unrelated systematically to one another or to those established by workers in different fields, and of a relatively low order of generality.

That the total body of verified theory which has resulted from sociological research compares unfavorably with that of anthropology in unity, in generality of application, in sheer quantity, and in potential significance for the integrated human science of the future would probably be admitted by most sociologists, and is certainly understandable in view of the special difficulties encountered. What is less generally recognized is that certain positive advantages have accrued from this experience which anthropology does not share and urgently needs to acquire. The very handicaps faced by the sociologist—confinement to a single society without the opportunity for cross-cultural validation, selection of his research areas by others than himself, and the compulsion to assess the numerous variables in complex situations—have exerted a highly salutary disciplinary effect. They have developed in him a high degree of awareness of the nature of scientific method, a respect for science comparable to that prevailing in the natural sciences, and an amazing ingenuity in adapting scientific means to scientific ends.

By comparison, anthropologists are extraordinarily naïve in scientific matters. Many frankly confess a humanistic rather than a scientific orientation, and not a few are openly antiscientific. Among those who are actually engaged in research problems which can be classed as scientific, only a handful are adequately grounded in scientific method, and many of these are committed to one method and are skeptical of others. Those who, like Kluckhohn, are both genuinely sophisticated and broadly oriented are rare indeed. In sociology, men with a flaming zeal for science are not uncommon. The writer thinks instantaneously of such diverse figures as Keller, Lundberg, and Stouffer, but he has rarely encountered such a man in anthropology. The low status of scientific interest and awareness in anthropology is assuredly the most serious handicap to the full participation of this discipline in the integrated human science of the future. Here, if anywhere, there is room for learning from both sociology and psychology.

The scientific superiority which sociology enjoys over anthropology is perhaps most obvious in the field of methodology. Anthropologists have, indeed, evolved the wholly admirable "genealogical method" for field research, which even sociologists could profitably adopt, but in general they have been uninventive. A striking example is provided by research in culture and personality with its almost slavish dependence on projective tests borrowed from psychiatry. When it comes to the formulation and testing of hypotheses, anthropologists reveal little comprehension of the requisites of viable scientific theory and even less of the methods which science has devised for putting such a theory to the test.

The misunderstanding of scientific method is perhaps most extreme in that group of anthropologists which makes the most vociferous pretensions to being scientific and comparative—the British structuralists headed by Radcliffe-Brown. The alleged "laws" of this school turn out, upon examination, to be verbal statements like "the equivalence of brothers" or "the necessity for social integration" which fail completely to specify the concomitant behavior of variables, and their proof invariably rests on the inspection of a single society with perhaps some reference to a small and utterly unrepresentative sample of other societies in British colonial territory. American anthropologists tend less to distort than to ignore the canons of science. They too have made excessive use of that crudest of all scientific methods, the "clinical method" in the broadest sense, which consists essentially in the intensive examination of single complex cases and depends on skill and experience alone to assess the influence of different variables. Little use has as yet been made of such relatively refined methods as experiment (not always impossible with human subjects), analysis of the crucial case (one selected because all variables occur naturally in the combination desired), and statistics (with its varied techniques for establishing covariance in large numbers of cases).

Even the most casual contact with sociologists, or with the literature they produce, reveals their superior scientific sophistication. Anthropologists cannot afford to rest on their laurels, contemplating with complacency their own impressive structure of culture theory and smugly treating the methodological efforts by which their colleagues in sociology attempt to cope with peculiarly difficult problems as a slightly ridiculous game of mental gymnastics. Even granted that these efforts are occasionally excessive, have the anthropologists been guilty of fewer excesses when they have faced equally knotty problems, as in trying to account for national character? If anthropology is to become a science, and to play an equal role with its sister disciplines in building the unified human science of the future, it has much to learn about science and scientific method from sociology.

We have now reviewed the history of the relationships between sociology and anthropology, assessed the respective strengths and weaknesses of each in relation to their differential problems and development, shown some of the more important contributions which sociology has made to anthropology in the past, and indicated some of the genuine achievements of the former which the latter has not yet adopted or taken full advantage of. It may not be amiss, in conclusion, to assume the role of prophet and, by projecting these trends into the future, attempt to visualize what may be the distinctive contributions of the two disciplines to a unified science of human behavior.

In the first instance, the relations of both to psychology will require some revision. Each will have to become reconciled to the near certainty that the basic mechanisms of behavior will be established primarily by psychological research rather than by their own efforts. Concepts like "the processes of social interaction," "the processes of cultural change," and "the socialization process" must be recognized as nothing more than psychological processes, such as those of perception, learning, and personality development, operating under the special conditions created by human social life. There must be no more reification of "culture" or "social structure" as causal forces, no more assumption of a special super-individual or superorganic level of phenomena characterized by a body of principles inaccessible to the psychologist.

Psychologists, in their turn, must desist from their efforts to explain social and cultural phenomena in terms of behavior mechanisms alone. All such attempts in the past have failed dismally, and they will fail equally in the future, for mechanisms, whether of learning or of personality, produce differential results depending upon the particular conditions of material environment, social organization, and culture prevailing in a given situation. It is the special province of the sociologist and the anthropologist to study such conditions and to determine what constellations thereof, in conjunction with behavioral mechanisms, produce this or that social or cultural manifestation. It is not enough that either side should admit the importance of the other's contribution. Both must recognize that each holds one indispensable key and lacks another, and that few if any of the rooms in the future mansion of human science can be unlocked without both.

The relations between anthropology and sociology promise to be somewhat different. The most crucial determinant would appear to be the fact that one holds most of the resources, the other most of the tools with which to exploit them. Anthropology has at its disposal, in the riches of ethnography, evidence concerning an immensely wider range of variation in human behavior than has any other discipline. It has access to thousands of nature-made experiments, combining conditions of social and cultural life that are utterly impossible to reproduce artificially. They provide the ideal ultimate testing ground for theories of human behavior. The human scientist of the future will certainly look with equal skepticism upon statements alleged to be generally valid for man when made on the basis of animal experiments unchecked with human subjects and when based on research in a single society unverified by a cross-cultural test. To us as citizens, of course, our own society looms as enormously important; as scientists, however, it remains an insignificant single case among thousands, and statements concerning it, no matter how firmly buttressed, can no more be accepted as true of mankind in general than could psychiatric observations on a single patient.

If anthropology appears qualified and even destined, by virtue of its superior resources, to become the final proving ground of behavior theory in the future, it sadly lacks the means to realize this potentiality. These means, among which by far the most important are sophistication in scientific theory and versatility in scientific method, are found in abundance in the sister discipline of sociology, where they lie for the most part unnoticed. Their utilization must follow one of two alternative courses. Either anthropology must go to school and learn thoroughly the skills which sociology has to offer, thereby equipping itself to perform the task, or sociologists will revive their nineteenth-century interest in ethnography, apply to it their wealth of new techniques, and succeed where Spencer, Durkheim, and Sumner failed in establishing a genuine cross-cultural science of man. The Human Relations Area Files would incomparably facilitate the latter.

Whatever the outcome, sociology will certainly retain one exceedingly important function. Though the general validity of theories about human behavior must depend ultimately upon cross-cultural checking, our own society offers obvious advantages as a preliminary testing ground. The costs in time and funds are minimal. The researcher commands the language of his subjects. As a participant, he knows their culture intimately, and can adapt his techniques with precision to the social situation as well as to the requirements of the problem. He can draw upon enormous resources of data gathered by others to augment those assembled by himself. There are, to be sure, certain scientific problems which can be tackled only in another cultural setting. For the great majority, however, our own society provides the ideal scene for exploratory work, for experimentation with novel techniques, for the formulation and revision of hypotheses, and for their thorough initial testing.

Anthropology, if it rises to the occasion, may ultimately become the final arbiter of the universality of social-science propositions and may even contribute, next to psychology, the largest share of really basic theory. Sociology, however, gives promise of greater creativity in respect to theories in the lower and middle ranges, and certainly in regard to methodology, and it is quite conceivable that in some areas, like that of small group research, it may yield scientific principles of substantial magnitude.

Developments in all three disciplines over the past quarter century give numerous indications that psychology, sociology, and anthropology are gradually merging their most important individual contributions to form what may some day become a unified science of human behavior. Serious obstacles remain to be overcome in each of the fields, and this writer has taken pains not to minimize them. Nevertheless, he is heartened by the fact that those who share the vision of ultimate common achievement include a very large proportion of those to whom their respective professional colleagues are accustomed to turn for leadership.

3

This paper, originally published in the *American Anthropologist* (53: 465-473, 1951), was written at the urging of a number of my American colleagues who felt, with me, that the range of interests and activities among British anthropologists had grown unnecessarily restricted. I had no intention of depreciating them, for I regarded—and still regard —those whom I have mentioned by name as constituting the ablest and most productive single group in the history of our science, with perhaps the immediate successors of Boas as their only close rivals. My colleagues and I felt that possibly a little "needling" might stimulate them to expand their perspectives. This hope is as yet unrealized. British social anthropology continues to mine essentially the same vein—to be sure, still a productive one—and even its younger members have discovered no new and promising lodes comparable to those now being exploited by such of their American contemporaries as Conklin, Frake, Geertz, Goodenough, Lounsbury, Romney, and Wallace.

Reprinted by permission.

British Social Anthropology

FOR a decade or more, anthropologists in other countries
have privately expressed an increasingly ambivalent attitude toward recent trends in British anthropology—a curious blend of respect and dissatisfaction. It is high time that the
reasons for this attitude be subjected to analysis. An opportunity
to do so is presented by the publication of *African Systems of
Kinship and Marriage* (Radcliffe-Brown and Forde 1950), which
contains an ambitious 85-page introduction by Radcliffe-Brown,
the acknowledged dean of the group, and substantial contributions
by nearly all of its leading members—Evans-Pritchard, Forde,
Fortes, Gluckman, Kuper, Nadel, Richards, Schapera, and Wilson. When this volume is carefully analyzed in relation to previous
works by the same authors, the reasons for both aspects of the
ambivalent attitude emerge with some clarity.

On the positive side, the ethnographic contributions to the vol-

36

ume reveal without exception a very high level of professional competence in field research and in the analysis of social structural data, equalled only by the work of the very best men in other countries. They will be indispensable to all Africanists and will be greeted by students of comparative social institutions as a valuable addition to the descriptive literature. As an example of how factual knowledge has been expanded we may cite the contributions of Fortes to this symposium (1950: 252-284) and to an earlier one (1949a). In the one he corrects Rattray by showing that patrilineal exogamy among the Ashanti extends only to quinary relatives and not to the entire *ntoro* group, and in the other he clarifies satisfactorily for the first time the complex situation in the same tribe with respect to residence rules and household composition.

Theoretical as well as factual knowledge is advanced. Nearly every contributor calls attention to internal relationships between structure and behavior or between different aspects of structure in the groups studied as suggestive of broader scientific generalizations. These suggestions are invariably thoughtful, whatever their ultimate validity may prove to be. Particularly impressive, for example, is the analysis by Richards (1950: 207-251) of the matrilineal systems which stretch across the continent from the mouth of the Congo to the Zambezi delta, together with her suggested correlations between bride-price, rule of residence, relative authority of father or husband and maternal uncle, and form of political organization.

Analysis of their content reveals that the African articles are particularly complete on unilinear and local aggregations of kinsmen and that property and inheritance are covered unusually well. In general, however, they present a less well-rounded picture of the systems they describe than do comparable works by other ethnographers.[1] Of the various contributors, for example, only Gluckman (Lozi) and Kuper (Swazi) give complete data on patterned behavior between kinsmen; only Forde (Yakö) and Richards (Bemba)

[1] E.g., the contributors in Eggan (1937).

specify clearly the relative frequency of intracommunity and inter-community marriages; only Forde (Yakö), Kuper (Swazi), and Wilson (Nyakyusa) satisfactorily equate family types with occu-pancy of dwellings and compounds; and only Fortes (Ashanti), Gluckman (Lozi and Zulu), Kuper (Swazi), Schapera (Tswana), and Wilson (Nyakyusa) indicate precisely which first cousins are marriageable and which are prohibited mates.

This does not mean that the omitted aspects of these social systems are neglected, for they have often been described in pre-vious works or will be covered in subsequent ones. The seeming incompleteness merely reflects an increasing tendency on the part of British social anthropologists to fractionate their descriptions and analyses of social systems. Firth was able to give a well-rounded and satisfying account of the social organization of Tikopia, as well as much other valuable information, in a single volume (1936). Fortes, however, requires two volumes (1945, 1949) to analyze Tallensi kinship structure alone. Evans-Pritchard parcels out in-formation with an even more niggardly hand. His much admired earlier analysis of Nuer lineages (1940), he now informs us (1950: 360-361), is not to be relied upon by students of kinship because he was then concerned exclusively with political structure and said nothing about "small lineages which have fewer branches and less depth than the dominant clans." The apparent incon-sistency of this fractionating tendency with functional theory could readily be corrected by prefacing a partial description with a brief statement indicating how its matter integrates with the total cul-ture. This would make it possible to use a source with confidence before the author's bibliography is complete.

Nonetheless, the descriptive and analytical writing of the British social anthropologists attains an average level of ethnographic competence and theoretical suggestiveness probably unequalled by any comparable group elsewhere in the world. This explains and justifies the respect so widely accorded them. Offsetting these merits, however, are a number of special limitations which many professional colleagues abroad find difficult to understand and im-possible to defend.

The British social anthropologists, in the first place, do not concern themselves with the entire range of cultural phenomena but concentrate exclusively on kinship and subjects directly related thereto, e.g., marriage, property, and government. To be sure, some of them, like Richards (1932, 1939), have dealt with economics and others, like Evans-Pritchard (1937), with religion. Nevertheless, it is an incontrovertible fact that such major aspects of culture as technology, folklore, art, child training, and even language are almost completely neglected.

A second limitation is geographical. For a generation hardly a single professional British ethnographer has worked with any society not located in a British colonial dependency. The authors of the volume under consideration are, strictly speaking, not Africanists but Anglo-Africanists. Though the editors claim (p. vi) that "the chief varieties of kinship organization occurring in trans-Saharan Africa are illustrated and considered," in actual fact only Richards has crossed a political boundary—to examine the structures of a group of tribes in the Belgian Congo.

A third limitation, related to the foregoing, is an almost complete disinterest in general ethnography—difficult to account for in a country which has produced a Tylor and a Frazer. Of the two or three thousand primitive societies in the world whose cultures have been recorded, the British social anthropologists as a group reveal a concern with and knowledge of not more than thirty. These include: (1) the Ashanti, Bemba, Lozi, Nuba, Nuer, Nyakyusa, Swazi, Tswana, Yakö, and Zulu, on which new or additional original materials are presented in the recent African volume; (2) the Azande, Tallensi, and a few other African societies previously studied by the same authors or congenial colleagues; (3) the societies of Malaya and Oceania described by such other British social anthropologists as Bateson, Firth, Fortune, and of course Malinowski and Radcliffe-Brown; and (4) the Nayar of India and the Minangkabau of Sumatra, whose exceptionally weak conjugal bonds have apparently drawn special attention to them. This restriction of interest, it should hastily be added, does not apply to Gluckman or Richards, who manifest a definite concern with the regional distribution of the social systems they describe, nor to Forde (1934), who has shown a broad ethnographic orientation in previous work.[2]

With these exceptions, however, the ethnographic knowledge of the Anglo-Africanists appears to be confined almost exclusively to the earlier sources on the tribes they themselves have studied and to the works of their contemporary British colleagues. They pay no attention to the descriptive literature on French West and Equatorial Africa, Liberia, Ethiopia, and (except Richards) the Belgian Congo, to the abundant German sources on Tanganyika, Cameroon, Angola, and (except Gluckman) South West Africa, or even to sources in English on British-ruled peoples whom they have not personally investigated. Sometimes important ethnographies in a foreign language are ignored even when they deal with the same people. Thus no British student of the Yao (even Richards) appears to have consulted the quite useful monograph by Weule (1908).[3] To the primitive world outside of Africa and the British domains in the Pacific there appears only an occasional oblique and often superficial reference, e.g., in the African symposium to the Hopi, the Ge, and the Bush Negroes. With this neglect of ethnography is associated, of course, a very weak comparative interest.

The British social anthropologists, in the fourth place, are as indifferent to the theoretical as to the descriptive writings of their colleagues in other lands. They refer repeatedly to one another on theoretical issues but almost never cite an anthropologist from continental Europe, the United States, or even the British dominions. In the African volume, for example, the only non-British theorist whose views are seriously discussed is Loeb.[4]

A fifth blind spot is the almost complete disinterest in history. This stems in part from Malinowski but even more directly from Radcliffe-Brown, who has reiterated his opposition to history for

[2] This interest is continued in his editorship of the important current series entitled *Ethnographic Survey of Africa.*
[3] Tew (1950), for example, includes an incomplete reference to this source in her bibliography but does not draw upon it in the text.
[4] Cited by Gluckman in Radcliffe-Brown and Forde (1950: 190-193).

more than a quarter century (see Radcliffe-Brown 1923), though
he has sought to disguise it by directing his shafts only at "pseudo-
history" with verbal bows to "genuine history" (equally unused in
actual fact). British social anthropology has traditionally been
concerned only with the synchronic analysis of functional interrelationships, never with the diachronic derivation of the latter. Schapera's contribution (1950: 140-165) to the recent African volume
constitutes the only exception known to the writer, for it manifests a
genuine curiosity—and incidentally also a refreshingly frank
puzzlement—about how to account for the development, prior to
the period of observation, of the differences noted in marriage
regulations and kinship behavior among the various Tswana
tribes.

From the neglect of history is directly derived a sixth limitation,
namely, a lack of interest in the processes by which culture changes
over time, such as invention, acculturation, secondary reinterpreta-
tion, selective elimination, integrative modification, and drift.
Other students of Radcliffe-Brown, e.g., Eggan (1950), have
succeeded in fusing functional analysis with an interest in history
and an awareness of process in a highly productive creative synthesis, but there is as yet no indication of any comparable development in British social anthropology.

A seventh limitation is a widespread indifference to psychology,
which is somewhat surprising since a number of the contemporary
British students have been strongly influenced by Malinowski,
whose functional approach is one of the roots of the modern
interest in "culture and personality." Of the contributors to the
African volume, only Nadel draws upon psychological science for
aid in coping with theoretical problems.

These various limitations reflect the overwhelming influence of
Radcliffe-Brown. In the history of anthropology it was Malinowski
who first related culture to the fundamental biological and psychological needs of man and to the organized groups of individuals who
carry it. It was Radcliffe-Brown, however, who explored the actual
structuring of human relationships within such organized groups

and demonstrated how social behavior is keyed to structure. In particular, he rescued kinship from the morass in which it had been left by Morgan and Rivers—as a set of survivals from which earlier forms of marriage and kin groupings could supposedly be inferred—and showed that nomenclature, patterns of kinship behavior, marriage rules, and aggregations of kinsmen tend to be related to one another in consistent ways within any social system. These contributions are as valid as they are important, they have been accepted with near unanimity by modern anthropologists, and they assure their author a permanent position of honor in the history of the science.

By no means, however, did these contributions come as an unmixed blessing. They were accompanied from the first by a rejection of all the genuine gains achieved by earlier generations of anthropologists: the comparative ethnographic method of Tylor, which was capable of refinement into a powerful scientific tool; the historical methodology of Boas, a necessary prerequisite for the development of a sound theory of cultural dynamics; even the functional approach of Malinowski, which would have held open the door to psychology. In addition, Radcliffe-Brown is responsible for two serious distortions of scientific method from which his followers have never freed themselves, namely, (1) the notion that universal "laws" are discoverable from the intensive study of a very few societies selected without reference to their representativeness and (2) the misconception that such laws can be adequately expressed by verbal statements which do not specify the concomitant behavior of variables.

These errors might not have proved serious had Radcliffe-Brown shown a disposition to learn from his colleagues or even his disciples. But unlike Malinowski, who continued to expand and revise his theories to the last year of his life, Radcliffe-Brown seems never to have corrected a mistake nor to have modified his theoretical position in any significant respect since its earliest formulation several decades ago. The informed reader of his introduction to the recent African volume, therefore, will find practically nothing not already over-familiar. He will, however, find all the old errors repeated and a few new ones added. Its interest is exclusively historical.

The younger Anglo-Africanists have substantially surpassed their mentor in the quality of their field and analytical techniques and in the skill with which probable correlations between different aspects of a social system are isolated. Only Richards and Schapera, however, give evidence of relaxing some of the major restrictions. The limitations in interest and outlook impose severe constraints upon the range of theory, and confine hypotheses to a relatively simple level of scientific abstraction. They also greatly increase the danger of reification. Once an adhesion or correspondence has been tentatively established, the ethnographer, being inhibited from seeking any connection through such factors as psychology or process, is tempted to convert his discovery into a cause-and-effect relationship. Gluckman (Radcliffe-Brown and Forde 1950: 193), for example, postulates "that the divorce rate is a reflex of the kinship structure itself." He here reifies structure in precisely the way that White (1949) reifies culture. Overlooking the fact that kinship structure is as definitely an aspect of social behavior as is divorce, he short-circuits a scientific interpretation of their concomitant manifestations by asserting that the one causes the other.

Its voluntarily assumed limitations give British social anthropology the characteristic earmarks of a "school." During the past three decades the mortality of schools in anthropology has been exceedingly high. The present writer knows of only one other of consequence which survives anywhere in the world, namely, the German-Austrian "culture historical school." It bears a strikingly close resemblance to the British school. Like the latter it emphasizes certain highly refined canons of method and narrowly limits its range of theoretical interests. At least some of its techniques, such as those employed in the criticism of sources, are wholly admirable, as are those of the British school. Its theoretical orientation, however, is even more restricted.

As one rereads more of the earlier works of the British school, one becomes increasingly dissatisfied with the common explanation of its distinctive characteristics in terms of the national stereotype of unconsciously assumed superiority, complacent self-satisfaction, and insular aloofness. If this were true, the work of its practitioners should be shoddy in spots, which it is not. It should reveal serious internal strains and inconsistencies, which it does not. On the contrary, the entire corpus of writings constitutes a perfectly logical, self-consistent system which provides answers, or techniques for securing answers, to a number of important scientific questions. It is obviously capable of giving intellectual satisfaction to a group of scholars who are content not to ask other questions, or who prefer to wait before doing so until they have answered most of those originally posed.

Sober reflection has led to quite a different explanation of the peculiarities of the British school, namely, to the conclusion that they are actually not anthropologists but professionals of another category. They meet very few of the criteria by which the field of anthropology is commonly differentiated from the other social sciences. The special province of anthropology in relation to its sister disciplines is the study of culture. Alone among the anthropologists of the world the British make no use of the culture concept. Assuming culture to be their province, most anthropologists feel free to explore its every ramification. The British school alone concentrates upon a few words of Tylor's classic definition and rules the rest out of bounds, including such aspects as technology and the fine arts. Having chosen to investigate culture, most anthropologists find themselves committed to study the processes by which it grows (culture change), is transmitted from one generation to the next (education and socialization), and is spread geographically (diffusion or culture borrowing), and are thus driven irresistibly to an interest in history, psychology, and geography. The British alone ignore these problems and the adjacent disciplines that might contribute to their understanding.

In all the above respects the anthropologists of continental

Europe, the United States, Latin America, and most of the British dominions meet on common ground. With the English, however, they can find no overlapping interest unless they happen to be concerned on a worldwide scale with a restricted range of cultural phenomena impinging directly upon kinship. With this exception the only claim of the British school to the name of anthropology rests on the fact that they conduct much of their field research in nonliterate societies.

In their fundamental objectives and theoretical orientation they are affiliated rather with the sociologists. Like other sociologists, they are interested primarily in social groups and the structuring of interpersonal relationships rather than in culture, and in synchronic rather than diachronic correlations. Like many other sociologists they are confident of their ability to discover valid laws by the intensive study of a single society, or at least of a very small and nonrandom sample of all societies, without any necessity of comparative or cross-cultural validation. If American sociologists commonly select for study the simpler segments of our body politic, such as small rural villages, Southern Negro or mountaineer communities, or immigrant clusters in our urban centers, it is equally logical for British sociologists to choose simple communities elsewhere in the Empire rather than the highly complex and homogeneous population of the home island. The indifference of British social anthropology to world ethnography and to the ethnographic and theoretical contributions of foreign anthropologists, incomprehensible in a group of professional anthropologists, is quite understandable in a group of sociologists. Our interpretation accords, of course, with the historical derivation of the British school from the sociologist Durkheim through both Malinowski and Radcliffe-Brown. It explains the latter's predilection for "sociologistic" verbalisms as a substitute for scientific laws. It even accounts for such oddities as the fact that the American sociologist MacIver is more frequently cited than such American anthropologists as Boas and Kroeber.

Though unmistakably to be classed as sociologists, the British social anthropologists should not be associated with contemporary sociology, which has absorbed so much from both psychology and anthropology that it has become almost indistinguishable from the latter in its fundamental theoretical orientation. The comparison should rather be with the sociological schools of an earlier generation, as is suggested by the choice of MacIver rather than Merton or Parsons as an authoritative reference. Indeed the writer would rank the British social anthropologists with the very best of the sociologists, e.g., Sumner, Pareto, and Thomas, whose theories were current in the 1920's.

Once the true status of British social anthropology as a specialized school of sociologists is recognized, anthropologists in other lands will discover that their ambivalence and uneasiness are quite unwarranted. They can then allow their British colleagues to select their own special fields of investigation, elaborate their own methods, and define their own scientific problems with the same unconcern with which they accord these rights to any other discipline. And they can examine the results with the same detachment with which they scrutinize other sociological writings, utilizing what seems sound and useful and rejecting the rest without undue concern.

One question alone remains. Will a group of anthropologists in the strict sense emerge from the British school? The African volume gives definite intimations of such a possibility. Richards has already overcome the limitation upon ethnographic exploration, has analyzed the literature for a wide area, and has constructed a typology with exceedingly interesting theoretical implications. Schapera shows an unmistakable restiveness about exclusively sociological interpretations and an open interest in historical problems. Forde was once an anthropologist and may not have been wholly converted to sociology. Nadel manifests an interest in psychology. Among the non-Africanists in the British group Firth appears far from completely committed. Perhaps Great Britain in the future, as in the past, will discover that it can support anthropology as well as primitive sociology. If this happens, the unquestionably high level of professional competence among its practitioners gives promise that British anthropology might again rise to a position of preeminence in the world comparable to that which it enjoyed in the era of Tylor and again in that of Rivers.

4

This paper was presented at a conference of the New York State Department of Health at Lake Placid in June 1951, and was subsequently published in the *American Journal of Public Health* (42: 7-11, 1952). The past decade has witnessed a marked expansion in the role played by anthropology and other behavioral sciences in the health professions.

Anthropology and Its Contribution to Public Health

THERE are many defintions of anthropology, but the one I like best is short and snappy: "Anthropology is the science of man—embracing woman."

Despite its libelous implications, this definition makes the essential point. Anthropologists are interested in everything concerned with man. We are so interested in man that we make a special effort to study the things about him that most other people overlook. The most important of these are bones, potsherds, and "gooks."

Those who study bones are the physical anthropologists. Dogs, too, like bones—but not when they are thousands of years old. A physical anthropologist, however, will go into ecstasies over a mess of old bones. Look at my friend Carleton Coon and the important bones he has just unearthed in Iraq. Bones, of course, show where man came from and how he has evolved from apelike ancestors into the various races that now inhabit the world.

The anthropologists who study potsherds are the archeologists. They dig into the ground to find the traces of earlier and simpler civilizations, and to reconstruct the history of man's social and intellectual development over the million years before writing was invented. From that point on, the historians take over.

The third main group of anthropologists, the one to which I belong, includes those who are especially interested in "gooks." I am here using the slightly depreciative term from World War II to designate the many grubby little peoples who inhabit the world's jungles, tundras, coral atolls, and other out-of-the-way places. They do not count much in international politics, but they make their living and order their lives in many interesting ways. The study of their diverse customs often sheds light on aspects of man's culture history not revealed by bones and potsherds. Even more important, it gives us a broad comparative perspective from which we can judge more objectively the behavior of people in our own complex society.

This ability to stand off and look at our society from the outside, as it were, often leads to new insights. My main purpose here is to indicate how our modern methods of coping with the problems of health and disease look from the broadest possible comparative and historical perspective, and to draw a few tentative conclusions from this examination.

This matter of drawing conclusions is a ticklish business. We anthropologists get so inured to examining objectively all sorts of odd and even nasty customs and discussing them freely among ourselves that we tend to forget that other people are much more sensitive about them. We often make remarks and draw conclusions that seem to us perfectly matter-of-fact and reasonable, but which strike Great Aunt Hepsibah and other decent people as inexpressibly shocking. We have thus come to be regarded in some quarters as the muckrakers of this generation.

I do not think I have anything particularly shocking to say here.

And I have only one very unimportant popular delusion that I want to disabuse you of. You have all heard tell of "the world's oldest profession." Well, the implications of this expression are wholly false. Prostitution, historically, is a relatively recent phenomenon. I have personally read accounts of many hundreds of primitive societies, and in not a single one of them is genuine prostitution reported. Many of them exhibit forms of sex behavior that we would regard as exceedingly lax, but such laxity does not take the specific form of prostitution except in the so-called "higher" civilizations.

The oldest profession is actually the one to which you yourselves belong. Specialized occupations are exceedingly few in the simpler societies, and with a single exception none occurs more than sporadically. This exception is the medical profession. Specialized practitioners of the healing art are found, to the best of my knowledge, in every known society, however primitive. The medicine man, in one form or another, is universal and hence must be regarded as the oldest professional specialist.

Universality is always significant to the anthropologist. Variation and differentiation in culture the world over is the rule, and whenever the anthropologist finds a custom, an activity, or an institution present in all societies from the simplest to the most complex he can only conclude that it is universal because it is genuinely useful or adaptive, so that all peoples have come by trial and error to adopt it. This is the case, for example, with such customs as the prohibition of theft, incest, and murder and with such institutions as marriage, the family, and religion. The medical profession, then, is ancient and universal because it has rendered important and useful services to mankind.

This statement, of course, is hardly likely to be questioned in a group of medical men. It has, however, important implications which I doubt many of you have ever considered. The primitive medicine man is important despite the fact that he never practices medicine in the sense which you accept as axiomatic. He administers no medicines and he performs no operations. His activities are confined almost exclusively to magical rites based on superstitious beliefs for which there is not a shadow of scientific verification. He is a witch doctor, an exorcist, a faith healer, or, if you wish, a quack, but he is in no genuine sense a physician or a surgeon.

I do not mean to imply that primitive peoples are entirely ignorant of rational medicine, for some of them have considerable valid knowledge. Their pharmacopoeias often include genuinely efficacious remedies, quinine being the best known example. And their surgical techniques are sometimes even more advanced. Only a few years ago, for instance, a major new method for the setting and rapid healing of fractured long bones turned out to be the very technique employed by certain Pacific Islanders from time immemorial. I might remark parenthetically that cannibalism offers exceptional opportunities for the learning of anatomy.

It is important to note that these rational skills, so far as they are found among primitive peoples, are not practised by the medicine men. They are known and used, sometimes by a few expert old men or women, sometimes by specialized herbalists or bonesetters, sometimes even by chiefs. One of my own colleagues, for example, while engaged in field work on an isolated island in Fiji, was stricken with a septic sore throat which left him delirious with a temperature in excess of 103°. His frantic wife had given up hope, but the local chief completely cured him overnight by administering a secret herbal decoction whose efficacy was later independently validated.

The medicine men rarely have anything to do with remedies or surgery, or even with massage or obstetrics. They operate almost exclusively with magic—invoking spirit helpers, going into trances, uttering abracadabra, practising ventriloquistic tricks, pretending to suck intrusive objects out of the patient's body, and going through all manner of other rationally quite useless performances. And yet their patients get well. Of this, the anthropological evidence leaves not the slightest doubt.

Magical therapy really works. This is proved by numerous well attested cases, as well as by its universality, which would otherwise be quite inexplicable. As to *how* it works, I do not think there is now very much mystery. The principle involved is that which operates in modern faith healing and in various more respectable forms of psychotherapy. I happen to be personally favorably disposed toward psychoanalysis, but I am quite prepared to admit that this technique still has a good bit in common with primitive magic. The success of both is attributable to the fact that many human ailments are of a so-called "functional" rather than "organic" character; that is to say, they are due to imaginary, psychological, or neurotic causes and not to parasitic microorganisms, malnutrition, or other biological causes. Organic illness, of course, will not respond to any amount of psychological treatment, but when a complaint is imaginary or functional it is likely to disappear if the patient is convinced that he is cured. Modern psychotherapy does this in one way; primitive magical therapy in another. They both have so much in common, as a matter of fact, that it is appropriate to regard the medicine man as the lineal ancestor not of the physician but of the psychiatrist.

If the medicine man with his magical therapy plays an important and genuinely useful social role in recent primitive societies, this must also have been the case during the long prehistoric period which preceded the dawn of civilization. To estimate this properly, we must look at the probable distribution of contagious diseases in prehistoric times.

The great trading and conquering nations of antiquity and the early Middle Ages carried previously localized diseases widely over the Eurasiatic continent. Thus plague, cholera, and other epidemic diseases periodically swept into Europe from Asia. During the great Discoveries Period this dissemination became worldwide. Syphilis, for example, made its first appearance in Europe, and the explorers carried with them the endemic diseases of Europe to the uttermost parts of the earth. Today many of the most serious contagious diseases tend to have a worldwide distribution except as quarantine and other public health measures are able to keep them under control.

Conditions must have been utterly different in prehistoric times. Before the development of extensive trade, travel, and empire building, the peoples and regions of the world were relatively isolated from one another. Diseases could spread only with difficulty and tended to be localized in particular areas where they were endemic.

Under such circumstances a double evolutionary process takes place. Human beings gradually develop a relative immunity through a process of natural selection which eliminates the most susceptible strains in each generation. The disease microorganisms undergo an opposite evolutionary development which favors the less virulent strains; the more lethal strains kill their carriers and thus tend to be eliminated. In time, as a result of this dual process, the endemic diseases of a region become less dangerous to its inhabitants and the latter become less susceptible to the diseases.

Under conditions of relative isolation, then, organic diseases gradually come to constitute less and less of a social problem. As a corollary of this, functional ailments come to assume more and more comparative importance. Only when we comprehend this can we understand why primitive medicine reveals so great an emphasis upon magical psychotherapy and so relatively slight a development of rational or scientific techniques. The reason is simply that the patients who resort to the primitive medicine man are largely victims of functional rather than organic complaints, so that his procedures are adjusted to the actual demand.

The Discoveries Period radically altered these conditions. Explorers, traders, and missionaries carried the endemic diseases of Europe to previously isolated regions, and the diseases of the latter to Europe and other areas. The result was that the number of contagious diseases was multiplied everywhere in the world and that everywhere the newly introduced diseases were extremely serious because of the lack of biologically acquired immunities.

There is no need of reviewing here the familiar historical facts about the introduction of smallpox, tuberculosis, and other Eurasiatic diseases to the American Indians and the Pacific Islanders and the tremendous depopulation which resulted. I would, however, like to call attention to the special case of measles. In Europe this disease has been endemic so long that the white race has acquired through natural selection such a degree of biological immunity that most people regard it as merely an inevitable nuisance of childhood. Physicians realize, of course, that it is more serious than is popularly thought. Nevertheless, it is rarely a direct cause of death amongst ourselves.

When introduced into the Pacific Islands, however, it was the greatest single cause of depopulation in many places. The same has been true in parts of the New World. I personally witnessed an example as late as 1932, when I was studying the Haida Indians of the Queen Charlotte Islands off the coast of British Columbia. The Haida had been protected from measles for a long time by their island isolation and by public health precautions. Three months before my arrival, however, a schoolgirl had been flown home by plane from the mainland with an incubating case of measles. The disease spread like wildfire throughout the native village and by the time of my arrival more than ten per cent of the entire population had died of its direct or indirect effects.

Cases like this, which could be multiplied almost indefinitely, demonstrate both the enormous differences in racial and regional immunity and the disastrous results of European exploration and colonization. The countereffects, of course, were felt in Europe itself. You know better than I how many of the contagious diseases now current in the Western world have been assembled from the far corners of the earth.

The consequence that I wish to impress upon your attention is this: The relative proportion of organic to functional diseases was enormously increased everywhere in the world. In backward areas magical psychotherapy, which had previously been quite well adapted to local needs and conditions, was incapable of coping with the new situation and came to be scorned by medical men as nothing more than savage superstition. In Europe the increasing predominance of organic diseases stimulated the rise of modern scientific medicine. The pendulum swung so far, indeed, that functional ailments were almost completely ignored, or even denied.

I have thus far tried to sketch for you two major epochs in the history of medicine as viewed from the broadest possible anthropological perspective. The first epoch, embracing all of human history to the end of the Middle Ages, was characterized by the relative predominance of functional disease and the emergence of primitive magical psychotherapy. The second epoch, from the beginning of the Discoveries Period to the present, has been characterized by the relative predominance of organic disease and the emergence of modern scientific medicine.

I now venture to suggest that we are standing today at the threshold of a third major epoch. Scientific medicine and the public health movement have now advanced so far toward the control of organic disease, as witness the amazing increase in life expectancy, that the imbalance of the second epoch has been largely corrected. The relative importance of functional disease—of neuroses and psychoses—is being increasingly brought to our attention and begins to present the principal challenge to scientific medicine. The development of psychiatry during the present century represents a response to this challenge. And this development promises to go very much farther.

There are many ways in which anthropology can contribute to the public health movement. It can, for example, advise as to how to adapt health programs to the culture and social structure of local communities so that they may be made more effective. It can render particular service in introducing sound health measures in economically or socially backward countries. And so on.

It has seemed to me, however, that one of the greatest potential contributions of anthropology is to make those who are professionally concerned with health problems aware of the broad sweep of culture history and of their position in it. If our anthropological perspective is correct, we may expect an increasing measure of concern in the future with health problems centering upon functional or psychosomatic illness. Forward-looking physicians and public health experts will wish to prepare in advance against predictable eventualities.

I am, of course, aware that there is already a flourishing mental hygiene movement in the United States. It would seem to me unfortunate, however, if it were to develop in isolation from the older public health movement. Health is a single indivisible social problem, albeit with many special aspects, and a joint cooperative attack offers the best prospects for success. History and anthropology seem to suggest that mental health deserves a more integral place in the public health movement of the future than it has occupied in the past.

THE NATURE OF CULTURE

II

5

This, my first published paper, appeared in the *American Anthropologist* (34: 200-215, 1932). It was written at a time when my graduate training, which was largely in sociology, was being fructified by extensive reading in anthropology and by my earliest personal contacts with such men as Wissler and Sapir. I had just become a member of the new Department of Anthropology at Yale University and had reached the decision to make anthropology my primary field of specialization. The paper presents rather clearly the theoretical orientation with which I began my professional career—a position subsequently modified somewhat, especially through personal associations with colleagues in psychology and anthropology at Yale.

The Science of Culture

SOCIAL anthropology and sociology are not two distinct sciences. They form together but a single discipline, or at the most two approaches to the same subject matter—the cultural behavior of man. This identity has been all too frequently overlooked—by the general sociologists in their mad pursuit of the alluring mirages of social philosophy, methodology, and utopianism, and by the anthropologists in their eagerness to unearth before it is too late the facts of ethnography from which alone a general science of culture can be developed. If the anthropologists in many cases have failed to see the forest for the trees, the majority of the sociologists have yet to learn that such a thing as a tree exists. Nevertheless, the leaders in the various branches of these two allied fields, working independently, have succeeded in accumulating a respectable body of general conclusions based on inductive research. It is no longer admissible to spin out new theories of society and culture from the cozy depths of an armchair. We must start from the facts, of which an imposing mass has been assembled, and from the existing body of conclusions derived from the facts and verifiable by them. When this is done, and the deductions of armchair theorists are treated with the neglect they deserve, the apparent inconsistencies in the results of the reliable investigators in the several fields seem to fade away, and the broad outlines of an actual science of culture stand revealed.

That culture, a uniquely human phenomenon independent of the laws of biology and psychology, constitutes the proper subject of the social sciences, is a proposition accepted with practical unanimity by social anthropologists today. A large and increasing proportion of sociologists hold substantially the same position, and agree with Willey (p. 208) that "the study of culture—the processes of its origin and its growth, its spread and its perpetuation—constitutes the study of sociology." As regards the exact definition of culture, however, and its precise relation to the data of the biological sciences, certain vagueness still prevails. Even the brilliant analysis of Kroeber (1917) has left the concept hanging in a rather mystical though splendid isolation. Recent studies in various fields, however, have shed new light on the subject, and there seems to be no longer any basis for the criticism that the concept of culture is baseless or "supernatural." The differences in interpretation that exist are more apparent than real. They are for the most part differences in emphasis only, resulting from the fact that some authorities have stressed one factor and others another. It is the thesis of this paper that the various approaches are, actually, not contradictory, but supplementary; that their adherents err, not in what they assert, but in what they deny; that, in short, a true conception of culture will flow, not from the rejection of divergent points of view, but from their acceptance and reconciliation. After all, culture is a complex subject, and oversimple, particularistic explanations have gone out of fashion in the social sciences. It is here maintained, then, not that the students of culture should unite on some new concept, but that they are already in substantial harmony and need only to recognize that an adequate picture of culture emerges from a mere synthesis of their conclusions.

There is, in the first place, universal agreement—if we except the extreme racialists, eugenists, and instinctivists—that cultural behavior is socially rather than biologically determined; that it is acquired, not innate; habitual in character rather than instinctive. Culture rests, in short, not on man's specific germinal inheritance, but on his capacity to form habits under the influences of his social environment: "Instinct and the capacity to form habits, while related functions, are present in any animal in inverse ratio" (Watson: 254). Habitual behavior, being more susceptible to modification as the result of experience, possesses a certain "survival value" which has led to selection in its favor during the course of organic evolution. Hence, in general, as we rise in the organic scale the proportion of specific instinctive reactions declines while adaptive behavior becomes correspondingly more prominent (Briffault 1:45). The higher the animal, the fewer its instincts and the greater its ability to profit by experience. Man stands in this respect at the head of the animal world; he is the habit-forming creature par excellence: "If we neglect the vegetative . . . and the direct life conserving functions, such as attack and defense, there are few complete and perfect instincts in man yet observed" (Watson: 254). Briffault (1: 96-110), following Fiske, has sought to explain the adaptability of man's behavior, its comparative freedom from fixation by heredity, by the immaturity of the human child at birth and the prolongation of infancy; the network of association fibers in the brain, he maintains, is organized under the influence of environmental factors before heredity, as it were, can complete its work. Be this as it may, however, no doubt exists of man's supreme habit-forming capacity and of its basic role in culture. The endeavor, fashionable among psychologists not long ago, to interpret cultural phenomena as the manifestations of an equipment of assorted instincts, is now completely outmoded, its coup de grâce having been dealt by Bernard (1924). Man's habit-forming capacity, of course, has an instinctive or hereditary basis.

The individual comes into the world equipped with a vast number of unorganized responses, which he gradually organizes into habits as the result of experience. It is through this "conditioning process" that cultural activities, like all other habits, are acquired. As Tozzer (p. 56) points out: "from the point of view of human culture we can eliminate everything but those characteristics of man which he learns from his fellow man."

The student of culture by no means denies the existence or importance of heredity. He accepts fully, and cordially welcomes, the immense strides being made by the science of genetics. He neither asserts nor denies that the laws of heredity, well established for anatomical and physiological traits, apply also to mental traits. This question, he believes, it is the province of psychology to decide. But he does deny that the laws of heredity can contribute to his understanding of cultural phenomena—phenomena which are in no respect hereditary but are characteristically and without exception acquired. The student of culture assumes heredity as a starting point, as a mere condition perhaps comparable to the geographic environment, and that is all.

Heredity merely underlies culture. It gives man the unorganized responses which are organized through the conditioning process into habits. It also furnishes him with the mechanism—the sensory, nervous, and motor apparatus—through which all behavior, acquired as well as instinctive, individual as well as social, finds expression. And finally, it probably provides him with certain basic impulses which urge him toward behavior that will satisfy them. The nature and number of these impulses, indeed their very existence, still need to be established by careful objective research. Nevertheless, the student of culture is probably justified in assuming them on the strength of their almost universal acceptance, although it is not his province to weigh the respective merits of the "wishes" of Thomas, the "dispositions" of Williams, the "drives" of Woodworth, the "socializing forces" of Sumner, the "residues" of Pareto, and the countless similar concepts of other writers. He assumes them, but he recognizes that neither they nor any of the

other contributions of heredity determine or explain cultural phenomena. At best they merely direct human activities into certain
main channels. Thus a sex impulse drives men to seek sexual
gratification, and presumably underlies the marriage relation, while
other impulses may similarly lie at the root of language, economic
organization, religion, etc. The complexes of habit patterns which,
in human society, surround the various impulses and their satisfaction are known as "institutions," which Allport (1927: 168) correctly regards as clusters of "similar and reciprocal responses of a
large number of individuals" rather than as entities in themselves
capable of acting upon and controlling individuals. The institutions of economic organization, marriage, religion, etc., which
recur in all civilizations because they presumably have their roots in
hereditary impulses or drives, constitute in their ensemble what
Wissler (1923: 73-97) has aptly termed the "universal culture
pattern."

It is of the utmost importance to note, however, that although
heredity probably establishes the broad outlines of the universal
culture pattern, it in no way determines the content of the latter.
Heredity may enable man to speak, but it does not prescribe the
particular language he shall employ. It may drive him to some
form of sexual association, but the impulse may find adequate
satisfaction in a wide variety of polygynous, polyandrous, and
monogamous relationships. In short, culture owes to heredity only
the number and general character of its institutions, not their form
or content. Here, where environmental influences alone are at
work, almost infinite diversity prevails. If we compare human
behavior to a fabric in which heredity furnishes the warp and habit
forms the woof, the warp remains everywhere much the same, for
the student of culture is forced to recognize the essential "equality
and identity of all human races and strains as carriers of civilization" (Kroeber 1915: 285). The woof, however, varies with the
number and variety of cultural influences. Since the warp remains
comparatively constant, cultural diversities are due solely to diversities in the woof. To continue the figure, in the lower animals,

whose behavior consists in the main of instinctive responses, the woof of habit is so thin and scanty that it scarcely ever conceals the strands of the warp. To this is due the unfortunate but natural tendency of biological scientists, familiar with the overwhelmingly important role of heredity in animal behavior and cognizant of man's animal ancestry, to assume that human behavior is necessarily similarly determined and to seek explanations of cultural phenomena in terms of race or instincts or other organic factors. They overlook the fundamental fact that, in man, habits, especially those of cultural origin, overlie the hereditary warp so thickly that it is extremely difficult to perceive the latter at all, as is evidenced by the endlessly conflicting attempts to reconstruct man's "original nature." The students of culture, on the other hand, agree that explanations in terms of heredity are inadmissible, and that an adequate analysis of culture must start with a recognition of the unique role of habit in human behavior.

Habit alone, however, is far from explaining culture. Many cultureless animals possess a considerable habit-forming capacity, and some of the mammals are in this respect not radically inferior to man. Social scientists agree, therefore, that culture depends on life in societies as well as on habit. Individual habits die with their owners, but it is a characteristic of culture that it persists though its individual bearers are mortal. Culture consists of habits, to be sure, but they differ from individual habits by the fact that they are shared or possessed in common by the various members of a society, thus acquiring a certain independence and a measure of immortality. Habits of the cultural order have been called "group habits" (Smith 1930: 82; Kroeber 1928: 330). To the average man they are known as "customs," and anthropologists sometimes speak of the "science of custom" (see Benedict 1929).

The process of custom forming [as Chapin: 178, correctly states] is similar to that of habit forming, and the same psychological laws are involved. When activities dictated by habit are performed by a large number of individuals in company and simultaneously, the individual habit is converted into mass phenomenon or custom.

To the anthropologist, group habits or customs are commonly known as "culture traits," defined by Willey (p. 207) as "basically, habits carried in the individual nervous systems." The sociologists, on the other hand, almost universally speak of them as "folkways" (see Sumner 1906). General agreement prevails, therefore, that the constituent elements of culture, the proper data of the science of culture, are group habits. Only the terms employed are at variance.

Of the several terms, "folkway" possesses certain manifest advantages. "Custom" lacks precision. Moreover, though it represents adequately enough such explicit group habits as words, forms of salutation, and burial practices, it scarcely suffices for implicit common responses, mental habits, or ideas, such as religious and magical concepts, which are equally a part of culture. The term "culture trait," though it covers both of these types of group behavior, is also used to include material objects or artifacts, which are not group habits, indeed not habits at all but facts of a totally different order. Artifacts are not themselves primary data of culture, as is shown by the recognized distinction between their dissemination by trade and the process of cultural diffusion proper.

Material objects are considered as the outgrowths of habits; the material culture is transmitted, in the long run, in terms of knowledge of how to make material objects [Willey: 207].

"Culture trait" thus suffers from a basic inconsistency which renders its use frequently misleading and conducive to confusion of thought. The inadequacy of the term is tacitly recognized by anthropologists when they point out the danger of considering artifacts apart from their cultural setting.

Articles of everyday use, which might seem identical to the museum worker, may be utilized for vastly different purposes by each of the several tribes which employ them and with entirely different emotional reactions [Herskovits 1926: 241].

The substitution of "folkway" for "culture trait" would obviate all these difficulties. The term has never been employed for artifacts themselves but only for the group habits which surround them—the processes of their manufacture, the styles of decorating them, the methods of using them, the current ideas about them, etc. The folkways, in short, supply the social setting. The acceptance of "folkway" by the science of culture would have the great advantage of reducing the data of the science to a single class of strictly comparable phenomena. These phenomena, moreover, are objective behavioristic facts susceptible of repeated verification—an absolute prerequisite for a scientific study. The attempt in certain quarters to build a sound scientific structure on the quicksand of unverifiable subjective facts, such as "attitudes," has proved singularly sterile. In Boas's (1928: 148) words, "A study of the behavior of man shows that actions are on the whole more stable than thoughts."

What differentiates the folkway from the individual habit is primarily the intervention of society. Nongregarious animals, whatever their habit-forming capacity, could not possibly possess culture. From this it results that culture is superindividual. Individuals, to be sure, are the carriers of culture; a culture has no real existence save as it is embodied as habits in the nervous organization of the individuals who compose the group: "A culture is a system of interrelated and interdependent habit patterns or responses" (Willey: 207). Nevertheless, culture does not depend on individuals. An ordinary habit dies with its possessor, but a group habit lives on in the survivors, and is transmitted from generation to generation. Moreover, the individual is not a free agent with respect to culture. He is born and reared in a certain cultural environment, which impinges upon him at every moment of his life. From earliest childhood his behavior is conditioned by the habits of those about him. He has no choice but to conform to the folkways current in his group. Culture is superindividual, also, in the fact that its constituent folkways have in every case a history of their own, a history of their origin and diffusion which is quite independent of the lives and qualities of individuals. Even in the case of invention—the formation of a new habit which becomes a folkway when adopted by others—the individual is little more than the agent of social and historical forces. The study of parallel inventions (Kroeber 1917: 196-208; Ogburn: 80-102) shows that cultural innovations spring, not full-fledged from the brains of their reputed inventors, but from the cultural background or "cultural base," in each case as a synthesis of many previous inventions (see Gilfillan 1927: 530).

While each step in an invention is made by a specific individual, no step can be taken until necessary antecedents have been established, no matter what the abilities of the inventor. Because the inventor utilizes the transmitted culture and is limited by it, . . . it may be said that invention is superindividual [Willey: 210].

This view does not deny or minimize genius, but simply maintains that it is irrelevant to culture. Even more clearly is the history of folkways superindividual. An innovation may spread or stagnate, have its rise and fall, undergo countless historical fluctuations and vicissitudes. But in any case, once launched into the stream of culture, it is beyond the power of any individual to control. Evolution in the folkways, as Keller (1915) has so overwhelmingly demonstrated, is governed by massive impersonal forces. Hence it is both possible and permissible to study the history of a folkway, or the evolution of culture in general, without reference to individuals or their organic and mental characteristics.

The fact that culture is superindividual lifts it beyond the sphere of psychology. As Lowie (1917: 25-26) has expressed it: "The principles of psychology are as incapable of accounting for the phenomena of culture as is gravitation to account for architectural styles." Psychology deals only with the individual. It can and does study his hereditary traits. It can also study the genesis of an individual habit, or of a group habit in the individual. As social psychology it can concern itself with the responses of the individual to his social and cultural environment. But it is powerless to explain the development of culture. No psychological laws can possibly account for the evolution of the radio, or the diffusion of the use of tobacco, or the spread of the commission form of municipal government. It is a matter of indifference to psychology that two persons, instead of one, possess a given habit, but it is precisely this fact that becomes the starting point of the science of culture.

Cultural phenomena, from their independence of the laws of biology and psychology, may be said to operate in a distinct realm—the "superorganic." The concept of the superorganic, though named by Spencer (1874, 1: 3-15), was first consistently adhered to by Lippert (1886-87), and first clearly formulated and analyzed by Kroeber (1917). According to this concept, the phenomena of nature fall into three great realms: (1) the inorganic, where the chemical and physical sciences study the phenomena of matter and energy; (2) the organic, where the sciences of biology and psychology study living organisms and their organic behavior; and (3) the superorganic, where the social sciences study cultural and historical phenomena. The superorganic, to be sure, rests upon the organic, precisely as the latter rests upon the inorganic. But the science of culture is just as distinct, as to subject matter, laws, and principles, from biology and psychology as the biological sciences are from those of the inorganic realm. This point of view does not deny the fundamental unity of all nature, nor the legitimacy in each realm of utilizing to the utmost the knowledge acquired in the realm immediately below it, nor the possibility or even probability that the superorganic may be ultimately resolvable into the organic, and both into the inorganic. It merely maintains that natural phenomena are divided into three realms of ascending complexity, and that the data of each may be most profitably studied by its own students with their own methods and instrumentalities.

Although it is society which intervenes between, and in large measure distinguishes, the organic from the superorganic, society alone, even in conjunction with habit, is insufficient to explain the existence of culture. As Kroeber (1928: 330) points out: "Something more than gregariousness is needed to produce culture; otherwise cattle would possess it." Society alone does not raise behavior to the superorganic plane, for, although many lower animals live in societies, none of them possesses culture. "In this respect a tremendous gulf separates man and the lower forms of life, the anthropoid apes and social insects not excepted" (Case 1924: xxix). The uniqueness of human culture is revealed by a comparison between man and the social but cultureless insects. A justly famous passage by Kroeber (1917: 177-178) will lose none of its luster by another repetition.

Take a couple of ant eggs of the right sex—unhatched eggs, freshly laid. Blot out every individual and every other egg of the species. Give the pair a little attention as regards warmth, moisture, protection, and food. The whole of ant "society," every one of the abilities, powers, accomplishments, and activities of the species, . . . will be reproduced, and reproduced without diminution, in one generation. But place on a desert island or in a circumvallation two or three hundred human infants of the best stock from the highest class of the most civilized nation; furnish them the necessary incubation and nourishment; leave them in total isolation from their kind; and what shall we have? The civilization from which they were torn? One tenth of it? No, not any fraction; nor a fraction of the civilizational attainments of the rudest savage tribe. Only a pair or a troop of mutes, without arts, knowledge, fire, without order or religion. Civilization would be blotted out within these confines—not disintegrated, not cut to the quick, but obliterated in one sweep. Heredity saves for the ant all that she has, from generation to generation. But heredity does not maintain, and has not maintained, because it cannot maintain, one particle of the civilization which is the one specifically human thing.

The social phenomena of the ants are instinctive rather than acquired, transmitted through the germ plasm rather than through tradition, in short, biologically rather than culturally determined. All analogies drawn by enthusiastic biologists between human and insect or other animal societies, fall to the ground on this point. However striking the similarities may appear, they are never more than superficial.

The oft-cited parallel between human marriage and forms of permanent mating among certain lower animals, especially the birds, furnishes an excellent illustration of this fallacy. When a male and a female bird associate in a seemingly monogamous relationship, they do so because they are impelled by a specific mating instinct. It is an organic rather than a superorganic fact. Man, on the other hand, marries because in the course of his cultural evolution he has developed around his sexual impulse certain conventional taboos and restraints which leave marriage as the proper and socially sanctioned form of sexual association. The only organic fact involved is the sexual impulse or drive; a specific mating instinct is lacking. The impulse urges man only to seek sexual gratification; it does not even predispose him to contract a permanent union; the form of expression it takes is determined by cultural factors alone (Sumner and Keller 3: 1495-98). The almost infinite variety of marriage forms precludes the possibility of a specific mating, much less a monogamous, instinct in man. As Lippert (1931: 69) so aptly phrases it: "The institution of human marriage is not a subject of natural history but of culture history." Nevertheless, the majority of writers on this subject have confused the organic and superorganic, perhaps none so persistently as Westermarck (1: 72) who thus states his major premise: "The marriage of mankind is not an isolated phenomenon, but has its counterpart in many animal species and is probably an inheritance from some pre-human ancestor." From such a premise he can only reach, for all his wealth of data and his serious scholarship, conclusions of the utmost unreliability. Yet many students of culture, with an amazing inconsistency, have accepted uncritically the results of a work which violates their every canon.

The analysis of social phenomena among the lower animals demonstrates that society, however essential, is insufficient in itself to explain culture. This fact needs to be stressed, for the danger is, not that the role of society may be overlooked, but that it may be overemphasized. Indeed, the tendency among sociologists in particular has been to single out society, not as an outstanding factor in culture, but as their very subject of study itself. Thus they commonly define their field, not as the science of culture, but as the "science of society." They ignore the fundamental distinction between the social and the cultural, which Stern (1929) has so clearly pointed out. Allport (1924 and elsewhere), too, though with a different object in mind, has repeatedly attacked what he calls the "group fallacy." Not society, but culture is the distinctively human phenomenon. Those sociologists who have overlooked this fundamental fact have spent their time seeking "social processes" common to ants, cattle, and men alike, and they have found little save abstractions distressingly suggestive of the "conation" and "cognition" which an outmoded psychology once accepted as realities. The sterility of their work, as reflected in the contempt for sociology manifested by scholars in other fields, shows that they have been on the wrong track. As a consequence, the social anthropologists, whose results have encountered anything but a contemptuous reception from historians and others, now find themselves joined by a rapidly increasing school of "cultural sociologists," who realize the proper study of sociology is culture.

If society does not suffice to explain culture, just what is it which, when added to social life, has made possible the development of culture in the human race? Numerous writers have suggested human intelligence as the answer to this question. It has frequently been pointed out that man's typical manner of adapting himself to his environment differs significantly from that of the lower animals. His characteristic mode of adaptation, it is suggested, is mental; that of the animals, physical. The development of one great physical adaptation, the human brain, has rendered unnecessary any further important physical specialization, since it enables man, for example, to invent fur clothing in the Arctic instead of developing a fur coat of his own, or to invent an airplane instead of growing wings. On the basis of this distinction Keller (p. 21) defines culture as the "sum or synthesis of mental adaptations." Biological scientists (e.g., Tilney 1931) go even further in stressing the importance of the human brain and human intelligence. But important as this factor unquestionably is, it by no means suffices to explain culture, and it has probably, like society, been considerably overemphasized. In Kroeber's (1917: 69) opinion "the distinction between animal and man which counts is not that of the physical and mental, which is one of relative degree, but that of the organic and social, which is one of kind." Recent studies (e.g., Köhler: 185-224; Yerkes: 575-576) have clearly demonstrated that the anthropoid apes possess intelligence, "insight," or "ideation," of an order comparable to that of man, inferior only in degree; that both apes and men, for example, solve problems by intelligent behavior as opposed to the mere trial-and-error learning characteristic of the rest of the animal world. Yet, in spite of their intelligence, the apes lack culture.

A realistic view of human culture indicates that the role of intelligence is smaller than many have assumed. It is a truism of psychology and almost a matter of general knowledge that the chief use of the human mind is the invention of reasons or justifications for our beliefs and actions. The science of culture has suffered much in the past from rationalization or wishful thinking, and it should be among the first to minimize the importance of intelligence in human affairs. Comparatively little intelligence is needed to acquire a habit or folkway, none to preserve it: "Most habitual responses occur on a relatively low level of consciousness" (Bernard 1926: 34). Intelligence probably plays a more prominent part in the life of the individual than in that of society. At any rate, practically the only social process in which it demonstrably plays a significant role is invention. Yet apes also invent.

With the ape inventive but cultureless, the question arises whether we have not perhaps hitherto exaggerated the importance of invention in human culture. We are wont to think of it as the creative or productive element in civilization. We tend to view the other processes in culture as essentially those of transmission, preservation, or decay. The idea of progress, which has so powerful a hold on the unconscious as well as the conscious thought of our day, may have led us to overemphasize the rôle of invention. Perhaps the thing which essentially makes culture is precisely those transmissive and preservative elements . . . [Kroeber 1928: 340].

While it would be absurd to deny intelligence any importance in culture, the evidence clearly suggests the need of a search for other factors.

"That which distinguishes man from animals," says Anatole France, "is lying and literature." This aphorism expresses, with a characteristic twist, a widely if not universally recognized truth. The underlying idea, in more prosaic terms, is that man differs from the animals in the possession of language, which undoubtedly goes far to explain his possession of culture as well as his propensity for both forms of storytelling. Kroeber (1923: 106-107) has shown that the lower animals completely lack true language. Their cries, unlike human speech, are instinctive rather than acquired, organic rather than social. They convey to other animals, not objective ideas such as most human words represent, but merely subjective emotional states, such as suffering or sexual excitement. Thus they are comparable only to such words as the "ouch" uttered by a man unexpectedly pricked with a pin.

Since culture is not innate, it must be acquired anew by each individual and transmitted from generation to generation. It is this transmission of folkways which insures the continuity of culture in spite of the impermanence of the individual. The folkways thus transmitted constitute what is called the "social heritage" of the group. But culture is not only continuous; it is also cumulative (see Tozzer: 9). New inventions and acculturations from without are added to the stream of culture in each generation, and in most cases the new does not displace the old. Thus we still retain wine in spite of the later invention of distilled spirits, and both in spite of Prohibition. The stream of culture, the social heritage, thus shows a definite tendency to grow richer and fuller with the passage of time. This does not mean that cultural acquisitions are never lost, but the "lost arts" of antiquity are few by comparison with the arts which have survived alongside newer inventions.

Both the transmission and diffusion of culture require some means of communication. Imitation alone seems insufficient. To be sure, certain songbirds, when reared in the nests of another species, are said to acquire and transmit the songs of their foster parents. But except for such crude germs, nothing resembling a social heritage exists among the lower animals. What gives language its importance in human culture is the fact that it alone, with its derivatives such as writing, seems to provide an adequate means of communication. It alone makes possible the transmission of folkways, the continuity and accumulation of culture, the very existence of a social heritage. Without language, man would be little better off than the animals, as is proved by studies of deaf-mutes and other speechless persons (Briffault 1: 23-40). In a society without language, each individual would have to begin exactly where his parents began; he could possess only individual habits, not group habits; his behavior, in short, would be confined to the organic level.

Many authorities have recognized this fundamental rôle of language in culture.

The cultural life of man as distinguished from the social life of sub-human groups is dependent on articulate language. . . . The most important influence of language on social life is derived through its making possible the accumulation and transmission of culture. Recent studies in sub-human animals, especially of anthropoid apes, reveal the presence of many factors upon which culture depends, learning, inventiveness, memory, even the beginnings of symbolic abstraction. But the absence of an articulate language prevents cultural life in the sense possessed by men [Stern: 267].

If the transmissive and preservative elements in culture are basic, says Kroeber (1928: 341),

then the indispensability of speech to the very existence of culture becomes understandable. It is the communications, perhaps, more than the thing communicated, that count. At any rate the fact that speech, to the best of our knowledge, is as thoroughly wanting among the anthropoids as is culture, tends to confirm this conception.

Four factors, as we have now seen, have been advanced by various writers, and have received wide recognition, as explanations of the fact that man alone of all living creatures possesses culture—namely, habit-forming capacity, social life, intelligence, and language. These factors may be likened to the four legs of a stool, raising human behavior from the floor, the organic level or hereditary basis of all behavior, to the superorganic level, represented by the seat of the stool. No other animal is securely seated on such a four-legged stool. Many live in societies. Some manifest no mean intelligence and habit-forming capacity. None, however, possesses language. Just as no one or two of these factors alone can suffice to explain culture, so no animal can maintain an equilibrium on a stool with but one or two legs. All four legs seem necessary to attain the level of the superorganic, and man alone possesses all.

The case of the anthropoid apes is particularly instructive. They possess three comparatively well-developed legs of the cultural stool, lacking only language. And they appear to hover on the very verge of culture. Köhler (1925) has described the fads which occur with great frequency in groups of chimpanzees. From time to time one of these restless and curious animals makes an invention or discovery, e.g., sucking water through a straw, painting objects with white clay, catching ants on a twig moistened with saliva, teasing chickens by offering bread in one hand and jabbing with a sharp stick held in the other, or climbing rapidly to the top of a pole planted vertically on the ground and jumping off before it falls. The rest of the group then takes up the innovation by imitation, and for days or weeks the new practice rages with all the vigor of a recent fashion among humans, only to disappear after its novelty has worn off. While the fad lasts, it is certainly a group habit, an incipient element of culture. Only the absence of language, apparently, prevents the retention and accumulation of such acquisitions and their transmission to succeeding generations as a social heritage. Chimpanzee fads, in short, differ from human folkways only in their impermanency. Kroeber (1928: 326) would therefore seem to be wrong when he states that they possess no "residuum of unmitigatedly cultural material." Little more than a time element differentiates the chimpanzee use of straws from the modern American folkway observable in soft-drink parlors, or the ape's use of the "jumping stick" from human pole vaulting. The chimpanzee seems to be in the position of a man insecurely perched on a four-legged stool of which one of the legs is wanting. He can preserve a precarious balance only for a short time before the stool overturns and plunges him and his incipient culture once more to the organic floor.

The well-informed reader will find little that is new in the foregoing, little indeed that is not already widely accepted among students of culture. But this is precisely the purpose of the article, namely, to demonstrate that an adequate conception of the nature and basis of culture already exists and needs only to be recognized. The various partial interpretations of culture, stressing some of the basic factors and neglecting or even denying others, turn out upon examination to be not mutually exclusive but complementary. The general recognition of this fact should go far toward clearing the air of dogmatism and laying the foundation for constructive cooperative effort in solving the manifold problems of the science of culture.

6

This paper is an abridgment of an article entitled "The Cross-Cultural Survey" published in the *American Sociological Review* (5: 361-370, 1940). It is included to document the progress in my thinking over the position taken in the previous paper—a change due in large measure to the interdisciplinary stimulation of the Institute of Human Relations.

Fundamental Characteristics
of Culture

CROSS-cultural research rests, at bottom, on the conviction that all human cultures, despite their diversity, have fundamentally a great deal in common, and that these common aspects are susceptible to scientific analysis. Its theoretical orientation may be expressed in a series of seven basic assumptions. These are not claimed to be original, since many of them are shared by all social scientists, and all of them by many.

1. *Culture is learned.* Culture is not instinctive, or innate, or transmitted biologically, but is composed of habits, i.e., learned tendencies to react, acquired by each individual through his own life experience after birth. This assumption, of course, is shared by all anthropologists outside of the totalitarian states, but it has a corollary which is not always so clearly recognized. If culture is learned, it must obey the laws of learning, which the psychologists have by now worked out in considerable detail. The principles of learning are known to be essentially the same, not only for all mankind but

also for most mammalian species. Hence, we should expect all cultures, being learned, to reveal certain uniformities reflecting this universal common factor.

2. *Culture is inculcated.* All animals are capable of learning, but man alone seems able, in any considerable measure, to pass on his acquired habits to his offspring. We can housebreak a dog, teach him tricks, and implant in him other germs of culture, but he will not transmit them to his puppies. They will receive only the biological inheritance of their species, to which they in turn will add habits on the basis of their own experience. The factor of language presumably accounts for man's preeminence in this respect. At any rate, many of the habits learned by human beings are transmitted from parent to child over successive generations, and, through repeated inculcation, acquire that persistency over time, that relative independence of individual bearers, which justifies classifying them collectively as "culture." This assumption, too, is generally accepted by anthropologists, but again there is an underestimated corollary. If culture is inculcated, then all cultures should show certain common effects of the inculcation process. Inculcation involves not only the imparting of techniques and knowledge but also the disciplining of the child's animal impulses to adjust him to social life. That there are regularities in behavior reflecting the ways in which these impulses are thwarted and redirected during the formative years of life, seems clear from the evidence of psychoanalysis, e.g., the apparent universality of intrafamily incest taboos.

3. *Culture is social.* Habits of the cultural order are not only inculcated and thus transmitted over time; they are also social, that is, shared by human beings living in organized aggregates or societies and kept relatively uniform by social pressure. They are, in short, group habits. The habits which the members of a social group share with one another constitute the culture of that group. This assumption is accepted by most anthropologists, but not by all. Lowie (1937: 235-236) for example, insists that "a culture is invariably an artificial unit segregated for purposes of expedience. . . . There is only one natural unit for the

ethnologist—the culture of all humanity at all periods and in all places. . . ." The author finds it quite impossible to accept this statement. To him, the collective or shared habits of a social group—no matter whether it be a family, a village, a class, or a tribe—constitute, not "an artificial unit" but a natural unit—a culture or subculture. To deny this is, in his opinion, to repudiate the most substantial contribution which sociology has made to anthropology. If culture is social, then the fate of a culture depends on the fate of the society which bears it, and all cultures which have survived to be studied should reveal certain similarities because they have all had to provide for societal survival. Among these cultural universals, we can probably list such things as sentiments of group cohesion, mechanisms of social control, organization for defense against hostile neighbors, and provision for the perpetuation of the population.

4. *Culture is ideational.* To a considerable extent, the group habits of which culture consists are conceptualized (or verbalized) as ideal norms or patterns of behavior. There are, of course, exceptions; grammatical rules, for example, though they represent collective linguistic habits and are thus cultural, are only in small part consciously formulated. Nevertheless, as every field ethnographer knows, most people show in marked degree an awareness of their own cultural norms, an ability to differentiate them from purely individual habits, and a facility in conceptualizing and reporting them in detail, including the circumstances where each is considered appropriate and the sanctions to be expected for non-conformity. Within limits, therefore, it is useful to conceive of culture as ideational, and of an element of culture as a traditionally accepted idea,[1] held by the members of a group or subgroup, that a

---

[1] From the point of view of behavioristic psychology, of course, an idea is merely a habit of a special sort, a tendency to react with implicit linguistic or symbolic behavior rather than with overt muscular responses. The underlying mechanisms, e.g., of learning, are similar if not identical. Fundamentally, therefore, our fourth assumption should be subsumed under our first—that culture is learned—as a special case thereof. In view of the importance of symbolic, especially linguistic, behavior in man, however, it has seemed advisable to segregate the ideational point for separate exposition.

particular kind of behavior (overt, verbal, or implicit) should conform to an established precedent. These ideal norms should not be confused with actual behavior. In any particular instance, an individual behaves in response to the state of his organism (his drives) at the moment, and to his perception of the total situation in which he finds himself. In so doing, he naturally tends to follow his established habits, including his culture, but either his impulses or the nature of the circumstances may lead him to deviate therefrom to a greater or lesser degree. Behavior, therefore, does not automatically follow culture, which is only one of its determinants. There are norms of behavior, of course, as well as of culture, but, unlike the latter, they can be established only by statistical means. Confusion often arises between anthropologists and sociologists on this point. The former, until recently, have been primarily preoccupied with ideal norms or patterns, whereas sociologists, belonging to the same society as both their subjects and their audience, assume general familiarity with the culture and commonly report only the statistical norms of actual behavior. A typical community study like *Middletown* and an ethnographic monograph, though often compared, are thus in reality poles apart. To the extent that culture is ideational, we may conclude, all cultures should reveal certain similarities, flowing from the universal laws governing the symbolic mental processes, e.g., the worldwide parallels in the principles of magic.

5. *Culture is gratifying.* Culture always, and necessarily, satisfies basic biological needs and secondary needs derived therefrom. Its elements are tested habitual techniques for gratifying human impulses in man's interaction with the external world of nature and fellow man.[2] This assumption is an inescapable conclusion from modern stimulus-response psychology. Culture consists of habits, and psychology has demonstrated that habits persist only so long as they bring satisfaction. Gratification reinforces habits, strengthens and perpetuates them, while lack of gratification inevi-

---

[2] The only exceptions are partial and temporary ones, with respect to elements of culture in the process of dying out or being supplanted.

tably results in their extinction or disappearance. Elements of culture, therefore, can continue to exist only when they yield to the individuals of a society a margin of satisfaction, a favorable balance of pleasure over pain.[3] Malinowski has been insisting on this point for years, but the majority of anthropologists have either rejected the assumption or have paid it but inadequate lip service. To them, the fact that culture persists has seemed to raise no problem; it has been blithely taken for granted. Psychologists, however, have seen the problem, and have given it a definitive answer, which anthropologists can ignore at their peril. If culture is gratifying, widespread similarities should exist in all cultures, owing to the fact that basic human impulses, which are universally the same, demand similar forms of satisfaction. The "universal culture pattern" propounded by Wissler (1923: 73-79) would seem to rest on this foundation.

6. *Culture is adaptive.* Culture changes; and the process of change appears to be an adaptive one, comparable to evolution in the organic realm but of a different order (see Keller 1915). Cultures tend, through periods of time, to become adjusted to the geographic environment, as the anthropogeographers have shown, although environmental influences are no longer conceived as determinative of cultural development. Cultures also adapt, through borrowing and organization, to the social environment of neighboring peoples. Finally, cultures unquestionably tend to become adjusted to the biological and psychological demands of the human organism. As life conditions change, traditional forms cease to provide a margin of satisfaction and are eliminated; new needs arise or are perceived, and new cultural adjustments are made to them. The assumption that culture is adaptive by no means commits one to an idea of progress, or to a theory of

---

[3] Culture is gratifying, of course, not in an absolute but in a relative sense. To a slave, for example, the submission and drudgery demanded by his status are not actually pleasant; relative, however, to the painful alternative of punishment or death for rebellious behavior, observance of the cultural requirements of his status is gratifying or "reinforcing." Agricultural labor, again, may not be enjoyable in itself, but it is gratifying because it brings rewards, e.g., in food.

evolutionary stages of development, or to a rigid determinism of any sort. On the contrary, one can agree with Opler (1937: 207-208), who has pointed out on the basis of his Apache material, that different cultural forms may represent adjustments to like problems, and similar cultural forms to different problems. It is probable, nevertheless, that a certain proportion of the parallels in different cultures represent independent adjustments to comparable conditions.

The conception of cultural change as an adaptive process seems to many anthropologists inconsistent with, and contradictory to, the conception of cultural change as an historical process. To the author, there seems nothing inconsistent or antagonistic in the two positions—the "functional" and the "historical," as they are commonly labeled. On the contrary, he believes that both are correct, that they supplement one another, and that the best anthropological work emerges when the two are used in conjunction. Culture history is a succession of unique events, in which later events are conditioned by earlier ones. From the point of view of culture, the events which affect later ones in the same historical sequence are often, if not usually, accidental, since they have their origin outside the continuum of culture. They include natural events, like floods and droughts; biological events, like epidemics and deaths; and psychological events, like emotional outbursts and inventive intuitions. Such changes alter a society's life conditions. They create new needs and render old cultural forms unsatisfactory, stimulating trial-and-error behavior and cultural innovations. Perhaps the most significant events, however, are historical contacts with peoples of differing cultures, for men tend first to ransack the cultural resources of their neighbors for solutions to their problems of living, and rely only secondarily upon their own inventive ingenuity. Full recognition of the historical character of culture, and especially of the role of diffusion, is thus a prime prerequisite if a search for cross-cultural generalizations is to have any prospect of success. It is necessary to insist, however, that historical events, like geographic factors, exert only a conditioning rather than a determining influence on the course of culture. Man adjusts to them, and draws selectively upon them to solve his problems and satisfy his needs.

7. *Culture is integrative.* As one product of the adaptive process, the elements of a given culture tend to form a consistent and integrated whole. We use the word "tend" advisedly, for we do not accept the position of certain extreme functionalists that cultures actually are integrated systems, with their several parts in perfect equilibrium. We adhere, rather, to the position of Summer (1906: 5-6) that the folkways are "subject to a strain of consistency with each other," but that actual integration is never achieved for the obvious reason that historical events are constantly exerting a disturbing influence. Integration takes time—there is always what Ogburn (1922: 200) has called a "cultural lag"—and long before one process has been completed, many others have been initiated. In our own culture, for example, the changes wrought in habits of work, recreation, sex, and religion through the introduction of the automobile are probably still incomplete. If culture is integrative, then correspondences or correlations between similar traits should repeatedly occur in unrelated cultures. Lowie (1920), for example, has pointed out a number of such correlations.

If the seven fundamental assumptions outlined above, or even any considerable proportion of them, are valid, then it must necessarily follow that human cultures in general, despite their historical diversity, will exhibit certain regularities or recurrences which are susceptible to scientific analysis, and which, under such analysis, should yield a body of scientific generalizations. A primary objective of cross-cultural research is to formulate and test generalizations of this sort.

7

This paper was originally published as a chapter in *The Science of Man in the World Crisis*, edited by Ralph Linton (New York, 1945, pp. 123–142). At the time it was written I was a reserve naval officer on active service, temporarily stationed at the School of Military Government at Columbia University. Here began a close personal and professional association with Ralph Linton, which continued after the war when he moved to Yale University and endured until his death in 1953. I found this relationship as stimulating as it was congenial and gratefully acknowledge its influence on my own later development.

The Common Denominator
of Cultures

MOST of anthropological theory has revolved about the interpretation of the similarities and differences between the various cultures of mankind. Cultural differences, perhaps because they are more immediately obvious, have received especially close attention. They have been variously explained in terms of distinct stages of postulated evolutionary series, of allegedly disparate racial endowments, of diverse geographic or economic conditions, of nonrepetitive historical accidents, of endlessly varying social contexts, of unique configurations of like or unlike elements, of divergent personality characteristics created by differential childhood training, and so on. Cross-cultural similarities have received theoretical consideration, in the main, only when they have been confined to a limited number of particular cultures, in other words, when they could be regarded as exceptions in a universe of cultural diversity. Such instances of similarity have been explained in terms of the transplantation of culture through migration, of cultural diffusion through contact and borrowing, of parallel development from similar cultural backgrounds, of convergent development from unlike backgrounds, of the independent burgeoning of hereditary potentialities, or of the allegedly determining influence of like geographical factors. In comparison, universal similarities in culture, the respects in which all known cultures resemble each other, have received relatively little theoretical treatment. It is this subject—the common denominator of cultures—with which the present paper will be exclusively concerned.

Early reports of peoples lacking language or fire, morals or religion, marriage or government, have been proved erroneous in every instance. Nevertheless, even today it is not generally recognized how numerous and diverse are the elements common to all known cultures. The following is a partial list of items, arranged in alphabetical order to emphasize their variety, which occur, so far as the author's knowledge goes, in every culture known to history or ethnography: age-grading, athletic sports, bodily adornment, calendar, cleanliness training, community organization, cooking, cooperative labor, cosmology, courtship, dancing, decorative art, divination, division of labor, dream interpretation, education, eschatology, ethics, ethnobotany, etiquette, faith healing, family, feasting, fire making, folklore, food taboos, funeral rites, games, gestures, gift giving, government, greetings, hair styles, hospitality, housing, hygiene, incest taboos, inheritance rules, joking, kingroups, kinship nomenclature, language, law, luck superstitions, magic, marriage, mealtimes, medicine, modesty concerning natural functions, mourning, music, mythology, numerals, obstetrics, penal sanctions, personal names, population policy, postnatal care, pregnancy usages, property rights, propitiation of supernatural beings, puberty customs, religious ritual, residence rules, sexual restrictions, soul concepts, status differentiation, surgery, tool making, trade, visiting, weaning, and weather control.

Cross-cultural similarities appear even more far-reaching when individual items in such a list are subjected to further analysis. For example, not only does every culture have a language, but all languages are resolvable into identical kinds of components, such as phonemes or conventional sound units, words or meaningful combinations of phonemes, grammar or standard rules for combining words into sentences. Similarly funeral rites always include expressions of grief, a means of disposing of the corpse, rituals designed to protect the participants from supernatural harm, and the like. When thus analyzed in detail, the resemblances between all cultures are found to be exceedingly numerous.

Rarely if ever, however, do these universal similarities represent identities in specific cultural content. The actual components of any culture are elements of behavior—motor, verbal, or implicit—which are habitual, in the appropriate context, either to all the members of a social group or to those who occupy particular statuses within it. Each such component, whether called a folkway or a cultural trait or item, can be described with precision in terms of the responses of the behaving individuals and of the stimulus situations in which the responses are evoked. Eating rice with chopsticks, tipping the hat to a woman, scalping a slain enemy, and attributing colic to the evil eye are random examples. Any such specifically defined unit of customary behavior may be found in a particular society or in a number of societies which have had sufficient contact to permit acculturative modifications in behavior. It is highly doubtful, however, whether any specific element of behavior has ever attained genuinely universal distribution.

The true universals of culture, then, are not indentities in habit, in definable behavior. They are similarities in classification, not in content. They represent categories of historically and behaviorally diverse elements which nevertheless have so much in common that competent observers feel compelled to classify them together. There can be no question, for example, that the actual behavior exhibited in acquiring a spouse, teaching a child, or treating a sick person differs enormously from society to society. Few would hesitate, however, to group such divergent acts under the unifying categories of marriage, education, and medicine. All of the genuinely widespread or universal resemblances between cultures resolve themselves upon analysis into a series of such generally recognized categories. What cultures are found to have in common is a uniform system of classification, not a fund of identical elements. Despite immense diversity in behavioristic detail, all cultures are constructed according to a single fundamental plan—the "universal culture pattern" as Wissler has so aptly termed it.

The essential unanimity with which the universal culture pattern is accepted by competent authorities, irrespective of theoretical divergences on other issues, suggests that it is not a mere artifact of classificatory ingenuity but rests upon some substantial foundation. This basis cannot be sought in history, or geography, or race, or any other factor limited in time or space, since the universal pattern links all known cultures, simple and complex, ancient and modern. It can only be sought, therefore, in the fundamental biological and psychological nature of man and in the universal conditions of human existence.

The fact that all cultures conform in structure to a single basic plan was already recognized by anthropologists of the nineteenth century. Morgan, Spencer, and Tylor not only established the broad outlines of the universal culture pattern but also filled in many of the details. No adequate understanding of the phenomenon was available, however, until a reasonably satisfactory integration of sociological and psychological theory with anthropological science was at last achieved during the third and fourth decades of the twentieth century.

Most attempts to explain the universal culture pattern have started with the "psychic unity of mankind"—with the assumption, now firmly grounded in social science, that all peoples now living or of whom we possess substantial historical records, irrespective of differences in geography and physique, are essentially alike in their basic psychological equipment and mechanism, and that the cultural differences between them reflect only the differential responses of essentially similar organisms to unlike stimuli or conditions. In its broader aspects this position is probably not open to serious challenge. However, the great majority of theorists have sought the unifying factor in a single facet of man's fundamentally similar psychology, namely, in the common impulse factors in behavior. All cultures are said to resemble one another because men everywhere are driven to action by an identical set of inborn impulses which direct their behavior along parallel lines.

Until some two decades ago these common impulses were widely regarded as instincts. The success and prestige of the biological sciences since Darwin's day led many, if not most, social scientists to equate human behavior with that of the lower animals and to explain social institutions as the expression of a series of universal instincts. Marriage was equated with animal mating, housebuilding with nesting behavior, government with the rule of the herd by the strongest male. The marked parallels between the social behavior of ants, bees, wasps, and termites and the cultural behavior of man appeared especially convincing. However, the progress of science began to show increasingly the importance of learning and habit, even among the lower animals, and anthropological research, in particular, demonstrated beyond possibility of rebuttal that human behavior shows infinite variation from society to society and perpetual change in any one society as it exists through time, instead of the identity and persistency demanded by an instinct theory. It became abundantly clear that the invariable association of a particular series of responses with a specific stimulus, which always characterizes an instinct, is not only not the rule in man's social behavior but is actually so rare as to be practically undiscoverable. Culture is in no respect instinctive; it is exclusively learned. Since the publication of Bernard's *Instinct* in 1924, it has been impossible to accept any theory of instincts as an explanation of the universal culture pattern, or indeed as a solution to any cultural problem.

As instinct theories lost scientific respectability, strenuous efforts at salvage were made. Admitting the importance of the habit-forming mechanism and recognizing that different forms of behavior may be associated, through learning, with an identical stimulus, many authorities clung to the impulse factor in instinct and com-piled various lists of "drives," "wishes," "needs," "dispositions," or "prepotent reflexes" which were asserted to underlie cultural be-havior in much the same way as instincts had previously been invoked. The principal distinction lay in the divorce of impulses from invariable behavioral expressions and in the recognition that different and even diverse forms of behavior may be evoked by the same impulse in consequence of learning under differential condi-tions. It was maintained nevertheless that the impulses, being fundamentally physiological in nature, could be allayed only by behavior which relieved the conditions which gave rise to them, so that various responses to the same impulse, however else they might differ, would resemble each other in this vital respect. Responses to the hunger drive, for example, must have the ingesting of food in common.

Many attempts have been made to interpret the universal culture pattern along these lines, explaining cross-cultural similarities in the basic plan, structure, or organization of cultures in terms of a series of fundamental drives or impulses. Among the best known are the division of all social institutions, by Sumner and Keller, into those of self-maintenance, self-perpetuation, self-gratification, and reli-gion on the basis of the four "socializing forces" of hunger, love, vanity, and fear, and the somewhat more complex functional analy-sis of institutions, by Malinowski, in terms of the satisfaction of certain basic "needs." Comparable but on the whole less satisfac-tory efforts are legion.

It is not the purpose of this paper to discredit such interpreta-tions. On the contrary, the author believes them to be suggestive and, within limits, sound. Modern psychology and physiology have established the existence of a number of basic impulses—those of ingestion (hunger, thirst, inhalation), of excretion (urination, defe-cation, exhalation, sexual emission, lactation), and of avoidance (pain, heat, cold). To these must certainly be added anger or aggression, induced by frustration of the expression of other drives, and anxiety or fear, induced apparently by situations resembling those in which pain or deprivation have been experienced. There can be little question but that these impulses or drives represent a common factor in the experience of all human beings, that they are aroused from time to time in all individuals of all societies, that the kinds of behavior that will allay them are universally limited by the fundamental biological and psychological nature of man, and that they consequently operate to channelize cultural as well as individual behavior. They certainly serve as a partial explanation of the universal culture pattern. There are, however, substantial grounds for believing that they do not provide a complete explanation.

In the first place, the impulses or drives that have been scientifically established do not account for all parts of the universal pattern in an equally satisfactory manner. It seems reasonably safe to attribute the food quest to the hunger drive, shelter to heat and cold avoidance, war to aggression, and marriage to the sex impulse. To what recognized impulses, however, can we assign such equally universal cultural phenomena as the arts and crafts, family organization, and religion? Defenders of the interpretation in question are prone to invent hypothetical impulses to meet such cases, postulating, for example, an instinct of workmanship, a parental drive, or a religious thrill. Such inventions, however, find no shred of support in physiological or psychological science. On the contrary, a fully satisfactory alternative explanation of the underlying motivations is available in the psychological theory of acquired or derived drives.

It is common knowledge that only a small proportion of men's actions in any society spring directly from any of the demonstrable basic drives. In most human behavior the motivation is exceedingly complex and derivative. Even in the case of eating, the widespread prevalence of food preferences and taboos reveals the importance of acquired appetites as contrasted with the inborn drive of hunger. We eat what we like, at hours to which we are habituated, in surroundings which we enjoy. Daily in our habitual eating behavior we satisfy appetitive cravings, but rarely in adult life are we driven by actual hunger pangs. In obeying the dictates of an acquired appetite we incidentally satisfy, of course, the hunger drive, and thereby reinforce the appetite, but the actual incentive is the derived and not the basic impulse.

What is true of eating is even more characteristic of other forms of behavior. Many of our sexual responses, for example, are also appetitive in character; acquired drives impel us to seek the company of persons of opposite sex on the basis of age, appearance and garb, social congeniality, and other factors irrelevant to physical sex, and to engage in conversation, dancing, and divers other activities short of copulation. In still other aspects of social behavior—for example, in religious ritual and the fine arts—the factor of basic-drive reduction shrinks to relative insignificance by comparison with derivative motivations, and may even become impossible to identify. In the case of those elements of the universal culture pattern which cannot readily be attributed, at least in part, to some recognized basic drive, it seems more scientific to ascribe them to derived or acquired drives, which naturally vary from society to society, than to invent hypothetical new drives for which no factual evidence can be advanced.

A second substantial reason for rejecting the impulse factor in behavior as the sole explanation of the universal culture pattern is the fact that most social institutions or culture complexes actually give satisfaction to several basic impulses as well as to a variety of derived drives. To attribute marriage to sex alone, for example, is greatly to oversimplify a complex social phenomenon. As Lippert was the first to point out clearly, the economic factor in marriage is at least as important as the sex factor. The latter can really account only for copulation; it is the conjunction of the former that produces an enduring marital association. The relation of the hunger drive to marriage is seen, for example, in the division of labor by sex, which characterizes marital unions in all societies and, in most of them, demonstrably increases, diversifies, and stabilizes the food supply available to each spouse. Even our own society, which emphasizes the sex factor in marriage to an exceptional degree, has enshrined the hunger factor in a proverb about the most direct way to a man's heart. Marriage gives expression to still another basic impulse in various forms of relief from anxiety—for example, escape from the social disapproval commonly encountered by celibates, economic security gained through union with a wealthy spouse or a good provider, and the personal solace achievable in an intimate relationship.

Similarly, war is motivated not alone by aggression but often in large measure by fear, by the desire for feminine approbation (derivative in part from the sex impulse), and by greed for gain (in which the hunger drive may be significantly involved). Religious behavior is often rooted in anxiety—in fear of the unknown and unpredictable, in dread of what the future may bring, or in a sense of personal inadequacy. In addition, it frequently has a strong erotic component, as psychiatrists have pointed out; or it expresses aggression, as in sorcery or religious intolerance; or it reflects the need for food or material comforts, as in magic or prayer. Analysis of almost any other large segment of cultural behavior would reveal a similar conjunction of diverse motives. This interlacing of basic drives, which is, of course, rendered infinitely more complex by the intervention of acquired motivations, makes it exceedingly difficult to segregate cultural phenomena according to their impulse components.

It must be conceded, therefore, that the analysis of collective behavior from the point of view of underlying motives, although suggestive, does not yield a fully satisfactory explanation of the universal culture pattern. Its principal defect seems to lie in the fact that it does not take into account the complete psychological mechanism involved in habitual behavior. Derived as it is from earlier instinct theory, it considers exclusively the impulse factor in behavior and ignores all else. When other aspects of the mechanism of habit formation and perpetuation are taken into account, a more adequate interpretation of the universal culture pattern emerges.

Fundamentally, all behavior is designed to mediate between two types of situations in which organisms find themselves, namely, those in which impulses are aroused and those in which they are satisfied. An organism encountering a situation of the first type is stimulated to activity; encountering a situation of the second type, it experiences a reduction in drive, and its activity ceases or is replaced by behavior in response to other stimulation. Once initiated by a drive, behavior in response thereto continues until satisfaction has been achieved, or a stronger drive intervenes to impel behavior in another direction, or unsuccessful responses have brought exhaustion and fatigue. In the last case, the drive-impelled behavior will recommence after an interval, and continue to appear until satisfaction is achieved or, if success is essential to life, until the organism dies.

Living organisms have evolved two distinctive means of adapting their behavior so as to transform situations evoking drives into those bringing about their reduction. The first, shared by all forms of life, is instinct, a precise organization of behavior developed through natural selection and transmitted through heredity. An instinct enables an organism to respond automatically to a drive-arousing situation by specific forms of behavior which have been established by the evolutionary process because they normally result in drive reduction. In cases where this does not happen, however, the individual organism is helpless; it is incapable of producing alternative forms of behavior. This defect is corrected by the second mechanism, that of habit formation, which is well developed in all the higher forms of life, including man. Through this mechanism, an individual can meet a drive-evoking situation for which the species has evolved no suitable instinctive response, by varying his behavior and by acquiring as a habit any new response which happens to lead to reduction of the drive. It is this second psychological mechanism upon which all cultural behavior depends.

Now it is significant that, in the process of establishing and maintaining habits, the crucial factor is not the source of the behavior in impulse or stimulus but its effect in drive reduction. It is the latter which fixes, reinforces, or perpetuates the responses that have occurred. Whenever a drive is reduced, the probability of the recurrence of the same behavior in a similar situation is increased. Mere repetition of the stimulation, in the absence of drive reduction, does not strengthen the ensuing behavior. On the contrary, it leads to its extinction and to the appearance of random responses of other kinds, that is, to trial-and-error behavior.

Whenever behavior results in the allaying of a drive, even though by sheerest accident, its effect is to connect that behavior not only with the impulse which produced it but with all the stimuli concurrently impinging upon the organism. With repetition, not only of the behavior but of its drive-reducing effect, certain of the concurrent stimuli, singly or in combination, gain the power to evoke the now habitual responses even though the original impulse is not present. Such stimuli which have gained the force of drives are essentially what is meant by "acquired drives." They are the product of learning as much as are the responses they evoke. It is in this way, for example, that the appetite for food can be aroused, in the absence of perceptible hunger, by the sight, the odor, or even the verbal description of a juicy steak.

The fact that the crucial factor in habitual behavior is its effect rather than its origin suggests that an explanation of widespread cultural similarities might more profitably be sought in an examination of cultural forms from the point of view of their relation to drive reduction or reward than in an analysis of their impulse components. The interplay of different motives in the same behavior and the problem of differentiating acquired from basic drives offer no obstacles to this type of interpretation. If a particular kind of behavior regularly results in drive reduction, any or every motive which may evoke it will be reinforced, and complex and derivative motivations are to be expected.

Since cultural behavior is always habitual in character, and since habits are maintained only so long as they bring rewards, every established element of culture is necessarily accompanied and supported by impulse satisfaction. The insistence of the "functionalists" in anthropology on this point has the full backing of psychological science. When traditional forms of behavior cease to gratify impulses, random responses supervene and cultural change is in the making. The present paper is not concerned, however, with cultural change. It takes cognizance only of cultural forms which are firmly entrenched and of widespread occurrence, and which consequently are regularly bulwarked by rewards.

Cultural behavior may be related to rewards in various ways. In some instances it leads directly and almost exclusively to the reduction of a basic drive. Thus the food quest leads directly to hunger satisfaction, the use of fire and clothing in northern latitudes to cold avoidance, and various sex practices to sexual gratification. The behavior must conform to conditions set by human physiology and psychology for the reduction of the drive in question, and the variant customs of different societies have in common the fact that they all meet these conditions. They can be regarded as alternative solutions to identical problems posed by original human nature. If this were the only relation of cultural behavior to rewards, analysis in terms of underlying impulse factors would provide an adequate explanation of the universal culture pattern.

Many cultural habits, however, instead of gratifying basic drives directly, serve only to facilitate their eventual satisfaction. Cultures contain an immense number of so-called "instrumental responses" which of themselves reduce no basic drives but merely pave the way for other acts which have rewarding results. Instrumental acts acquire in time, of course, the support of learned or derived drives, but they are seldom innately rewarding in themselves. Making a spear or a pot, for instance, gratifies no basic impulse, although at some future time the result may serve to lessen the interval or the expended effort between the onset of the hunger drive and its reduction. The reciprocal habits embodied in social and economic organization represent another outstanding example of instrumental behavior. Through interpersonal relationships and organization, individuals are enabled to use other individuals as instruments to facilitate eventual impulse gratification in much the same way as technology enables them to use artifacts.

Instrumental responses do not become established because they themselves bring gratification but because of a particular characteristic of the learning mechanism. Any response which reduces the elapsed time or the expended effort intervening between drive and reward is reinforced and strengthened, and thus tends to be repeated under similar conditions until it becomes fixed as a habit. Such responses become as readily associated with attendant external stimuli as with whatever drives are operative, and in this way they tend to become supported by derivative rather than primary motivations. Since acquired drives can differ widely from society to society, it is unsafe to attribute cross-cultural similarities in instrumental responses to identical basic impulses. Resemblances are more likely to be due to the particular characteristics of the instrument, whether artifact or social arrangement, or to similarities in the conditions under which reward occurs.

A like situation prevails with respect to a third and very large category of cultural habits, namely, those in which behavior is followed by rewards that bear no relation, or only an incidental one, to the impulses prompting the behavior. A gambling spell may be followed by a lucky fall of the dice, or rainmaking magic by a providential thunderstorm, and thus become entrenched as a habit. Neither action, however, either produced the rewarding situation or facilitated it in instrumental fashion. Such cultural responses can survive frequently nonsuccess because of the psychological fact that a habit is commonly strengthened by a single successful exercise more than it is weakened by several failures.

Another example is seen in instances where behavior motivated by one drive results in the gratification of other drives not actually involved in the particular response. A superstitious fear of blood may motivate a tribe to isolate its women after childbirth, but this action may incidentally achieve the fortunate results of assuring postparturient mothers of a needed rest period and of preventing the spread of puerperal fever or other infections, and these may be at least as rewarding as the effect in relieving anxiety. Similarly, even though marriage may often be prompted in large measure by the sex drive, the matrimonial relationship brings other rewards—food, physical comforts, and security—without which, as we have seen, the institution would be difficult to explain.

All cultures, moreover, exhibit numerous adaptive responses which are not directly supported by primary impulse satisfactions. Some authors have attributed these to "social needs," which are defined as depending not upon drives but upon requirements which must be met if groups of individuals and the cultures they bear are to survive in competition with other societies bearing other cultures. One example is the so-called need of education. A culture cannot persist unless it is transmitted from generation to generation, and a society cannot survive without culture, which embodies in the form of collective habits the successful experience of past generations in meeting the problems of living. Hence every society is said to be characterized by the need of educating its young. Unlike reproduction, which is assured in large measure by the sex impulse, education is supported by no primary drive. The immense effort which must be expended by parents and teachers over so many years to inculcate in the young the full cultural equipment of adults is not in itself rewarding but must be bulwarked with auxiliary rewards.

Similarly every society is said to have a "need" for government—for a political organization sufficiently developed to provide for effective common action against potential enemies, to maintain internal order against dangerous interferences with the routine of social living, and to furnish necessary social services not achievable in other ways. Public service is not self-rewarding. Men cannot be depended upon to devote themselves to the common weal through altruism alone. Every society consequently surrounds the holders of political positions with prerogatives and dignities.

The concept of social needs, though useful as a first approximation, is a loose and not wholly satisfactory solution of the scientific problem presented by the universality of certain social institutions or culture complexes which are not directly maintained by specific primary impulse gratifications. It seems preferable to state rather that they have their origin in the ordinary processes of cultural change and their support in the gratification of complex and derivative impulses. Under the pressure of frustration and nonsuccess, behavior is altered. Certain responses, either random in their origin or borrowed from contiguous societies which appear to have achieved greater success, are tried out. If they chance to be followed by rewards of any sort, or even by a lesser degree of discomfort than attends alternative responses, they tend to be repeated and to become established as habits. The situations under which they arise acquire increasing power to evoke them. Learned or derivative impulses develop in support of them, and primary impulses which chance to be satisfied incidentally are pressed into their service, until they become amply fortified with auxiliary rewards.

In the case of education, acquired drives such as pride, prestige, identification, and parental love spring to the support of instruction. The primary drives of pain and anxiety are mobilized in the form of social sanctions for nonconformity. The children themselves, as they become socialized and acquire skills, reciprocate with materially rewarding behavior in ever increasing measure, and in many societies become actual economic assets at an early age. In divers ways an adjustment is evolved whereby the effort expended in education is balanced by a complex system of commensurate rewards.

In the case of government, through a similar process of adaptive cultural change, chiefs are induced to assume war leadership, maintain public order, and perform other social services by according them deference, the right to exact tribute, the privilege of polygyny, or other rewards. Feudal lords receive rents and services, municipal officials enrich themselves by graft, legislators secure jobs for their relatives or special favors for themselves and their business associates, and so on. Actually, of course, the power and pelf of political office are usually sufficiently great to attract a plethora of applicants, and the social problem is more commonly that of keeping exploitation within moderate limits—by revolution or "voting the rascals out"—rather than that of finding somebody who will assume the responsibilities. Only the naïve expect good government at no cost.

The process by which adaptive behavior that is not obviously expressive of basic drives or rewarded by their gratification becomes established in human cultures has been likened by some authors to the process of organic evolution in biology. Human societies enter into competition, it is alleged, as do subcultural organisms, and as they succeed or fail in the competition for life their customs are perpetuated or eliminated. The chances of success are enhanced to the extent that the customs are adaptive, irrespective of whether or not they are rationally devised. Within the same society, moreover, alternative customs—old and new, native and borrowed—compete with one another, as it were, and over time the fitter tend to survive. There is thus operative in cultures, it is asserted, a selective process analogous to natural selection on the biological plane by which adaptations in culture are brought into being and perpetuated.

This theory has been received with scant respect by American anthropologists, who have dismissed it as an unwarranted analogy from biology. In the opinion of the present writer the dismissal was not wholly justified. Despite certain deficiencies, the theory represented a distinct advance over the crude invention-diffusion hypothesis inherited by the critics via Boas from the French sociologist, Tarde. Its real defect is not its derivation from biological science, for a scientist may legitimately seek his hypotheses anywhere, and it in no way confuses the cultural and the organic. Nor is it necessarily invalidated by the epistemological criticism of circular reasoning, namely, that adaptation and survival are defined in terms of each other. Its principal fault appears to be that it attempts to explain too much.

It is difficult to escape the conclusion that cultural change depends upon conflict and survival in certain extreme instances. Thus Carthaginian culture certainly disappeared and Roman culture spread as a consequence of the extirpation of the Carthaginians in the Punic Wars. Since the Discoveries Period, moreover, native cultures have been exterminated with their bearers in various parts of America and Oceania, and replaced by European civilization. It is also probable that cultures have occasionally disappeared from the stage of history in consequence of maladaptive practices pursued until the entire society became extinct, much as numerous animal species have failed to survive because they were unable to produce adaptive mutations when needed.

On the other hand, the obliteration of a culture through the elimination of the entire society that bears it is by no means the rule in human history. If defeat in war or depopulation from maladaptive practices leaves any survivors, cultural change comes about through another and far less drastic mechanism. Prompted by discomfort and frustration, the survivors try out innovations in behavior, invented or borrowed, and through successful trial and error arrive at new cultural adjustments. They may end up, to be sure, with a culture much like that of their more successful neighbors. However, this result has not been produced by a pseudobiological process of selective elimination and replacement of culture bearers, but through the ordinary psychological process of learning, undergone on a mass scale. All normal cultural change proceeds in precisely the same manner. The usual adaptive mechanism in human history, then, is neither that of biological evolution nor yet one that is unique to man. Instead of a new phenomenon in nature, that of social or cultural evolution, there is simply the age-old phenomenon of habit formation, operating under the distinctive conditions of human society and culture.

The essentially psychological character of the processes and products of culture change suggests that we look into the principles of learning for an interpretation of the universal culture pattern. One factor, that of basic drive or impulse, has already been isolated and found helpful, though not sufficient in itself to provide a complete explanation. A second factor is that of stimulus or cue. Any recurrent element or pattern of elements in the situations in which particular responses occur and are rewarded may acquire the power to evoke those responses, even in the absence of the original impulse. Any prominent stimuli that are of worldwide occurrence might thus be expected to be associated with cultural responses in numerous societies. Among the stimuli of this type are night and day, the heavenly bodies, widespread meteorological and geographical phenomena, certain animals and plants, and the features of human anatomy and physiology. As a matter of fact, nearly all peoples have cultural beliefs about, and cultural responses to, such phenomena as the sun and moon, darkness, rain, thunder, the ocean, mountains, streams, blood, hair, the heart, the genitals, sneezing, breathing, menstruation, childbirth, sickness, and death. Although these cultural forms need have nothing in common save their stimuli, the principle of limited possibilities and the psychological factor of generalization, not to mention cultural diffusion, often result in striking similarities among different populations. In any event, widely occurring natural stimuli provide a useful auxiliary basis for classifying and interpreting cultural universals.

A third important factor in learning is that of prior habit. Since preexisting habits greatly affect behavior in a learning situation, experimenters in animal learning always use naïve subjects, that is, those as free as possible from unknown prior habits that might predetermine their behavior. It is perhaps for this reason that the psychologists themselves have been so uniformly unsuccessful in their attempts to interpret cultural behavior, for no adult human being in any society ever enters naïvely into a situation of cultural learning—on the contrary, men carry into every learning situation a battery of cultural habits in comparison with which the prior conditioning of the most maze-wise experimental rat appears infinitesimal.

From the point of view of the universal culture pattern, prior habit becomes important especially in connection with the psychological factor of generalization, by which is meant the tendency of any learned response to be repeated under similar conditions of drive and stimulus. In consequence of generalization, a response

adapted to one situation will tend to reappear in another in proportion to the elements of similarity between the two. Cultures provide
innumerable examples. Supernatural beings are regularly anthro-
pomorphized and dealt with in ways that have proved successful in
human relations—by supplication (prayer), gift (sacrifice), aggression (exorcism), flattery (laudation), self-abasement (asceti-
cism), or etiquette (ritual). Political organization commonly
follows the model of the family, with which it has an authoritarian
element in common. Departed spirits are often assimilated to the
breath, which also leaves the body in death. Menstrual and lunar
phenomena are frequently equated because of their similar period-
icity. Numerous indeed are the cross-cultural similarities which
result from generalization.

A final important factor in learning is that of limitation in the
range of potential responses. In any learning situation the number
of possible responses an organism can make is always limited. No
animal can respond with an act for which it is not physically
adapted. A man cannot jump or fly to the top of a tree to gather its
fruits; his responses are limited to such acts as climbing, cutting
down the tree, or employing a pole or a missile. Prior habits or
their lack sharply limit the range of possible behavior. Familiar
situations tend to evoke familiar responses and inhibit novel ones,
and complex responses, like speaking a new language or making an
important invention, are impossible until a whole series of prerequisite habits have been acquired. Limitations are also set by the
structure of the situation in which behavior occurs. Under identical conditions of drive, reward, and prior conditioning, an experimental rat will behave differently in two mazes of different shape,
and a human being in two differing social situations. The limiting
conditions of geographical environment have often been pointed
out: a Samoan cannot build an igloo or an Eskimo prepare kava.

The most important of limitations on the possibilities of response
are probably those set by the nature of man himself and of the
world in which he lives, as these are known to science. Technological activities must conform to the physical and chemical properties

of the materials with which men work. There are relatively few ways, for example, in which fire can be generated or a pot constructed. Customs in hunting and animal husbandry must conform not only to the physical but also to the biological and behavioral characteristics of the animals concerned. Human physiology and psychology set limits to the ways in which disease can be cured or a child brought into the world. Habit and custom must be observed in social relations. Successful responses—and all established cultural responses are successful, that is, normally rewarded—must cope with all the conditions under which they take place. These conditions introduce into culture the principle of limited possibilities, which is of extreme importance in determining the universal culture pattern.

Where the limitations on potential responses are slight, the variation in detail between unrelated cultures may be immense, even though traits be fundamentally related through a common drive, stimulus, or other universal factor. Thus, though every society has a language with a vocabulary, the words for any universal phenomenon, such as water, walk, or woman, may be and are formed by an almost infinite variety of phonetic combinations among the different peoples of the earth. Folktales, taboos, and ceremonials reveal a similar variety in detail. In nearly all such cases, specific similarities are reasonably attributable to an historical connection.

In other instances the limitations are greater and the possible responses can be exhausted in a short list. Every society affiliates a child with a group of relatives through a rule of descent. Only three alternatives are known, namely, patrilineal, matrilineal, or bilateral descent, and every culture incorporates one of these rules or some combination thereof, such as optional, alternating, or double descent. Again all societies have to deal with the corpses of the dead, and face therein a limitation in practicable possibilities. Among these the most prominent are abandonment of the place of death, feeding the corpse to carnivorous animals or birds, inhumation, rock burial, water disposition, tree or scaffold burial, cremation, mummification, and embalming. In such cases it is to be expected that different and even historically unconnected peoples will frequently chance upon the identical solution to the same problem.

The extreme situation is encountered in those instances where the number of practicable or satisfying responses is limited to one. When this happens, cultural uniformities are not of pattern or structure only but of content as well. Disparities in actual behavior become minimal. Perhaps the most striking example is seen in family organization.

Complex family forms, such as polygynous and extended families, are variable, but all known societies have the same fundamental form, the nuclear family of father, mother, and children. This may stand alone, as in our own society; it may be complicated in particular cases by the inclusion of other relatives; or it may exist as a distinguishable unit within a more complex social grouping. Extended families, for example, normally consist of a number of nuclear families united by a common line of descent, and polygynous families typically include several nuclear families in which the same man plays the role of father in each. In contrast to many lower animals, the father is always a member of the human family—presumably because education is one of the family's universal functions and only a man is capable of training a male child in masculine cultural skills.

In all societies the nuclear family is established by marriage, and the relationship between its adult members is characterized by a division of labor according to sex. Sexual intercourse is always permitted between father and mother, but invariably prohibited as incestuous between father and daughter, mother and son, brother and sister. Seeming exceptions, such as dynastic incest, pertain only to small groups of peculiar status, never to an entire society. The nuclear family is always an economic unit, and it is universally charged with the functions of child rearing, socialization, and early education. The family may gather to itself other functions in particular societies, but throughout history and ethnography it is invariably the focus of the sexual, economic, reproductive, and educational relationships indicated above. This coincidence of behavior is truly remarkable in view of the diversity of responses in other departments of culture.

The explanation is not far to seek. The sex drive accounts for cohabitation, and indirectly for reproduction. Its satisfaction tends to give at least some permanence to sexual association, during which the advantages inherent in a division of labor have an opportunity to manifest themselves. Primary sex differences channelize economic pursuits, and economic rewards fortify the sexual association. Children make their appearance in this context, and are bound to the mother through lactation. Their care and training are more naturally assigned to the mother and her sexual and economic partner than to anyone else. In so far as derivative motivations are required to support the parents in these tasks, they will be supplied in the manner previously outlined.

At no point in this development are the initial responses so difficult as to lie outside the range of probable occurrence in any society. Factors of drive, stimulus, and circumstances sharply limit alternative possibilities. Finally, the particular constellation of relationships provides individuals with such powerful rewards and solves at once so many problems of vital importance to society that, once made, the responses are certain to be fixed and perpetuated. Man has never discovered an adequate substitute for the family, and all Utopian attempts at its abolition have spectacularly failed.

The only universal characteristics of the family that have proved difficult to explain are its associated incest taboos. Freudian psychology offers the most hopeful lead, but the problem is too complex for consideration here. It is of interest to note, however, that Freud chose this particular cultural universal, the family, as the keystone of his entire theoretical system. Reversing the usual scientific practice of making psychology an underlying discipline in relation to the social sciences, Freud founded his psychology on a cultural fact, though he used the terminology of instinct. Whereas behaviorists look primarily to the inherited mechanism of learning for the interpretation of behavior, Freudians look to the conditions of learning, and in particular to the structure of family relationships under which the earliest human learning occurs in all societies. Both approaches are presumably sound, and the psychology of the future will doubtless result from their amalgamation.

An attempt to present a complete analysis of the universal culture pattern, with a full consideration of the factors underlying each category, would far exceed the limits of the present paper. The author's primary purpose has been to indicate the general lines along which such an analysis might be undertaken and to present a few illustrative examples. The principal conclusion has been that the common denominator of cultures is to be sought in factors governing the acquisition of all habitual behavior, including that which is socially shared. Among these the most important are those which bear directly upon the incidence of reward. To the extent that these conclusions prove valid, one brick will have been added to the scientific edifice of the future, in which anthropological and psychological theory will be united in a broader science of human behavior.

DYNAMICS OF CULTURAL CHANGE

III

8

This paper was originally published as a chapter in *Man, Culture, and Society,* edited by Harry L. Shapiro (New York, 1956, pp. 247-260). I have long been interested in, and have frequently taught courses on, the dynamics of cultural change, but my views have largely been derived from the work of others rather than from intensive personal research.

How Culture Changes

IT is a fundamental characteristic of culture that, despite its essentially conservative nature, it does change over time and from place to place. Herein it differs strikingly from the social behavior of animals other than man. Among ants, for example, colonies of the same species differ little in behavior from one another and even, so far as we can judge from specimens embedded in amber, from their ancestors of fifty million years ago. In less than one million years man, by contrast, has advanced from the rawest savagery to civilization and has proliferated at least three thousand distinctive cultures.

The processes by which culture changes are by now reasonably well known to science. They cannot be understood, however, without a clear comprehension of the nature of culture, and this must be summarized here even at the risk of some repetition.

Culture is the product of learning, rather than of heredity. The

113

cultures of the world are systems of collective habits. The differences observable among them are the cumulative product of mass learning under diverse geographic and social conditions. Race and other biological factors influence culture only in so far as they affect the conditions under which learning occurs, as when the presence of people of markedly different physique operates as a factor in the development of race prejudice.

Culture is learned through precisely the same mechanism as that involved in all habit formation. Hunger, sex, fear, and other basic drives, as well as acquired motivations, impel human beings to act. Actions encounter either success or failure. With failure, especially when accompanied by pain or punishment, an action tends to be replaced by other behavior, and its probability of recurring under similar conditions is diminished. Success, on the other hand, increases the tendency of responses to occur when the same drive is again aroused in a like situation. With repeated success, responses are established as habits, and are progressively adapted to the situations in which they are appropriate.

A culture consists of habits that are shared by members of a society, whether this be a primitive tribe or a civilized nation. The sharing may be general throughout the society, as is normally the case with language habits. Often it is limited to particular categories of people within the society. Thus persons of the same sex or age group, members of the same social class, association, or occupational group, and persons interacting with others in similar relationships commonly resemble one another in their social habits, though diverging behaviorally from persons in other categories.

The social sharing of habits has several causes. The fact that the situations under which behavior is acquired are similar for many individuals conduces in itself to parallel learning. Even more important is the fact that each generation inculcates in the next, through education, the cultural habits which it has found satisfying and adaptive. Finally, the members of any society exercise pressure upon one another, through formal and informal means of social control, to conform to standards of behavior which are considered right and appropriate. This is particularly true of behavior in interpersonal relationships, where the success or failure of an action depends upon the reaction of another person to it, rather than, for example, upon its adaptiveness to the innate qualities of natural objects. Once one has acquired a limited number of stereotyped patterns of social behavior one is equipped to cope successfully with widely diversified social situations, and is provided with a body of reliable expectations regarding the probable responses of others to one's own behavior. This gives confidence and spares the individual an immense amount of individualized learning, which is ever a painful process. It is with good reason, therefore, that every society lays great stress on social conformity.

The habits that are variously shared within a society, and which constitute its culture, fall into two major classes, namely, habits of action and habits of thought. These may be termed, respectively, "customs" and "collective ideas." Customs include such readily observable modes of behavior as etiquette, ceremonial, and the techniques of manipulating material objects. Collective ideas are not directly observable but must be inferred from their expression in language and other overt behavior. They include such things as practical knowledge, religious beliefs, and social values. Moreover, they embrace a mass of rules or definitions, which specify for each custom the persons who may and may not observe it, the circumstances in which it is and is not appropriate, and the limits and permissible variations of the behavior itself. Collective ideas also include a body of social expectations—anticipations of how others will respond to one's own behavior, especially of the sanctions, i.e., social rewards and punishments that can be expected from conformity and deviation. With every custom and with every organized cluster of customs, such as "culture complex" or "institution," there is ordinarily associated a mass of collective ideas.

Actual social behavior, as it is observed in real life, must be carefully distinguished from culture, which consists of habits or tendencies to act and not of actions themselves. Though largely determined by habits, actual behavior is also affected by the physiological and emotional state of the individual, the intensity of his drives, and the particular external circumstances. Since no two situations are ever exactly alike, actual behavior fluctuates considerably, even when springing from the same habit. A description of a culture is consequently never an account of actual social behavior but a reconstruction of the collective habits which underlie it.

From the point of view of cultural change, however, actual or observable behavior is of primary importance. Whenever social behavior persistently deviates from established cultural habits in any direction, it results in modifications first in social expectations, and then in customs, beliefs, and rules. Gradually, in this way, collective habits are altered and the culture comes to accord better with the new norms of actual behavior.

Changes in social behavior, and hence in culture, normally have their origin in some significant alteration in the life conditions of a society. Any event which changes the situations under which collective behavior occurs, so that habitual actions are discouraged and new responses are favored, may lead to cultural innovations. Among the classes of events that are known to be especially influential in producing cultural change are increases or decreases in population, changes in the geographical environment, migrations into new environments, contacts with peoples of differing culture, natural and social catastrophes such as floods, crop failures, epidemics, wars, and economic depressions, accidental discoveries, and even such biographical events as the death or rise to power of a strong political leader.

The events which produce cultural change by altering the conditions under which social behavior proves adaptive, i.e., is or is not rewarded, are invariably historical, i.e., specific with respect to time and place. Events occurring at different places and times may resemble one another, however, and exert parallel influences upon different cultures. It is thus possible to view changes in culture either in relation to their spatial and temporal setting or in relation to comparable events wherever and whenever they have occurred. The former or "historical" approach answers such questions as what? when? and where? The latter or "scientific" approach, by illuminating the processes by which change occurs, answers the question how? Both approaches are valid and completely complementary.

Historical anthropologists commonly discuss particular traits of culture, such as the use of tobacco, the wheel, the domesticated horse, the alphabet, or money, treating of their "invention" at specific times and places and of their "diffusion" from the points of origin to other parts of the world. Since our problem is to describe *how* culture changes, we must abandon the bird's-eye view of the historian and examine the processes within societies by which all changes, and not merely particular ones, take place. These processes may be conveniently grouped under the terms "innovation," "social acceptance," "selective elimination," and "integration."

Cultural change begins with the process of INNOVATION, the formation of a new habit by a single individual which is subsequently accepted or learned by other members of his society. An innovation originates through the ordinary psychological mechanism of learning, and differs from purely individual habits only in the fact that it comes to be socially shared. It is nevertheless useful to distinguish several important variants of the process.

An innovation may be called a *variation* when it represents a slight modification of preexisting habitual behavior under the pressure of gradually changing circumstances. The slow evolution in the forms of manufactured objects over time usually represents an accumulation of variations. In the same manner, tattooing can be extended over a wider area of the body, additional barbs may be added to a harpoon, skirts may be lengthened or shortened, folk tales may grow by accretion, or ceremonial may become increasingly elaborate and formalized. Variation occurs in all cultures at all times. The individual increments of changes are often so slight as to be almost imperceptible, but their cumulative effect over long periods may be immense.

When innovation involves the transfer of elements of habitual behavior from one situational context to another, or their combination into new syntheses, it is called *invention*. At least some degree of creativeness is always present. Most of the important techno-logical innovations are of this type. Thus the invention of the airplane involved the synthesis of such elements as the wings of a glider, an internal-combustion engine from an automobile, and an adaptation of a ship's propeller. Though less well known, inven-tions are equally common in the nonmaterial aspects of culture. The city-manager plan, for example, represents an obvious transfer of techniques of business management to the sphere of local gov-ernment, and most forms of religious worship are modeled on behavior toward persons of high social status, e.g., sacrifice upon bribery, prayer upon petitions, laudation upon flattery, ritual upon etiquette.

Since invention always involves a new synthesis of old habits, it is dependent upon the existing content of the culture. A synthesis cannot occur if the elements which it combines are not present in the culture. It is for this reason that parallel inventions so rarely occur among unconnected peoples of differing culture. With the exception of such simple and obvious combinations as the hafting of tools, anthropologists know of only a handful of genuine inven-tions that have been arrived at independently by historically unre-lated peoples. Among them perhaps the most famous are the fire piston, invented by the Malays and a French physicist, and the dome, developed by the ancient Romans from the arch and inde-pendently invented by the Eskimos for their snow igloos.

Among peoples of the same or related cultures, on the other hand, parallel inventions are extraordinarily common. The culture provides the same constituent elements to many people, and if one person does not achieve the synthesis others are likely to do so. The Patent Office furnishes thousands of examples. In one famous instance, the telephone, applications for a patent were received on the same day from two independent inventors, Bell and Gray. An-other noted case is the independent formulation of the theory of natural selection by Darwin and Wallace. So common is this phenomenon that scientists often live in dread of the anticipation of their discoveries by rivals. Parallel invention thus appears to be frequent and almost inevitable among peoples of similar culture, though so rare as to be almost nonexistent among peoples of different culture.

A third type of innovation may be called *tentation*. Unlike the previous types, which merely modify or recombine elements of habit already in existence, tentation may give rise to elements that show little or no continuity with the past. The mechanism by which these are acquired is that which psychologists call "trial-and-error learning." Tentation may occur in any situation in which established habits prove ineffective and individuals are so strongly motivated that they try out other modes of behavior in a search for an adequate solution to their problems. They will ordinarily try out first a number of variations and recombinations of existing habitual responses, but if all of these fail they will resort to "random behavior," in the course of which they may accidentally hit upon some novel response which solves the problem and thereby becomes established as a new cultural element.

Crises are particularly conductive to tentation. In a famine, for instance, people try out all sorts of things that they have never eaten before, and if some of them prove nutritious and tasty they may be added to the normal diet. An epidemic similarly leads to a search for new medicines, and both primitive and civilized peoples have discovered useful remedies in this way. War also leads to improvisation, as do economic crises. The New Deal in the recent history of the United States, for example, reveals numerous instances of tentation. Scientific experimentation, it should be pointed out, is often a form of controlled tentation, as when a new series of chemical compounds are systematically put to test. The saying that "necessity is the mother of invention" applies more forcefully to tentation than to invention proper.

When accidental discoveries lead to cultural innovations, the process is commonly that of tentation. The origin of the boomerang in aboriginal Australia will serve as an example. Over much of that continent the natives used curved throwing sticks to kill or stun small animals, and in a limited part of the area the true boomerang was used for this purpose. Almost certainly the first boomerang was produced by sheer accident in the attempt to fashion an ordinary throwing stick. Observing the unique behavior of the particular stick in flight, the maker and his fellows doubtless attempted to duplicate it. They must have resorted to tentation, or trial-and-error behavior, until they eventually succeeded, and thereby established boomerang manufacture as a habit. The history of modern "inventions" is full of such instances, the discovery of the photographic plate by Daguerre being one of the most familiar examples.

Tentation also accounts for a type of cultural parallel which is distinct from genuine independent invention. There are certain universal problems which every people must solve and for which there are a limited number of easy and obvious solutions, so that peoples in different parts of the world have often hit upon the same solution quite independently. Rules of descent provide a good illustration. In all societies, each individual must be affiliated with a group of relatives to whom he regards himself as most closely akin and to whom he can turn for aid in time of need. There are only three possibilities: patrilineal descent, which relates an individual to kinsmen in the male line; matrilineal descent, which affiliates him with relatives through females; and bilateral descent, which associates him with a group of his closest relatives irrespective of their line of descent. Every society must choose one of these alternatives or some combination thereof, and, since the possibilities are limited to three, many peoples have, of necessity, arrived independently at the same cultural solution. Funeral customs present another example, since there are only a limited number of feasible ways of disposing of a dead body. In all such instances, if a society is compelled for any reason to abandon its previous custom it will inevitably, through tentation, arrive at an alternative solution which other peoples have independently adopted.

The fourth and last type of innovation is *cultural borrowing,* which is what the historical anthropologist, with his bird's-eye view, calls "diffusion." In this case the innovator is not the originator of a new habit, but its introducer. The habit has previously been part of the culture of another society; the innovator is merely the first member of his social group to adopt it. From the point of view of psychology, cultural borrowing is merely a special case of the learning process known as "imitation." The innovator, faced with a situation in which the shared habits of his own society are not fully satisfactory, copies behavior which he had observed in members of another society, instead of resorting to variation, invention, or tentation to solve his problem.

Of all forms of innovation, cultural borrowing is by far the most common and important. The overwhelming majority of the elements in any culture are the result of borrowing. Modern American culture provides a good illustration, as can be shown by a few random examples. Our language comes from England, our alphabet from the Phoenicians, our numerical system from India, and paper and printing from China. Our family organization and system of real property derive from medieval Europe. Our religion is a composite of elements largely assembled from the ancient Hebrews, Egyptians, Babylonians, and Persians. Metal coinage comes from Lydia, paper money from China, checks from Persia. Our system of banking, credit, loans, discounts, mortgages, etc., is derived in its essentials from ancient Babylonia, with modern elaborations from Italy and England. Our architecture is still largely Greek, Gothic, Georgian, etc. Our favorite flavors in ice creams, vanilla and chocolate, are both borrowed from the Aztecs of Mexico and were unknown to Europeans before the conquest by Cortez. Tea comes from China, coffee from Ethiopia, tobacco from the American Indians. Our domesticated animals and plants, virtually without exception, are borrowed. If the reader were to make a list of absolutely everything he eats during the next week, analysis would probably show that one-third are products that were already cultivated in Neolithic times and that at least two-thirds were being raised at the time of Christ, and it would be surprising if the list contained any item that was not cultivated for food somewhere in the world when Columbus sailed for America.

Our own culture is not unique in this respect, for it is doubtful whether there is a single culture known to history or anthropology that has not owed at least 90 per cent of its constituent elements to cultural borrowing. The reason is not far to seek. Any habit that has become established in a culture has been tried out by many people and found satisfactory. When a society finds itself in a dilemma, therefore, the chances that an element already present in the culture of another people will turn out to be an adequate solution to its own problem are vastly greater than those of any random and untested innovation of another type. Cultural borrowing is thus highly economical, and most peoples tend to ransack the cultural resources of their neighbors for adaptive practices before they resort to invention or tentation.

Cultural borrowing depends upon contact. Obviously the opportunity for borrowing is lacking in the case of a completely isolated society. Other factors being equal, the extent to which one culture will borrow from another is proportionate to the intensity and duration of the social intercourse between their bearers. Contact need not always be face-to-face, however, for there are numerous instances of cultural borrowing at a distance through the medium of written language or through copying of articles received by trade. By and large, however, societies borrow mainly from their immediate neighbors, with the result that the products of diffusion are ordinarily clustered in geographically contiguous areas.

Trade, missionary enterprise, and political conquest create conditions conducive to cultural borrowing. Peculiarly important, however, is intermarriage, for this brings individuals of differing culture together within the family, where children can learn from both parents. Diffusion then proceeds through the socialization process, which produces far more perfect copying than does cultural borrowing on the adult level. The American "melting pot" operates largely through this mechanism. Primitive peoples practicing local exogamy, i.e., requiring individuals to obtain spouses from another village or band, commonly reveal considerable cultural uniformity over wide areas, as in aboriginal Australia and among the Indians of the Northwest Coast. By contrast, in areas like Melanesia and Central California where marriage normally takes place within the community, even villages a few miles apart may differ strikingly in dialect and customs. In the one case, culture is diffused through the same process by which it is transmitted; in the other, even adult contacts tend to be restricted to a minimum.

Incentive—a need or drive—is an essential in cultural borrowing as in other types of innovation. A people rarely borrows an alien cultural element when they already possess a trait which satisfactorily fills the same need. Thus the blubber lamp of the Eskimos was not borrowed by the Indians to the south, who had plenty of wood for fires to heat and light their dwellings. On the other hand, the extraordinarily rapid diffusion of tobacco over the earth after the discovery of America reflected the general absence of competing traits. It has been observed that the first individuals in a society to borrow alien customs are likely to be the discontented, underprivileged, and maladjusted. Thus in India Christian missionaries have made many more converts among the "untouchables" than in the higher strata of society, and in our own country fascism and communism attract an unduly high proportion of unsuccessful and neurotic people.

The presence in a receiving society of some of the habit elements involved in a new trait greatly facilitates borrowing. It is for this reason that diffusion occurs most readily among peoples of similar culture, who already share many elements of habit. Thus Englishmen and Americans borrow more frequently and easily from each other than from Russians, Chinese, or Hottentots. Conversely, aboriginal peoples are greatly handicapped in taking over the complex technology of modern civilization. They cannot, for example, begin to manufacture the steel products which they want without also taking over such things as blast furnaces and rolling mills.

Cultural borrowing will occur if the new habit is demonstrably rewarding. The native quickly adopts steel knives and axes from the white man because their superiority to his former stone implements becomes immediately apparent. On the other hand, Europeans were slow to borrow paper manufacture from the Chinese because the advantages of paper over parchment appeared very slight at first. The Chinese and Japanese have not yet adopted the alphabet from western civilization because, however great its ultimate advantages, it would impose heavy burdens and discomforts upon all literate persons during the necessary period of readjustment. Geographic and climatic factors may prevent diffusion by withholding or reducing the possibilities of reward, and social prejudices such as ingrained conservatism may counterbalance potential advantages by inflicting disapprobation upon innovators.

Borrowing need not be exact. Oftentimes, indeed, all that is borrowed is the external "form" of a custom and not its "meaning," i.e., the collective ideas associated with it. The familiar caricature of the cannibal chief wearing a silk hat provides a good illustration. Frequently an imperfect copy is quite adequate. Thus when the Plains Indians took over horses and riding equipment from the Spaniards they omitted the horseshoe, which was quite unnecessary on the prairie. Sometimes changes are imposed by the conditions of the geographical environment. When the Iroquois Indians adopted the birchbark canoe from their Algonkian neighbors, for example, they altered the material to elm bark because of the scarcity of birch trees in their habitat. Frequently cultural factors favor a modification. The original Phoenician alphabet lacked characters for vowels, the nature of their language being such that consonant signs sufficed for the identification of words. Since this was not true of the Greek language, when the Greeks borrowed the Phoenician alphabet they converted characters for which they had no need into symbols for vowels.

Modifications are so common in cultural borrowing that authorities like Malinowski have regarded the process as scarcely less creative than other forms of innovation. Often, indeed, it is inextricably blended with invention or tentation. This is well illustrated in instances of "stimulus diffusion," in which only the general idea of an alien cultural trait is borrowed, the specific form being supplied by improvisation. Thus a famous Cherokee chief named

Sequoyah, though an illiterate man, had noticed that white men could somehow understand messages from pieces of paper on which peculiar marks were inscribed, and he came to the conclusion that this would be a useful skill for his own people to acquire. He therefore set himself the task of devising a system of marks by which the Cherokee language could be written. Inventing some signs of his own and copying some from pieces of printed matter—numbers and punctuation marks as well as letters, upside down or on their sides as often as upright—he produced a novel form of writing, a syllabary rather than an alphabet, which his tribesmen learned and still use.

The second major process in cultural change is SOCIAL ACCEPTANCE. So long as an innovation, whether original or borrowed, is practiced by the innovator alone in his society, it is an individual habit and not an element of culture. To become the latter it must be accepted by others; it must be socially shared. Social acceptance begins with the adoption of a new habit by a small number of individuals. From this point it may spread until it becomes part of the subculture of a family, clan, local community, or other subgroup, or until it becomes a "specialty" characteristic of persons belonging to a particular occupational, kinship, age-graded, or other status category, or until it becomes an "alternative" widely but optionally practiced. Eventually it may even become a "universal," shared by all members of the society. The term "degrees of cultural saturation" has been proposed for the various steps in social acceptance.

The learning mechanism involved in social acceptance is imitation, as in the case of cultural borrowing, but the model whose behavior is copied is a member of one's own rather than another society. So similar are the two processes that the term "diffusion" is often applied to both; social acceptance is called "internal" or "vertical" diffusion to differentiate it from cultural borrowing, which is termed "external" or "horizontal" diffusion. With minor exceptions, most of what has previously been stated about the latter process applies equally to the former. Since close contact and similarity of culture can be taken for granted, however, copying is usually far more exact, and this is accentuated by social control.

A factor of considerable importance in social acceptance is the prestige of the innovator and of the group which is first to imitate him. Changes advocated by an admired political or religious leader are readily adopted, whereas few will follow an unpopular or despised innovator. Clothing styles accepted by "the four hundred" quickly diffuse throughout the masses, but the "zoot suit" does not spread from the taxi dance hall to the ballroom. Women imitate men more readily than vice versa. In our own society, for example, many women have adopted masculine garments, smoking and drinking habits, and occupations, but there appears to be no concerted movement among men to wear skirts, use cosmetics, or apply for positions as nurses, governesses, or babysitters.

SELECTIVE ELIMINATION constitutes a third major process of cultural change. Every innovation that has been socially accepted enters, as it were, into a competition for survival. So long as it proves more rewarding than its alternatives a cultural habit will endure, but when it ceases to bring comparable satisfactions it dwindles and eventually disappears. The process superficially resembles that of natural selection in organic evolution. It should be noted, however, that cultural traits do not compete directly with one another but are competitively tested in the experience of those who practice them. Oftentimes the competition is carried on between organized groups of people with contrasting customs and beliefs, as between nations, political parties, religious sects, or social and economic classes, and the issue is decided indirectly by the victory of one group over the other. By and large, the cultural elements that are eliminated through trial and error or social competition are the less adaptive ones, so that the process is as definitely one of the survival of the fittest as is that of natural selection.

Few of the genuine gains of culture history—the achievements of technology, of science, of man's control over nature—have ever been lost. The so-called "lost arts of antiquity" are largely mythical. To be sure, particular peoples have declined in civilization, but not until they have passed on their contributions to others. What man has lost, in the main, is a mass of maladaptive and barbarous practices, inefficient techniques, and outworn superstitions. New errors arise, of course, in each generation, but it is comforting to realize that the mortality of error is vastly greater than that of truth.

It is the genuine achievements of man that anthropologists have in mind when they say that culture is cumulative, comparing culture history to the growth of a snowball as it is rolled down a hill. Even achievements that are superseded rarely disappear. Today the electric light has proved superior to earlier methods of lighting, but the gas mantle, the kerosene lamp, and the tallow candle still survive in out-of-the-way places or under special conditions. Survival is often assured through a change in function. The use of outmoded weapons has been preserved, for example, in athletic sports like fencing and archery and in boyhood toys such as the sling and the peashooter. Other ancient usages survive in legal, religious, and adacemic ceremonial. Written records, of course, preserve much of the culture of the past from oblivion. Our libraries bulge with the puerilities as well as the achievements of history.

The fourth and last important process in cultural change is that of INTEGRATION. The shared habits that constitute a culture not only fluctuate in their degree of social acceptance, and compete for survival, but they also become progressively adapted to one another so that they tend to form an integrated whole. They exhibit what Sumner has called "a strain toward consistency." Every innovation alters in some respect the situations under which certain other forms of habitual behavior occur, and leads to adaptive changes in the latter. Similarly it must, in its turn, be adjusted to modifications elsewhere in the culture. While each such change is in itself, of course, an innovation, their reciprocal interaction and cumulative effect deserve special recognition as an integrative process.

The history of the automobile during the present century in our own culture provides an excellent example. A similar story could be told for other modern innovations such as the telephone, the airplane, the radio, and electrical household gadgets, and all of them pale before the potentialities of atomic energy.

Certain anthropologists have erroneously assumed that the elements of any culture are in a state of nearly perfect integration, or equilibrium, at all times. Actually, however, perfect equilibrium is never achieved or even approached. The adjustment of other elements of culture to an innovation, and of it to them, requires time—often years or even generations. In the meantime other innovations have appeared and set in motion new processes of integration. At any given time, therefore, a culture exhibits numerous instances of uncompleted integrative processes as well as examples of others which have been carried through to relatively satisfactory completion. What we always encounter is a strain toward internal adaptation, never its full realization.

The period of time which must elapse between the acceptance of an innovation and the completion of the integrative readjustments which follow in its train Ogburn has aptly called "cultural lag." During such a period of lag people attempt, through variation, invention, tentation, and cultural borrowing, to modify old customs and ideas to accord with the new, and to adjust the new to the old, so as to eliminate inconsistencies and sources of friction and irritation. In a modern democratic society, politics is a major scene of such efforts.

The net effect of the various processes of cultural change is to adapt the collective habits of human societies progressively over time to the changing conditions of existence. Change is always uncomfortable and often painful, and people frequently become discouraged with its slowness or even despair of achieving any genuine improvement. Neither history nor anthropology, however, gives grounds for pessimism. However halting or harsh it may appear to participants, cultural change is always adaptive and usually progressive. It is also inevitable, and will endure as long as the earth can support human life. Nothing—not even an atomic war—can destroy civilization.

9

This paper reproduces part of a chapter entitled "Evolution in Social Organization" originally published in *Evolution ond Anthropology: A Centennial Appraisal,* edited by Betty J. Meggers (Anthropological Society of Washington, 1959, pp. 126-135). As a graduate student I was strongly indoctrinated with a modified form of the unilinear evolutionism prevalent in sociology and anthropology during the late nineteenth century. With considerable resistance I was gradually persuaded, through increasing familiarization with the theoretical and descriptive literature of anthropology, that this position was fundamentally untenable and I arrived at the negative conclusions presented here.

Reprinted by permission of the Anthropological Society of Washington.

Cultural Evolution

THERE were theories of organic evolution prior to Darwin, but it was the *Origin of Species* which first lifted the concept of evolution from the level of philosophy to that of science. Darwin postulated, and proved by a massive array of evidence, that living organisms, from their first appearance in the primeval sea, have differentiated into their present multitudinous forms through a single universal process of change involving natural selection and the survival and perpetuation of the more adaptive among naturally occurring variations. Subsequent research has confirmed his hypothesis, and modern genetics has refined it by discovering the precise mechanisms of variation and transmission. With inconsequential exceptions, all competent biologists today accept the Darwinian theory of evolution, thus refined, as valid. It has withstood a succession of onslaughts, many of which have sought to inject into it some metaphysical or theological principle such as vitalism, orthogenesis or predetermination, teleology or purpose. Despite attempts at disproof and perversion, it stands impregnable—perhaps the most imposing single achievement in the history of science.

Even before Darwin's work appeared, attempts were made to transfer the concept of evolution from the realm of living organisms to that of human cultural phenomena. The publication of the *Origin of Species* and the *Descent of Man,* and their enthusiastic reception by biologists, provided an enormous stimulus to such efforts, and, as is well known, anthropological theory became so permeated with evolutionary ideas during the balance of the nineteenth century that this period is now generally designated by historians of our subject as that of "evolutionism."

It appeared self-evident to these early anthropological theorists that biological evolution came essentially to a halt once it had produced in man an organism with the capacity for culture. They argued that culture provided man with a buffer against natural selection, so that the mode of adaptation shifted largely to the level of cultural achievement. In other words, cultural evolution carried on where biological evolution left off. Although all aspects of culture were considered, special attention was given by such men as Bachofen (1861), Lippert (1886–87), Lubbock (1870), McLennan (1865, 1876), Morgan (1871, 1877), Spencer (1874–96), and Tylor (1865, 1889) to evolution in social organization. They agreed in general that early man lacked a family organization and lived in loose bands practicing sexual promiscuity, and that subsequent cultural developments brought about successively a matrilocal family organization with matrilineal descent, then the patriarchal family with polygyny and patrilineal descent, and finally the monogamous nuclear family with bilateral descent. With certain qualifications, especially in Morgan and Tylor, all these theorists conceived of cultural evolution as essentially unilinear in character. In other words, they assumed the parallel and independent development of historically unrelated cultures through a series of essentially similar stages.

The expansion of ethnographic knowledge and the resulting recognition of the role of diffusion in culture change made these unilinear theories increasingly suspect during the early decades of the twentieth century, and they are now, of course, universally discredited by competent scholars. Childe (1951), Steward (1949, 1953, 1955, 1956), and White (1943, 1945, 1949) have recently made energetic attempts to salvage the concept of evolution for cultural anthropology, Childe and White by relating it to culture as a whole rather than to particular cultures, and Steward by dealing with similar developmental sequences in historically unrelated cultures. We shall return to them shortly.

The problem of the applicability of the concept of evolution to cultural phenomena raises some basic questions. Is the concept of social evolution merely another sterile analogy from the field of biology, or has it genuine utility? Do the recent attempts to resuscitate it offer real promise for the future of anthropological theory? If not, what are the prospects that some other formulation may prove useful? Before attempting to answer these questions, it will be advisable to take a close look at precisely what the biologist means when he uses the term "evolution."

As Mayr (1959: 2) has so aptly expressed it, the biologist since Darwin views evolution from the point of view of populations, not of types. He sees each species as occupying a definite geographical range and ecological niche, and its members as harboring a pool of genes. A gene is a highly complex chemical unit, and is subject to mutation. For the sake of simplicity we shall ignore certain kinds of mutations, such as changes in the number or chromosome arrangement of genes, and concentrate upon what is apparently the commonest kind, namely changes in the chemical composition of particular genes. These occur spontaneously, that is, for reasons not yet fully comprehended, and with a relatively low though by no means negligible frequency. They seem usually to involve minor chemical modifications and to be random. The same mutations of any gene may occur repeatedly, but of course no mutation can appear in the absence of the gene of which it is a specific modification. Thus whenever a gene pool looses a particular gene, mutations that represent chemical modifications of that gene can no longer occur; conversely, when a gene pool is enriched by a new mutant gene, additional possibilities of modification are opened up. Since mutations are random, they are in overwhelming proportion deleterious in their effects and only occasionally advantageous. Evolution, however, depends on the occurrence of beneficial mutations under situations in which the individuals who carry them will enjoy improved chances for survival, and upon the accumulation over time of such adaptive mutations.

As Dobzhansky (1957) points out, sex is the supreme adaptation in the history of organic evolution. It shuffles genes in endlessly novel combinations, and spreads all mutations that are not definitely deleterious widely in any gene pool or population. With as few as 100 gene differences in a species, the possible gene combinations in the next generation amount to 3^{100}. Only an infinitesimal fraction of these can ever actually occur. It thus happens that in any sexually reproducing species every individual, except for identical twins, is genetically unique. This genetic diversity provides the raw materials upon which natural selection operates to produce evolutionary changes.

The environment in which a species lives plays a fateful role. This is passive rather than active; the influence exerted is limiting rather than determining. The environment does not evoke mutations but sets the conditions for survival of those that happen to occur. Environments fluctuate, as climate changes and other species that prey upon, provide food for, or otherwise affect the life conditions of the one in question, wax or wane in numbers, appear or disappear, or themselves undergo evolutionary modification. Successive states of the environment determine which individuals of the species, or more basically which particular genes and gene combinations, shall survive and which shall perish without offspring. If none happens to have the genetic endowment to survive, the species becomes extinct, and its entire complement of unique genes is lost. If some chance mutation, or combination thereof, hap-

pens to enable particular individuals to make a novel adaptation or
fill a new ecological niche, these individuals will tend to survive, to
produce an increased number of offspring with the same adaptive
characteristics, and perhaps ultimately to evolve into a new species. This is basically what is meant by natural selection and the
survival of the fitter. The process must be viewed statistically, in
terms of the probabilities at any given time that particular genes
occurring in the population's pool will survive and ultimately give
rise to new mutations, or will be selected out and become permanently lost. In no respect is the process predetermined or purpose-
ful, but is entirely unpredictable. It is, nevertheless, magnificently
creative.

From this brief summary we may now abstract what seem to be
some of the most outstanding general characteristics of evolution as
it is envisioned by the biologist. Four of these seem particularly
worth stating in the form of as many propositions. They are:

1) That evolution is an actual process of change, not a classificatory characterization of sequences.

2) That evolution consists of real events, not of abstractions
from events, so that evolutionary development is historical
in the strictest and most literal sense.

3) That the course of evolution is fundamentally divergent or
multilinear. When parallel development occurs in more than
one evolutionary line, the sequences and results are similar
only in a typological sense, and are never in any respect
identical.

4) That evolution operates by a purely fortuitous mechanism,
and is neither predictable, predetermined, nor purposive.

If we now turn to the concept of evolution as it has been applied
to cultural phenomena by three principal groups of anthropological
exponents, we note that only rarely does any of our four general
statements hold true. Whatever these anthropologists are talking
about, it is certainly not evolution in the sense used by biologists.
The divergence does not consist merely in the fact that biologists
and anthropologists apply the term evolution to different bodies of

phenomena—a self-evident point acknowledged by everyone. The discrepancy lies far deeper. The anthropologists commonly assign to the term a totally different and basically noncomparable kind of meaning.

To the nineteenth-century theorist, evolution was not a process of change but a typology of sequence, thus contradicting Proposition 1. It was not historical in the sense of a record of specific events, but rather a conceptual abstraction from many independent historical sequences, thus contradicting Proposition 2. It was unilinear instead of multilinear, in contravention of Proposition 3. And it was universal and inevitable, and hence predetermined and predictable, thus contradicting Proposition 4.

White's conception of cultural evolution also does violence to all four statements. It departs from that of the early evolutionists chiefly in its explicit divorce of evolution from all historical events —a complete inversion of Proposition 2. Instead of isolating similarities in the actual culture history of different peoples, White transfers the concept to the rarefied abstraction of culture in general. He is impressed by such facts as that food-gathering economies have everywhere preceded food-producing ones, that simple techniques and institutions have preceded complex ones, and in particular that man's per capita control of energy has been uninterruptedly increasing throughout human history. The present writer finds himself agreeing with Steward (1953: 317) that White's "postulated sequences are so general that they are neither very arguable nor very useful." They are comparable to such facts in the biological realm as that unicellular organisms preceded multicellular ones or that living forms first became adapted to a marine environment and only later became capable of living on the land and still later in some instances acquired the power of flight. These facts are so obvious, so trite, and intellectually unstimulating that biologists mention them only in passing and never become involved in scientific controversies over them.

Steward, unlike White, equates cultural evolution with the actual culture history of the various peoples of the earth. Moreover, he not only admits but emphasizes that its course is multilinear rather than unilinear. He is impressed, however, by evidences that some culture historical sequences of some historically unrelated peoples exhibit substantial similarities. He is not content, like most of his predecessors, merely to assert parallel evolution as a fact and to support his assertion with examples. On the contrary, the fact poses for him a scientific problem and sends him on a search for causes, on a quest for the scientific laws that govern such regularities. His task may perhaps be compared to that of the biologist who seeks to comprehend and account for the similarities in the development and form of the various vertebrate species that have adopted, for example, either a cursorial, an arboreal, a burrowing, or an aquatic mode of life. In any event, he has clearly chosen an important and not a trivial problem.

In the conduct of his research Steward must, like any scientist, analyze and classify his data, and in so doing he naturally abstracts from historically independent sequences of development the classificatory resemblances with which he wishes to deal. It is only in this respect, however, that his work appears to have anything in common with that of either White or the nineteenth-century evolutionists. Unless I completely misread him, he considers all cultural evolution to be basically multilinear and regards cases of parallel development as exceptions demanding special investigation. If this is the case, it is not Steward who uses the term in a sense fundamentally different from that of the biologists, but rather the people who incorrectly assume that he equates it with parallel development who do so.

Our analysis has shown that the most common application of the term and concept of evolution in anthropology, namely, in reference to typological parallels between historically independent sequences of cultural forms, represents a serious distortion of, and a false analogy to, its fundamental biological meaning. If this is so, we may inquire whether there is any observed phenomenon on the cultural level that does bear a genuine resemblance to organic evolution and might thus be regarded as a true analogy. The answer is not only affirmative but very obvious. The group of processes usually designated collectively as those of culture change, and on which we possess an immense literature (see Keesing 1953), corresponds closely in practically every respect to the processes of organic change known to the biologist as evolution. Culture change meets exactly the criteria embedded in our four statements. It refers to actual processes of change, not to abstracted typological sequences. Its events are historical in the most literal sense, and in their totality constitute culture history. Its course or direction is fundamentally multilinear. And it operates in a fortuitous, not in a predictable or predetermined manner. Moreover, it is adaptive, producing cultural adjustments to the geographical environment and to the other basic conditions of life. It even fulfills the specification of Mayr (1959: 2) that evolution deals with populations rather than types. The populations are, of course, societies rather than species, and the reservoirs of change are pools, not of genes but of culture traits.

Anthropologists have long dimly sensed these similarities, and have not hesitated on occasion to use "cultural evolution" in a sense synonymous with culture change. The latest instance to come to my attention is a recent article by Goodenough (1957) entitled "Oceania and the Problem of Controls in the Study of Cultural and Human Evolution." Both Keller (1915) and Childe (1951) have noted marked parallels between the processes of cultural change and those of organic evolution, equating innovation or invention with variation or mutation, imitative learning with heredity, and the selection of adaptive norms through experience with natural selection. Some of these processes on the cultural level have received detailed analysis from anthropologists, notably innovation by Barnett (1953), and all of them have been repeatedly assessed in somewhat summary fashion, e.g., by Beals and Hoijer (1953), Gillin (1948), Kroeber (1948), Linton (1936), and Murdock (1956). The only extended and systematic treatment to date, however, remains that by Keller (1915), now seriously antiquated.

The analogy between the processes of culture change and those of organic evolution breaks down at only a single point, namely, in respect to diffusion. The elements of culture are capable of leaking, as it were, from one trait pool to another, whereas this is possible to only an extremely limited extent with the elements of gene pools. One society can borrow traits from another whose culture history has previously followed a quite different line of development, whereas one species cannot ordinarily acquire genes from another. There are, of course, minor exceptions in the latter case, notably instances of natural hybridization, but they are extremely rare as contrasted with the frequency of interfertilization in cultural evolution. The branching tree-like figure by which we commonly represent organic evolution would have to be modified, in the case of cultural evolution, by allowing the various limbs and twigs to meet and fuse with one another in a highly complicated interlacing network. The genetic relationships of any culture, consequently, cannot be traced back along a single line of development, like those of a species, but must be followed through many lines which diverge and then often merge again.

The distinctive process of diffusion does not, of course, render the concept of evolution wholly inapplicable to culture change. It merely introduces a new dimension. In particular, it does not negate the genetic character of culture change, for, as is well known, the content and organization of any culture largely determines which elements will be borrowed from other societies and which will be rejected. Furthermore, the subprocess of integration assures that both borrowed and traditional elements will gradually become fused into a harmonious whole. In recent years, moreover, it has become increasingly clear that diffusion does not operate with equal facility in all aspects of culture. In some areas it occurs with extreme ease, and is overwhelmingly the principal process by which change takes place. In other areas, however, borrowing is relatively difficult, and most changes are brought about by the gradual modification of existing cultural patterns, in other words, by a genetic process more directly comparable to that of organic evolution. The difference appears to lie in the extent to which the aspect of culture in question is socially structured, that is, in the extent to which the behavior of one individual is dependent upon, and interdigited with, the reciprocal behavior of his fellows. This may be illustrated by an example chosen from either extreme.

The smoking of tobacco is a cultural trait that is socially structured to only a very slight extent. One person can take up smoking, or drop it, or shift from a pipe to cigarettes regardless of whether or not other members of his society do likewise. The functions and satisfactions of smoking are largely individual, and rarely do social sanctions constitute a serious deterrant to a change in habits. Hence an individual in a nonsmoking society can readily borrow the smoking practices of another culture, and these practices can spread equally easily from one person to another within the society until smoking has become firmly established as a new culture pattern. Hence tobacco smoking has been able to diffuse from its American Indian inventors throughout much of the New World and then ultimately over practically the entire earth.

At the opposite pole, in respect to diffusibility, stands language, whose functions are primarily social rather than individual. If one member of a society learns an alien language, this may prove useful in trade or travel but it will not facilitate communication with other group members unless many or most of them also acquire it. Hence one language replaces another only under special circumstances, notably those of conquest and colonization. Individual words may be borrowed from another language, to be sure, but they are usually those associated with new or borrowed elements of culture for which no names have previously existed. Replacement of native by borrowed words is much less common, especially in the area of basic vocabulary. The diffusion of grammatical forms occurs even more rarely. For these reasons, changes in language are largely genetic, consisting of gradual divergent modifications of existing forms, and the whole science of historical linguistics rests on this foundation.

Linguistic change parallels biological evolution even in minute particulars. Just as a species consists of a population characterized by a particular gene pool, so a language is exhibited by a population possessing a pool of speech elements, such as phonemes, morphemes, and lexemes, assembled in distinctive combinations. Both types of populations have geographical distributions with definite boundaries. However much the representatives of a species may vary throughout its range, they constitute a unit insofar as adjacent variant forms everywhere interbreed with each other. Similarly, varying dialects constitute a single language insofar as adjacent ones are everywhere mutually intelligible. Within a language, as within a species, the elements of a pool are readily diffusible. They spread to a very limited extent, however, across boundaries where mutual intelligibility does not exist, just as genes do not spread across barriers to interbreeding. When separated by such barriers, both language and species pursue divergent lines of evolution. Hence to the historical linguist the figure of a branching tree serves to represent the relationships of cognate languages just as adequately as it serves the biologist to represent the genetic relationships of species and genera, and for closely similar reasons.

Like language, "the forms of social organization seem singularly impervious to diffusion" (Murdock 1949: 196). They are characteristically structured so that the behavior of every member of a society is reciprocally intermeshed with that of his fellows in a strikingly interdependent fashion. Although anyone may borrow from another culture such a trait as the smoking of tobacco, no individual can adopt an alien social status, a lineage organization, or a joking relationship. Such behaviors can be acquired from another society only by general consensus, or at the very minimum by a group of individuals acting in concert. Since the conditions under which such direct transfer can occur are highly exceptional, change in social organization ordinarily comes about, like that in language, through a dynamics of internal development. Influences from outside the society make themselves felt, not through direct cultural borrowing, but by altering the conditions of social life in such a way as to stimulate changes in interpersonal interaction, which may then crystallize in new social structural norms. The pro-

cesses of cultural variation and differentiation in social organization, as in language, are thus primarily genetic in character, and
can therefore be appropriately designated as evolutionary in the
most precise sense.

Evolution in social organization appears, on the surface, to differ
from linguistic evolution in one striking respect. In language, the
process is notably divergent, producing a very wide variety of forms
in both structure and vocabulary, whereas in social organization it
is often convergent, producing a finite number of typologically
similar structures under not only comparable but often quite different situations. It is, of course, this tendency toward parallelism
that misled the early evolutionists and caused them mistakenly to
arrange the parallels in a chronological sequence of stages. A more
satisfactory explanation is now available. Convergence in social
organization, as we have shown elsewhere (Murdock 1945), results
from an inherent limitation in practicable possibilities, such as does
not prevail to any comparable extent in the realm of language. In
kinship organization, for example, there are only a limited number
of basic configurations that possess sufficient internal coherence to
give them a measure of relative stability. Each represents a point
of equilibrium, as it were, and when this equilibrium is seriously
disturbed for whatever reason, one change precipitates another in a
series until the social system again comes to rest at some one of the
alternative stable configurations.

Social organization does not, however, stand alone in this respect. Cases of convergence have frequently been noted in organic
evolution, for example, the similarities in form achieved independently by the pterodactyls, birds, and bats in acquiring the power of
flight. They also occur in the development of languages, as witness
the interest formerly shown by linguists in such typological classifications as agglutinative, isolating, inflectional, and polysynthetic.
And we have already alluded to the preoccupation of Steward
(1949) with independent similarities in the growth of complex
civilizations. The difference is merely that convergence of forms
and parallel sequences of change seem to occur with greater fre-

quency and to exhibit more striking typological resemblances in the development of social organization than in other processes of evolution, either organic or cultural.

Save in rare cataclysmic instances, evolutionary change proceeds, not by alternating phases of disorganization and reorganization, but by a smooth process of small adaptive modifications. At all points in such a development the subject of the evolutionary process, whether a biological organism, a language, or a social system, maintains a sound functional balance. In organic and linguistic evolution such change is more or less continuous. In social organization, however, it seems to be interrupted by long periods of relative stability when particular configurations are attained whose elements are not only functionally integrated but are characterized by a deeper internal consistency that tends to preserve them in equilibrium until forces of unusual strength initiate a new series of gradual changes toward another stable configuration.

If the term evolution is to have a legitimate place in the technical vocabulary of anthropology, it must designate, like its biological prototype, not some nebulous abstraction, but a very concrete process of orderly adaptive change.

10

This paper has not previously been published. It was read in an original draft at the annual meeting of the American Sociological Association in 1960. In its present form it has benefited by suggestions made by William F. Whyte, which are gratefully acknowledged.

Cultural Relativity

F
OR some years I have felt increasingly uncomfortable about the concept of cultural relativity. It seems to me to contain elements of both good sense and scientific nonsense, and I will make some attempt to disentangle them in my remarks, which will necessarily be tentative and exploratory.

Cultural relativity, in any version, is less than a century old. To the ancient Greeks, to the Chinese, and to most other known peoples, one's own culture was taken as the standard against which all others were judged. To the extent that alien customs and values differed from one's own, their adherents were "barbarians" deserving only of scorn, if indeed they were even considered human beings at all.

This ethnocentric point of view still characterized the earliest anthropological field workers. They were interested in the curious and bizarre features of other cultures, in the constrasts which the

144

customs of "savage" and "barbarous" peoples presented to those of "civilized" European Christendom. In consequence, they were more concerned with the construction of evolutionistic schemes than with the systematic or even the sympathetic understanding of other ways of life.

This early "believe-it-or-not" period came to an end with Sir Edward B. Tylor. With rare perspicacity, Tylor rejected all the older reports of men with tails, of societies without language or marriage or religion, and accepted as valid only what seemed to him to make reasonable sense. Subsequent research has proved his judgment to have been remarkably sound. By the end of the nineteenth century anthropologists and sociologists had generally come to recognize that all cultures make sense, even though this sense, in the opinion of some authorities like Levy-Bruhl, might follow a logic alien to our own.

It was William Graham Sumner, in *Folkways* (1906), who first explicitly formulated the conception of cultural relativity. He rejected not only the ethnocentric mode of judging other cultures in relation to our own but also denied the validity of any absolute standard, moral or otherwise, for evaluating cultural phenomena. A culture and its component parts, he insisted, can be appropriately assessed only in terms of its own context—geographical, historical, and societal. He shocked his contemporaries by asserting that even practices like infanticide, slavery, cannibalism, human sacrifice, and religious prostitution, that are anathema to us, are comprehensible in the light of their settings, representing adaptations to particular sets of circumstances. As such, they must be accepted as justified, as right in an objective or scientific sense, and even, from the standpoint of their practitioners, as moral. "The mores can make anything right."

Sumner's still remains the most forceful and objective definition of cultural relativity in the literature of social science. Since he recognized himself as a sociologist, is claimed by sociologists, and has received scant recognition from anthropologists, it comes as a bit of a surprise to find Herskovits, in *Man and His Works* (1948),

claiming cultural relativity as "anthropology's greatest contribution." Let us examine for a moment the subsequent history of the
concept in anthropology.

The most famous statement of the anthropological position is
probably that formulated by Ruth Benedict in her *Patterns of
Culture* (1934). Benedict held, not only that cultures must be
viewed in the context of the situations faced by the societies that
bear them—a position with which few modern social scientists
would quarrel—but also that they must be viewed as wholes. To
her, every culture is a unique configuration and can be understood
only in its totality. She strongly implied that the abstraction of
elements for comparison with those of other cultures is illegitimate. An element has no meaning except in its context; in isolation
it is meaningless. I submit that this is nonsense. Specific functions, of course, are discoverable only in context. Scientific laws or
propositions, however, can be arrived at, in anthropology, as in any
other science, only by abstracting and comparing features observable in many phenomena as they occur in nature.

Another form in which the concept of cultural relativity is expressed in the anthropological literature is the allegation, e.g., by
Herskovits, that all cultures must be accorded equal "dignity" and
equal "validity." This seems to me to be not only nonsense but
sentimental nonsense. It is one thing to respect the organization,
integration, complexity, and adaptiveness of cultural systems, but
quite another to insist that all are equally admirable or even equally
adaptive.

This, like most other versions of cultural relativity, seems to pay
homage to the status quo, and, as critics have pointed out, to take a
position opposed to cultural change. It reflects, I suppose, a sentimentality to which we anthropologists are peculiarly prone. We
feel an obligation to record descriptions of the thousands of indigenous cultures of the world, yet we see these cultures changing or
disappearing before our eyes and realize the sheer impossibility of
placing them all on record before they alter unrecognizably. Unconsciously, if not conciously, we would like to slow this process of

change. Many American anthropologists, for example, favor an Indian policy which would preserve, as far as possible, the traditional cultures of our indigenous population, and these views have had a measure of administrative support. The objective, to put it bluntly, is to convert our Indian reservations into human zoos. Theories of cultural relativity probably reflect in some measure this essentially sentimental prejudice against change—in simple or exotic cultures, it should be noted, not in our own.

It is curious that all modern versions of cultural relativity—from the hard-boiled one of Sumner to the sentimental one of Herskovits—rest on the implicit assumption that "what is, is good." This is either a moral judgment and, as such, scientifically irrelevant, or, if the moral element is eliminated, it reduces to the proposition that "what is, is"—in other words to a meaningless tautology. From the point of view of science, in short, we have scarcely advanced over the old ethnocentric assumption of our own culture as the standard by which others are to be judged or the alternative of adopting from ethics or religion some universal philosophical standard of judgment.

Are we then to abandon cultural relativity outright as a useless or spurious concept? Not, I think, before we make another try, and see if we cannot find some formulation that is both valid and useful. Perhaps the fault of previous attempts lies in their static quality—in their implicit commitment to the status quo and their failure to reckon with the fact of cultural change. After all, change is a universal phenomenon; no recorded culture has ever remained static, even during relatively brief periods of observation. The analysis of cultural change constitutes a major field of anthropological research, and we know a great deal systematically about the processes by which change occurs and about the factors which induce, accelerate, retard, and channelize it. Possibly cultural relativity can be adapted to this body of knowledge and interpreted in accordance with it.

The prevailing theory of cultural change rests on the assumption that every culture consists of learned or habitual patterns of thought

and action current in a particular society, distributed among its
members in accordance with the prevailing structure of social statuses, and transmitted with relatively modest modifications from
each generation to the next. These modifications are conceived of
as occurring through the following processes:

1) INNOVATION (invention): the origination of a new response
   pattern by some member of the society.
2) BORROWING (diffusion): the adoption of a new pattern by
   imitation from members of another society among whom it
   has been current.
3) INTERNAL DIFFUSION: the spread of a new pattern from
   the individual innovator or borrower to other members of
   his society, i.e., its social acceptance.
4) INTEGRATION: the adaptation of a new pattern to the cultural context and the concurrent modification of preexisting patterns to accord with the new element.
5) SELECTIVE ELIMINATION: the loss of cultural patterns
   formerly prevalent in a society as a result of replacement
   by others or of their failure to provide satisfactions.
6) SOCIALIZATION (education): the transmission of culture
   patterns to each succeeding generation within a society, a
   social process in which replication is seldom exact.

These several processes correspond precisely to the processes of
individual learning as these have been laid bare by psychologists.
They simply represent learning in the context of social life—collective learning or social learning in the sense of Miller and Dollard,
Social Learning and Imitation (1941). They involve no new principles, but they are channelized, of course, by the conditions of life in
society—cooperation, differentiation of functions, social control,
and the like.

Modern psychology has disproved the old assumption, typified
by Bagehot's "cake of custom" and by the views of Boas and his
followers in American anthropology, that culture has a sort of
inertia, its elements tending to persist unless actively impeded or
counteracted. Psychology supports rather the view of Malinowski,

expressed in *Crime and Custom in Savage Society* (1926), that elements of culture are supported by their success in subserving human needs and by reciprocity in social interaction. This is, of course, the expression on the societal plane of the famous reinforcement principle of individual psychology.

The culture of any society at any time embraces an assemblage of elements from many sources—inheritance from the historical past, recent innovations and borrowings, and integrative readjustments —all of them tested or in the process of being tested by group experience. Sumner was doubtless correct in his assumption that any such assemblage can be regarded as the best one, that is the most adaptive and satisfactory one, achievable under the prevailing conditions.

This by no means implies, however, that it is the best conceivable assemblage under comparable circumstances. It only represents the best possible choice among the alternatives actually available to the society in question, not the best possible selection from among all conceivable alternatives, including elements not yet invented and those exhibited by remote peoples. Killing the aged, cannibalism, slavery, magical therapy, and simple artifacts of stone and wood may represent admirable adjustments in societies whose cultural heritage and that of their neighbors provide only an extremely limited range of choice. But to assert that such usages should be accorded a "dignity" and a "validity" equal to that of adequate old age security, animal husbandry as a source of meat, voluntary free labor, scientific medicine, and metal artifacts is an absurdity.

Ethnography demonstrates that, when faced with expanded possibilities of cultural choice, all peoples reveal a preference for steel over stone axes, for quinine and penicillin over magical therapy, for money over barter, for animal and vehicular transport over human porterage, for improvements in the food supply which enable them to rear their children and support their aged rather than killing them, and so on. They relinquish cannibalism and head-hunting with little resistance when colonial governments demonstrate the material advantages of peace. Such evidence indicates that different cultural adjustments to similar needs are by no means of equivalent utility or practical worth. Some must manifestly be superior to others in at least a pragmatic sense if they are always chosen in preference to the latter when both alternatives are available.

Not only do all peoples readily accept certain kinds of cultural innovations when an opportunity is provided; many of them are actively "in the market" for changes that offer promise of improvements in their manner of life. A "revolution of rising expectations" is observable throughout most of the world. Many of the choices made or sought accord with Western conceptions of what is "modern" or "progressive." To generalize from this, however, would be to fall into the old ethnocentric fallacy. On the other hand, to withhold opportunities by challenging our own right to recommend changes in the cultures of others would be sheer sentimentality.

What we urgently need is systematic scientific knowledge about the choices for change which peoples do and do not make when presented with an opportunity, the criteria according to which such decisions are made, and the modes of implementing them effectively. This could conceivably yield an empirically tested, scientific yardstick for measuring the adaptive value and satisfaction-yielding quality of different ways of life and their component elements. Governments, missionaries, educators, and others concerned with programs of planned cultural change could surely find such a yardstick more useful than absolute standards derived from philosophy, religion, or ethnocentric prejudice. There seems no inherent reason why valid cross-cultural generalizations cannot be established in the area of cultural change as well as in that of synchronic integration within social and cultural systems.

The proposed pragmatic standard cannot, of course, be applied at once. It must be worked out by painstaking scientific research in the records of cultural change. It is a standard to be discovered, not adopted. Perhaps the best augury of its potentialities lies in the fact that it would be derived from science, not imposed upon science.

11

This paper, originally published in the *Southwestern Journal of Anthropology* (11: 361-370, 1955), expresses my satisfaction at evidences indicative of a shift from a static or synchronic to a dynamic or diachronic emphasis in social structural studies.

Reprinted by permission.

Changing Emphases in Social Structure

Whorf/no...

W HEN scientists approach a new subject, their first task, after that of raw description and preliminary ordering, is to discover which descriptive features of the phenomena under observation are particularly useful for grouping or differentiation, and to initiate classification on the basis of such criteria. Their next task is to determine which features isolated according to one set of criteria coexist with features isolated according to other useful criteria. In this way they arrive at larger typological classifications which bring a measure of systematic order into what had first seemed sheer descriptive chaos. Noteworthy examples in other sciences include the Linnaean classification of living organisms and the periodic system of classifying chemical elements devised by Mendelyeev.

In anthropology, the initial classificatory task has by now been substantially accomplished in the field of social structure. Through the contributions of men like Morgan, Tylor, Rivers, Kroeber, Lowie, Linton, Spier, Kirchhoff, Radcliffe-Brown, Steward, and Eggan we now possess satisfactory criteria for differentiating types of family organization, kin and local groups, and kinship terminology and behavior patterns. Moreover, the work of Rivers, Lowie, Radcliffe-Brown, and many others, including the present writer, has shown how these features are combined with one another in particular ways to produce a finite number of types of social organization, which in their totality represent a systematic classification comparable to those of Linnaeus and Mindelyeev.

However useful, and indeed indispensable, is this task of classification, it is by no means the ultimate goal of science. Any typological system is, by its very nature, static in character. It takes on full meaning only when scientists are able to demonstrate the dynamic processes which give rise to the phenomena thus classified. The Linnaean system, for example, came alive only after Darwin had discerned the processes of variation and natural selection, and especially after the geneticists had laid bare the dynamic mechanisms of heredity.

It is the contention of this paper that the anthropological study of social structure has gradually been emerging from its classificatory or typological phase, and that the changing emphases which we can currently observe are characterized for the most part by a common concern with dynamics or process. Before examples are cited, it will be well to review briefly the cardinal facts about human behavior which must be fully recognized before a genuine dynamic orientation becomes possible.

First of all, we must be fully aware that man is an animal, a mammal, and a primate with all the potentialities with which the processes of organic evolution have endowed him, including in particular the capacities for perception, learning, and personality development which have been the special study of psychology.

Secondly, we must recognize that man always lives in societies and be fully cognizant of all the implications of this fact, as they have long been known to sociologists. Unlike the ants and bees, man is not biologically a social animal equipped by heredity with prepotent capacities for complex associative life, but in every individual case must be bent and broken to group living through the arduous process of socialization and be kept in the paths of conformity through the imposition of social controls. The first anthropologist fully to appreciate this basic fact was Malinowski (1932: 23-27) with his emphasis upon the factor of "reciprocity" in the maintenance of norms of social interaction.

Thirdly, we must realize that every human society has a culture, that cultures are acquired and transmitted exclusively by learning, that their elements are only in part shared by the entire society, being largely distributed according to the prevailing system of social relationships in association with ascribed and achievable "statuses" (see Linton 1936: 113), and that the norms of man's social interaction are as definitely a part of culture as are the norms of his reactions to the external material world. It is for this reason, incidentally, that the writer prefers the term "cultural anthropology" to "social anthropology," even for the study of social organization.

Fourthly, we must always remember that cultures change with time, and therefore always have histories. They reflect the opportunities and limitations presented by the habitat of the particular society and the accidents of epidemics, crop failures, and natural calamities, of discoveries and inventions, of intergroup contacts, wars, conquest, and migration, of strong and weak political leadership, and innumerable others. It is thus quite clear that the form and content of any culture at any particular time will reflect its form and content at an earlier period as well as the forces and influences playing upon it at the moment. Equally crucial is the recognition that cultural change, like organic evolution, proceeds, not haphazardly, but according to a definite dynamics. Among the specific processes involved, three basic ones are today generally recognized: (1) the process of cultural innovation, most recently analyzed by Barnett (1953); (2) the process of cultural borrowing, whose dynamics has been most clearly set forth by Dollard (Miller and

Dollard 1941: 253-273); and (3) the process of readjustive integration (e.g., see Linton 1936: 347-366).

Applying these crucial findings of our science to the special field of social structure, we can observe the static yielding to the dynamic approach along at least two distinct continua. The first is the time continuum. We have succeeded in combining the historical and functional points of view so thoroughly that we are showing increasing skill in interpreting historical changes in social organization as adaptive modifications reflecting the processes of innovation, borrowing, and integration. The second continuum is that of the life history of the individual. We are beginning to view social systems from the point of view of the individuals who live through, uphold, and modify them—fitted to a preexisting system through the process of socialization, learning the appropriate motivations and goals, occupying successive statuses through age ascription and individual achievement, yielding to the pressures for social conformity, and yet facing and creatively solving problems as they arise in such a way that the social norms are themselves gradually changed.

The emerging dynamic approach to social structure contrasts sharply with all earlier approaches. Among the more important of these, one substituted for history and process a single inevitable and universal succession of structural forms, with matrilineal descent everywhere yielding in time to patrilineal and the clan to the family, with no conception of the individual except as the slave of custom, and with no comprehension of the nature of social interaction. A second saw matrilineal and patrilineal complexes striding around the world in seven-league boots, stressing history without process, and dismissing man as uninventive and society as irrelevant. A third treated, and sometimes still treats, social structure as a series of abstract forms, for all the world like a high school mathematics teacher's blackboard demonstration of a theorem in geometry, rejecting even processless history along with all psychology and even culture, and reducing man himself to an automaton actuated by stresses flowing from structural principles. If this latter approach enjoys more respect today than the other two, it is largely because its proponents stress field research and have produced an unusual number of excellent descriptive studies. In its theoretical orientation, however, it seems no less sterile than the others, and as even more devoid of dynamic quality.

Let us now look at some concrete examples of the changing emphases in social structure. The trend begins with the students of Boas, who professed to be primarily concerned with history but who nevertheless recognized clearly that history operates through process. A single instance must suffice—an acute article by Spier (1922) in which he used data from Havasupai social organization to illuminate the dynamics of the development of unilinear kingroups.

The greatest stride forward, however, was initiated by Eggan, who for the first time succeeded in effectively fusing the historical and the functional approaches, first in his work on the Southeast and subsequently on the western Pueblos (see Eggan 1950). In the writer's opinion, Eggan deserves far more credit as a creative innovator than has as yet been accorded him. He was followed in the Southeast by Spoehr (especially 1947), who laid bare the similar steps by which a series of kinship systems independently adjusted to the transition from matrilineal to bilateral descent. The writer (1949: 198-259) has attempted to show that cultural change in the realm of social structure is not random but is controlled by a principle of limited possibilities.

A considerable proportion of the recent work on social organization by American anthropologists reflects a comparable awareness alike of history and of process. Two representative examples will serve as illustrations. Both are as yet unpublished articles [1] which have recently been brought to the writer's attention—one by L. C. Faron entitled "Araucanian Patri-Organization and the Omaha System" and the other by R. F. Murphy entitled "Matrilocality and Patrilineality in Mundurucú Society." Both compare the findings

[1] Both articles were published in 1956; see the Bibliography.

of recent field research in South America with published reports from an earlier period, and reconstruct the course and dynamics of change with admirable sophistication. If, as the writer believes, these papers are typical of recent trends, the next decade may well see noteworthy advances in the dynamics of social organization.

Not only can a knowledge of history and process illuminate our understanding of social structure, but the reverse is also true. Features of social organization can frequently yield clues to the mechanisms of culture change. One illustration may be cited. It has long been observed that some regions of the world, like aboriginal Australia and the Northwest Coast of North America, exhibit marked cultural homogeneity over wide areas, whereas others, like Melanesia and central California, reveal sharp differences from tribe to tribe and even from village to village within the tribe. Different branches of the Pomo tribe, for example, have kinship systems belonging to types as widely different as Hawaiian, Crow, and Omaha—a divergence within one tribe greater than that within an entire culture area in such surrounding regions as the Northwest Coast, Plateau, or Great Basin.

Comparative evidence suggests that such contrasts may often be explained by differential features of social organization, notably the presence or absence of a rule of local exogamy. Where local communities, as in native Australia or the Northwest Coast, are regularly exogamous, whether organized as localized clans or as what the writer has called "patri-demes," every marriage brings together in the family two persons of at least somewhat variant cultural backgrounds, and their children grow up exposed to both. This accomplishes two things. It exposes every individual in the region—not merely an occasional trader or traveler—to conditions favorable for acculturation. Even more important, perhaps, it results in accomplishing cultural borrowing during the period of early socialization, when imitative learning is much more perfect than in later life. It puts the socialization process to work, so to speak, in support of the diffusion process. Culture is borrowed through the very mechanism by which it is transmitted. Diffusion thus proceeds with extreme ease over the entire area where local exogamy prevails, and widespread culture similarities are the inevitable result.

In default of a rule of local exogamy, most marriages take place between members of the same community. Hence culture borrowing can occur only on the adult level, and even this tends to be inhibited by the fact that kinship ties between different communities are few and weak. Under such circumstances the processes of cultural differentiation are likely to outrun the leveling influence of diffusion, so that even neighboring villages of the same tribal group may exhibit marked cultural divergences, as in Melanesia and central California.

Conceivably the very wide geographical distribution of many early archaeological cultures in both the Old and the New World may reflect exogamous practices rather than meagerness of the cultural base. Small local bands tend to exogamy because composed of near kinsmen. Perhaps local endogamy became common only after technological advances had paved the way for local groups of substantial size. If such be the case, marked regional differentiation may be more characteristic of later than of earlier phases of cultural development.

It may be remarked parenthetically that the features ascribed by Redfield to "folk societies" seem to be particularly associated with peoples practicing local endogamy. Those characterized by local exogamy, even where extremely backward in culture, often exhibit a relatively cosmopolitan world outlook.

The potential contributions of social structure to an understanding of cultural change are also illustrated in an important paper by Bruner (1955) on Mandan-Hidatsa kinship. Bruner is able to demonstrate, on the basis of completely recorded genealogies, that every member of the community studied who follows the European, i.e., Eskimo, pattern of kinship terminology is descended from a mixed marriage in either the first, second, or third ascending generation. In other words, acculturation in kinship usage has taken place only when mediated by the socialization process, never on the basis of adult interpersonal contacts alone.

All in all, the static view of social structure which seeks explanations exclusively within the existing framework of a social system on the highly dubious assumption of cultural stability and nearly perfect functional integration seems clearly to be giving way, in this country at least, to a dynamic orientation which focuses attention on the processes by which such systems come into being and succeed one another over time. A second dynamic approach is also discernible, though less well advanced. This views a social system from the standpoint of the life histories of the individuals who move through it.

One line of attack is to clothe the dry bones of formal structural analysis with the living tissues of personality dynamics as these are coming to light through our developing knowledge of culture and personality. Some challenging suggestions along this line appear in the papers prepared in 1954 for the Social Science Research Council Summer Seminar on Kinship, in which Aberle, Basehart, Colson, Fathauer, Gough, Sahlins, and Schneider participated.

A second line of attack consists in following the lead of Linton (1940) and examining not only the familial and kin groupings of a social system but also the age statuses which individuals of each sex successively occupy during a normal lifetime and which often prescribe shifting goals and differential behavior.

An excellent example of the new insights which such an approach can yield is provided in a forthcoming paper by Goodenough (1955) reappraising residence rules. Noting that he and another competent anthropologist, John Fischer, working in the same community in Truk at nearly the same time and using the same intensive methods of genealogical recording and household censuses, reached markedly different conclusions as to the statistical incidence of matrilocal and patrilocal residence, Goodenough properly concludes that the discrepancy could only flow from differing definitions of the two residence rules. In seeking a clarification, he then turns to his own field data from the Nakanai of New Britain in Melanesia, and demonstrates that for this society even the most accurate census data are incapable of revealing the residence pattern.

Among the Nakanai, a man normally lives with his father until the latter's death, then removes to the hamlet of his maternal uncle. If, however, his father dies before he himself marries, he goes to live with a father-substitute, who may be related to him in a variety of ways, who may live in the same or another hamlet, and who may be succeeded by other father-substitutes. Even the most careful household census among the Nakanai can reveal nothing but a bewildering chaos of residential practices, since the number of cases of residence with a father-substitute is high and their variety immense. No pattern whatsoever emerges until attention is focused on the lifeline of the typical individual. Then it becomes clear that the rule of residence is definitely what we might call patri-avunculocal, i.e., preferably patrilocal in the early years of marriage but in later years preferably avunculocal in the hamlet of the man's maternal uncle. The diverse other instances are resolved by recognition of the fact that the Nakanai regard living with a father-substitute as merely a variant of the initial patrilocal norm forced by the unfortunate circumstances of one's own father's premature death.

A comparable and even more complex case is provided by the Ashanti of West Africa. When I was writing my *Social Structure,* the chief sources available on the Ashanti were the works of Rattray, and I encountered extreme difficulty in typing the social system of this society. Since then, new data have been presented by Fortes (1949) which provide a basis for resolving the difficulty.

What Fortes reveals is an extraordinary complexity with regard to rules of residence and forms of family organization. Patrilocal, avunculocal, neolocal, and even a form of matrilocal residence all occur with considerable frequency, as do independent nuclear families, independent polygynous families, and extended families of patrilocal, avunculocal, and mixed types. No one residence pattern or type of family organization enjoys any overall preference or occurs with sufficient statistical frequency to justify setting it up as the prevailing social norm. Ordinary synchronic structural analysis, consequently, leaves us with no alternative except to characterize the system as fluid and patternless. Such a conclusion, however, would be completely erroneous. In actuality there is a high degree of patterning, but this becomes apparent only when we follow Ashanti men and women through their typical life histories in terms of the successive statuses which they occupy and the shifting norms which characterize these statuses.

In the first place, husband and wife do not ordinarily live together during the early years of married life. Each remains with his own relatives, although the wife cooks for her husband and sends the food to him daily by couriers from her household. From the point of view of the children born during this period, residence is matrilocal, i.e., with the mother and her kinsmen.

After a few years, however, the wife leaves home and joins her husband—presumably about the time when her oldest children require a father's participation in their socialization. During this second period of life, residence, from the point of view of the child, is patrilocal, i.e., with the father and his relatives.

At some time during late childhood or adolescence, or occasionally even later, children of both sexes normally leave their father's home and go to live with a maternal uncle. In other words, they shift to avunculocal residence.

The residence pattern in later life varies with circumstances. A minority of adult males remain with their fathers in patrilocal residence, and are ultimately joined by their wives and children. The majority, however, live with their maternal uncles after they marry and produce a family. A nephew who is to succeed his uncle will normally continue in avunculocal residence permanently. For those who are not prospective heirs, however, lifelong dependence is disapproved, and it is the goal of every successful man to establish an independent household.

This is accomplished in either of two ways. If the man's mother is still alive, he feels obligated to establish her in an independent household as its head. In this case, she naturally leaves her husband, and is joined by some of her sisters and daughters as well as by the son who has provided the new home. From the point of view of this son, though not of his mother, wife, or children, residence is matrilocal. True matrilocal residence, where a husband lives with his wife and her kinsmen, is disapproved and rare.

If the man's mother is dead, his goal is to leave his maternal uncle and to establish neolocal residence in an independent household of his own. Here he brings his wife and children, who are gradually replaced by his sisters' children as he and they grow older. Thus, when we follow an Ashanti man throughout a normal life career, we find him ultimately the head of an avunculocal extended family, either as the successor to an uncle or other matrilineal relative or as the founder of an independent household.

In societies like the Nakanai and Ashanti, where goals and behavior shift with age statuses in such a way as to complicate the structuring of social groups, the basic patterns may often be better revealed by the life histories of reasonably successful individuals than by demographic analysis. Ashanti society may, with considerable justification, be classed as fundamentally avunculocal because headship of an avunculocal extended family is the life goal toward which every Ashanti male strives and is in fact achieved with sufficient frequency to maintain goal-directed behavior at all levels. The fact that only a minority of the men have actually attained this goal at any given moment, or even ever attain it, seems less important than that the great majority accept the goal and direct their behavior accordingly.

This mode of analysis can even yield new insights into the structure of our own society. With us, of course, status is achieved primarily through advancement in the social class system rather than by age or succession to family headship. Any individual can, through energy, skill, or luck, rise during his lifetime from any point of origin in the social class hierarchy to a secure position in the upper middle class. At any one time, of course, not more than perhaps twenty percent of the total adult population actually enjoy such a favored status. Nevertheless, the flow of immigration has assured steady increments at the bottom of the class structure, and our differential birth rate, expanding economy, and increasing standard of living have continuously opened up new positions at the top, so that a considerable number of people actually do rise from humbler origins to the upper middle class—a number sufficient at least to maintain effort directed toward this goal in a very much wider segment of the population.

This confers upon our society a basically upper-middle-class orientation, despite the fact that the members of this class never actually constitute more than a minority. We lack a strong aristocratic tradition in part because membership in our small upper class is not generally attainable through individual effort and its goals are therefore not widely accepted, and in part because the position of this class is not buttressed by feudal land tenure or any comparable source of overwhelming economic or political power; every study of the American class structure, indeed, has shown per capita wealth to be greater in the upper-middle than in the upper class. Nor are we committed to socialism with its upper-lower or working-class orientation, which tends to be accepted in societies like Australia, New Zealand, and the Scandinavian countries where there are insufficient openings at the top to reward and thus maintain upper-middle class goals throughout the population.

In conclusion, it should be emphatically reaffirmed that the static approach to the analysis of social structure has been a valuable and necessary first step in the development of this branch of our science. We should not forget its substantial contributions as we move in the direction of increasing dynamism and catch glimpses of the greener pastures which lie ahead.

SOCIAL ORGANIZATION

IV

12

This paper was originally published in the *American Anthropologist* (42: 555-561, 1940). It reflects the influence of W. E. Lawrence, whose analytical creativity and encyclopedic knowledge of aboriginal Australian social systems provided one of the major stimuli which led me to specialize in the field of kinship and social organization.

Double Descent

I N the theoretical literature of social organization, two primary
types of descent are commonly distinguished, namely, "bilateral descent" and "unilinear descent." Under the former,
social affiliation corresponds to actual genealogical relationship,
being traced equally through all lineal relatives of a given ascending
generation without regard to the sex of the relative or of connecting
relatives. Under unilinear descent, on the other hand, the line of
affiliation through one parent and through lineal ascending and
descending relatives of the same sex is emphasized, yielding either
matrilineal or patrilineal descent, and other possible lines of affiliation are disregarded. It is the purpose of this paper to call attention
to the third primary type of affiliation, "double descent," which has
been reported by recent ethnographers for a number of widely
separated areas, but which has thus far escaped extended theoretical consideration.

167

Double descent is essentially a combination of matrilineal and patrilineal descent, the two modes of affiliation being followed concurrently. It is thus not unilinear but bilinear.[1] It is not, however, bilateral, since it does not treat all possible lines of affiliation equally but emphasizes two lines and disregards others. The distinction between the three modes of descent can be illustrated by considering the affiliation of Ego with his grandparents. Under unilinear descent, Ego is affiliated with only one of them—the maternal grandmother under matrilineal descent and the paternal grandfather under patrilineal descent. Where double descent prevails, Ego is affiliated with both his maternal grandmother and his paternal grandfather but not with his maternal grandfather or his paternal grandmother.

It would seem advisable to reserve the term "double descent" for cases where both unilinear rules apply at the same time for the same individual, and to distinguish cases where either rule may apply but not both together. Instances of the latter type are too numerous to recount. For Indonesia alone, for example, Kennedy (1937: 291) mentions four variants in a single paragraph: matrilineal affiliation by ambil-anak in patrilineal societies when a family has a daughter but lacks sons; "a sort of reverse ambil-anak" in matrilineal societies; affiliation of daughters with their mothers, and of sons with their fathers, in Sula; and the affiliation of the first, third, and other odd-numbered offspring with their mother, and of even-numbered progeny with their father, among the Macassar and Buginese of Celebes.

Descent is not, of course, synonymous with relationship. Scores of ethnographers have attested, for example, that in patrilineal societies the mother and her siblings are often considered as closely akin to Ego as are the father and his siblings, and that the converse is true in many matrilineal societies. Moreover, patrilineal descent is clearly recognized by certain peoples, e.g., in Australia, who

[1] The term "bilinear descent" might have been used except for the possibility of confusion with "bilateral descent." A third alternative, "dual descent," was similarly rejected because it might suggest a connection with "dual organization."

are reported to be ignorant of the relationship between father and child. Descent means, as Rivers (1924: 86) pointed out, not relationship itself, but affiliation with a particular group of relatives.

Where descent is bilateral, i.e., where no single line of kinsmen is singled out for special emphasis, the kingroup with which an individual is typically affiliated from birth is the "kindred" (cf. Rivers 1924: 16), a group consisting of his closest actual relatives in whatsoever line. In our own society, for instance, it is the kindred which assembles on Christmas and Thanksgiving and at weddings and funerals. Since the kindred centers around an individual, its composition will rarely be the same for any two persons, except in the case of own siblings. In any society, kindreds overlap endlessly; the kindreds of two first cousins, for example, will coincide in half their membership (the relatives of the parents who are siblings) and will differ in the other half. It is impossible to segment a society into discrete kindreds. Whenever, then, forces are present which operate through historical processes to divide a society into discrete subgroups on the basis of kinship ties, one line of affiliation must be given preference and others disregarded. The product is unilinear descent, with either a matrilineal or a patrilineal bias depending upon a complex of factors. Among these, a fixed rule of residence in marriage, either matrilocal or patrilocal, seems often to have been especially influential. Unilinear descent yields discrete kingroups of several orders of magnitude. For certain of these, anthropology has an accepted terminology. They are called "lineages" when they are composed of persons who can trace actual common descent according to the preferred unilinear mode of affiliation, "sibs" when membership is extended to persons whose common descent is only traditional and not actually traceable, and "moieties" when the extension has reached the maximum point consistent with exogamy and the entire society is divided into halves on a kinship basis. In this brief sketch the innumerable local variants must be ignored.

Where double descent prevails, there are necessarily at least two coexistent and intersecting sets of kingroups—lineages, sibs, or moieties—the one matrilineal and the other patrilineal. A person must belong at the same time, for example, to a matrilineal sib which includes his mother and her relatives through females, but which includes his father, and to a patrilineal sib which excludes his mother and her relatives. Under certain special circumstances, as we shall shortly see, double descent gives rise to compound kingroups of a distinctive type, such as the so-called "marriage classes" of Australia.

Before reviewing the evidence for double descent, we shall gratefully accept a refinement in terminology suggested by Lawrence (1937: 319-320). To avoid the constant repetition of the long adjectives "matrilineal" and "patrilineal," otherwise necessary in referring to any kingroup under double descent, we shall employ "matri-" and "patri-" as prefixes and speak of matrilineages and patrilineages, matrisibs and patrisibs, and matrimoieties and patrimoieties.

The existence of double descent was first called forcefully to the attention of anthropologists less than two decades ago by Rattray (see especially 1923: 77-78) in his work on Ashanti.[2] As is now well known, the Ashanti have both matrisibs (abusua) and patrisibs (ntoro). The former are based on "blood," which is believed to descend in the female line only; the latter, on "spirit," which is transmitted exclusively through males. Both types of sibs are exogamous, totemic, and characterized by distinctive food taboos. Inheritance and succession to authority follow the female line and the avunculate exists, but residence is patrilocal and the household consists of a patrilineal extended family. The matrisibs, which are on the whole more important, are not localized but are united by a common ancestor cult and special funerary and other ceremonies in addition to the bonds of blood, property, and authority already mentioned.

The Ashanti system apparently has considerable regional extension. According to Herskovits (1937: 287), for example, "this

---

[2] See the immediate preceding paper in the present volume for a more accurate analysis of Ashanti social structure based on the work of Fortes.

type of social organization not only characterized the Ashanti and the peoples of the coastal region of the Gold Coast, such as the Ga and Fanti, but is also found in at least one group of New World descendants of these Gold Coast folk, the Bush Negroes of Dutch Guiana." Among the Nankanse of the Ashanti hinterland, Rattray (1932: 232-233, et passim) reports exogamous, nontotemic, and nonlocalized matrilineages (soo) as well as exogamous, totemic, localized, and politically organized patrisibs (bute). Here, however, the bias is definitely patrilineal, for residence is patrilocal and both inheritance and succession follow the male line.

Double descent is also reported from a geographically and culturally distinct area in Africa, namely, among the cattle-raising Southern Bantu. The Herero (Luttig 1934: 58-67), for example, have nonlocalized matrisibs (omaanda) as well as localized patrisibs (otuzo). Although both are exogamous and totemic, the matrisibs are primarily social in character and the patrisibs religious. Inheritance, like descent, is double, ordinary property being transmitted matrilineally to the brother or sister's son while sacred property is inherited in the male line. For the Venda, Stayt (1931: 185) reports the existence of patrisibs, which "were at one time exogamous and of a totemic character," but which are now broken down. Their functions are still preserved, however, by their constituent patrilineages, which are exogamous and localized. "Although descent, succession, and inheritance are reckoned through the father, every individual is also a member of a parallel lineage on the mother's side, very important in social and religious life. This group has a particular significance for the individual, exerting a stronger emotional and personal influence than the more formal patrilineal group." These matrilineages are linked primarily with the ancestor cult.

As is widely known from the classic work of Rivers (1906: 540-542, 556, 183, et passim), the Todas of southern India are organized into two endogamous moieties, each of which is subdivided into exogamous, localized, nontotemic patrisibs. The latter are corporate units, each with its own lands, its patron divinity, and its headman. Inheritance is patrilineal, and residence patrilocal. Rivers (1906: 546) climaxes his description of a rigidly patrilineal society with the categorical statement: "Descent among the Todas is always reckoned in the male line." In view of the reputation of Rivers as an outstanding authority on social organization, it came as a distinct shock to anthropologists, to learn, in 1937, that the Todas are really characterized by double descent. This spectacular discovery was made by Emeneau (1937: 103-112) during the course of his linguistic investigations. Rivers had mentioned a group called the püliol, without understanding its nature. Emeneau conclusively demonstrates that the püliol is a fairly typical matrisib, between the members of which marriage and sexual intercourse are strictly forbidden. Toda society is thus seen to consist of two endogamous moieties, each a complex of intersecting matrisibs and patrisibs. The discovery of double descent among the Todas suggests the desirability of reexamining other reputedly unilinear societies to ascertain whether or not an unsuspected second mode of affiliation may be present.

The interpretation of social organization in Australia, especially in the wide area where "marriage classes" are found, has long been a bone of contention among specialists. Howitt (1904: 103-119, 199-240) and others have sought to distinguish some Australian tribes as patrilineal in descent, others as matrilineal. Mathews (1900: 120; 1908: 89) ascribed matrilineal descent to the Aranda and other Central Australian tribes while Baldwin Spencer (1905: 380-381) insisted strenuously that the rule of descent in these same tribes is really patrilineal. These and other difficulties are easily resolved when it is recognized that the class area of Australia is actually characterized by double descent, by a combination of coexisting matrilineal and patrilineal modes of affiliation. The whole situation has been clarified by Lawrence (1937: 319-354) in a penetrating analytical study. "Three factors . . . must coexist to provide the common denominator of all Australian class systems, viz.: (1) marriage by sister exchange; (2) matrilineal descent in exogamous moieties; and (3) patrilineal descent in exogamous patriclans . . . Within the class area . . . all three factors are invariably present; the distinction between matrimoieties, sections, and subsections rests upon the elaboration of the third element, patrilineal descent, i.e., upon whether it is confined to patri-clans or is extended to aggregations or to divided aggregations of patri-clans" (p. 344).

In a two-class Australian system, as Lawrence points out, the localized patrisibs or "hordes" are bisected in alternating generations by two matrimoieties. In a four-class system the patri-sibs are aggregated into two patrimoieties, which are crosscut by the two matrimoieties, yielding four "sections." From the point of view of any individual, his own class or section will include all persons who are related to him both matrilineally and patrilineally, i.e., who belong both to his matrimoiety and to his patrimoiety; among them are always his siblings, his parallel cousins, and his paternal grandfather and maternal grandmother. A second class will include all persons of Ego's matrimoiety but of the opposite patrimoiety, e.g., a man's mother and his sisters' children. A third class will include patrilineal relatives of the opposite matrimoiety, e.g., a man's father and son. The fourth class or section numbers all those not related to Ego by either matrilineal or patrilineal descent, and it is from this group that he must always take his spouse. An eight-class system is differentiated by the addition of a third moiety dichotomy which intersects both the matrimoieties and the patrimoieties, yielding eight "subsections," but its analysis does not fall within the province of this paper. It is sufficient to note, in summary, that double descent is found throughout Australia with the exception of four or five tiny areas at the extreme margins of the continent.

In North Ambrym in the New Hebrides, Deacon (1927: 325-342) noted a form of social organization closely paralleling that of Australia. There are three exogamous patrisibs (bwulim), possibly localized, which are bisected in alternating generations by two exogamous matrimoieties (batatun). The combination yields six marriage classes or sections. Marriage, which takes place by exchange of sisters, is closely restricted. A man may not marry a woman of his own matrimoiety, of his own patrisib, or of his mother's patrisib; his choice is thus confined to the women of a single section of the opposite moiety.

Double descent also appears elsewhere in Oceania, but without the refinement of marriage classes characteristic of Australia and Ambrym. In Manus, for example, Mead (1933: 206-236) found small, exogamous, localized, nontotemic patrisibs and unnamed, exogamous, nonlocalized matrilineages; the latter, however, include only lineal, not collateral, relatives. For Ontong Java, Hogbin (1931: 407-408) reports landowning patrilineages and houseowning matrilineages. Marriage prohibitions, however, apply bilaterally. Residence is mixed—more often matrilocal in poor families and patrilocal in rich families. In Pukapuka, the Beagleholes (1938: 221-233) found a variety of kingroups: bilateral kindreds; nonexogamous and only slightly functional matrimoieties; four nonlocalized, nonexogamous matrilineages (wua), headed by the eldest member, with functions in fishing, sporting contests, and life-crisis feasts; seven localized, nonexogamous, landowning patrilineages (po), each with a chief, priest, and cemetery; exogamous matrilineal sublineages, controlling taro beds and functioning in cases of homicide; and nonexogamous patrilineal sublineages with cemetery plots. Residence is patrilocal, succession to chiefship patrilineal, and inheritance generally patrilineal but matrilineal with regard to certain taro beds.

Our survey [3] has revealed the unquestionable existence of double descent in six widely scattered culture areas: West Africa, Bantu South Africa, India, Australia, Melanesia, and Polynesia.[4] This should suffice to establish it as a recurrent feature of social organization. Thus far we have unearthed no report of its occurence in the New World, except among the transplanted Bush Negroes of

---

[3] Conducted mainly in the files of the Cross-Cultural Survey at the Institute of Human Relations, Yale University.

[4] For a more recent and comprehensive compilation of attested cases, see J. Goody, "The Classification of Double Descent Systems," *Current Anthropology*, 2: 3-25, 1961. The appended critical comments by R. B. Lane on Goody's basis of classification deserve special attention.

Dutch Guiana. Once the possibility of double descent is recognized, it may be discovered by future field work even in North America. The Todas may not be the only well-described tribe among whom it has been overlooked.

Although our cases are too few to yield statistically reliable results, analysis of them reveals certain suggestive uniformities. Except in Ontong Java and Pukapuka, exogamy is everywhere associated with both patrilineal and matrilineal kingroups. Inheritance and succession, where reported, are everywhere patrilineal, except among the Ashanti, where they are matrilineal, and in Ontong Java and among the Herero, where inheritance is mixed. With Ontong Java again a partial exception, residence is in all cases patrilocal, and it is always the patrilineal kingroups, and never the matrilineal, which are localized and politically organized on a local basis. This suggests a possible origin for double desent. If, as has been suggested by many anthropologists, a regular rule of residence is an important factor in the development of unilinear kingroups, double descent would result when a people with strongly functional exogamous matrilineal kingroups comes to adopt patrilocal residence and to organize politically on a local basis in consequence either of outside contact or of internal adjustment.

13

This paper was originally published as a chapter in *Social Structure in Southeast Asia,* which I edited (*Viking Fund Publications in Anthropology,* no. 29, 1960, pp. 1-14)—a symposium of contributions by anthropologists of seven different nationalities presented at the Ninth Pacific Science Congress in Bangkok in November 1957. My own paper, written after the Congress as an introduction to the published symposium, was stimulated by the contributions of my fellow participants, by significant earlier papers by Davenport and Goodenough, and by penetrating discussions by Eggan, Firth, Fortes, and others during the course of a seminar on nonunilinear kinship systems held in 1958-59 at the Center for Advanced Study in the Behavioral Sciences in Palo Alto. In a very real sense, therefore, this paper represents a collective effort.

Cognatic Forms of Social Organization

T HE various forms of social groups which have in common the fact that membership is acquired through one parent only—either exclusively through the father or exclusively through the mother, not through both at the same time nor optionally through either—are today universally called "unilineal." This term embraces the two alternative categories of "patrilineal" and "matrilineal" as well as so-called "double descent," which is not an independent rule of affiliation but refers to societies which have two or more types of kingroups, some of which are characterized by parilineal and others by matrilineal descent. There is also widespread acceptance of "lineage" as the most general term applicable to all consanguineal groups resulting from unilineal descent. Unilineal kingroups are differentiated as "patrilineages" or "matrilineages" in terms of the two alternative organizing principles, and as "minimal," "minor," "major," or "maximal" lineages in terms of their increasing generation depth from the common ancestor of their members. A maximal lineage with geographically dispersed membership, with few if any corporate characteristics, and with an unknown or merely postulated or traditional common ancestor is often distinguished as a "sib" (in British usage a "clan"). If an entire society is divided into two very large sibs, these are called "moieties."

Since lineages are almost universally characterized by exogamy, their members can rarely reside together as a local group. Localization necessitates some compromise between the prevailing principle of unilineal descent and the fact of coresidence. In the overwhelming majority of unilineal social systems this compromise is achieved through adherence to a "unilocal" rule of residence—patrilocal, matrilocal, or avunculocal—which is consistent with the rule of descent. What results is a local group having as its core the adult members of a lineage of one sex only, to whom are added the inmarrying spouses of these members and from whom are subtracted their adult siblings of opposite sex who have departed to join their spouses in other local groups. British social anthropologists have not recognized or named this very important type of kingroup. I have elsewhere (1949: 65-78) suggested reserving for it the term "clan," and have named the three alternative forms in which it occurs "patriclans" (with patrilineal descent and patrilocal residence), "matriclans" (with matrilineal descent and matrilocal residence), and "avunctuclans" (with matrilineal descent and avunculocal residence).

At least a third of the societies of the world are not unilineal, in the sense that they do not employ either patrilineal or matrilineal descent as a major organizing principle in the grouping of kinsmen. Despite significant pioneer efforts, notably by Davenport (1959), Firth (1957), Freeman (1958), and Goodenough (1955), there still exists no solid consensus regarding organizational principles, typology, or terminology comparable to that achieved for unilineal social systems. This paper will attempt a clarification on all these points.

First of all, there is need of a general term, contrasting with "unilineal," which can be applied to any grouping of kinsmen organized by genealogical ties without particular emphasis on either patrilineal or matrilineal connections. The term "nonunilinear," employed by Davenport and Goodenough, has the disadvantages of being negative rather than positive in its connotations and of not implying kinship affiliation; any voluntary association is "nonuni-linear." The "multilineal" of Parsons (1943: 24) is inappropriate since, as will be indicated below, many such systems, including the American, are not in fact "lineal" in any sense. The "ambilineal" of Firth and the "bilateral" of current American usage seem better reserved for special subtypes of nonunilineal systems. I therefore propose the adoption of the one remaining familiar alternative, "cognatic," which is also the choice of Freeman and Leach. The word connotes appropriately "akin by birth." Its sole disadvan-tage, a minor one, is its former secondary meaning of "related on the mother's side," for which "uterine" is today the preferred synonym.

Analysis of cognatic social systems may begin with a considera-tion of five of those described in this symposium (Murdock 1960), which share a very large number of common features that align them with a recognized and widespread subtype, called "Eskimo" (Murdock 1949: 226-228). In all of them a small domestic unit is the most important social, economic, and landholding group—fully corporate in every sense. The Iban, Sagada, and Yami observe strict monogamy, and the Javanese and Subanun, though permit-ting polygyny, practice it to only a very limited extent. The do-mestic unit is an independent nuclear family in three instances, a stem family in two; one child continues to reside after marriage with his or her parents among the Iban and Javanese. Extended families occur in none of the five societies. Residence is ambilocal [1]—more often patrilocal than matrilocal among the Yami, more often matri-

[1] The writer has previously used "bilocal," but "ambilocal" is clearly pref-erable for a rule of residence which permits a choice between two unilocal alternatives, the one uxorilocal (matrilocal), the other virilocal (patrilocal or avunculocal).

local among the Javanese, equally balanced among the Iban, Sagada, and Subanun, never strictly unilocal. Neolocal residence also occurs as an alternative among the Javanese and as the norm in later life among the Subanun.

The Javanese and Sagada possess functionally insignificant ambilineal descent groups of a type to be analyzed later, but the only important grouping of kinsmen other than the dominant small family unit is the aggregation of near relatives to which Rivers (1924: 16) gave the name "kindred." All five of the societies in question possess kindreds, and in every case these embrace close lineal and collateral kinsmen regardless of whether the connecting links are male or female. The collateral range of the kindred varies. It embraces first but not second or remoter cousins among the Yami, but among the Iban the kindred includes fourth cousins though its effective range usually terminates with second cousins.

The domestic unit is always exogamous, the kindred only rarely so. The Iban, Javanese, and Subanun permit marriage with a first cousin; the Sagada and Yami forbid such unions but allow marriage with any second cousin. No group makes any distinction between cross- and parallel cousins. The same holds true of the kinship terminology, which clearly reflects the influence of both the family and the kindred. One set of terms is typically confined to members of the family unit, and a different set is employed for collateral relatives who are members of Ego's kindred but not of his family. This results in lineal terminology on the first ascending generation and in Eskimo terminology for cousins. The five societies reveal only two exceptions, both partial. The Javanese employ lineal terminology only for uncles, extending the term for mother to maternal and paternal aunts, and Frake reports that the Subanun apply either Hawaiian or Eskimo terminology to cousins depending upon the "level" of discourse. The two remaining principles of classification—bifurcate merging and bifurcate collateral (Lowie 1928)—find no expression in any of the five societies.

The two types of kingroups—the small family and the kindred—whose relative importance in the social structure characterizes these and other societies of the Eskimo type, demand meticulous analysis. A family is created by marriage, a universal human phenomenon, which establishes an affinal link between husband and wife and indirectly between their respective consanguineal kinsmen. A child acquires membership in a family by birth, or more technically and accurately by "filiation," which Fortes (1959: 206) defines as "the relationship created by the fact of being the legitimate child of one's parents" and correctly characterizes as "universally bilateral." Rules of inheritance, succession, and descent are compounded out of filiation links, usually by some selective preference for "patrifiliation" or "matrifiliation." For present purposes, however, the important point is that the small domestic unit is fundamentally a bilateral kingroup. It must therefore be defined in such a way as to exclude any lineal principle. Of the various forms of the family or household recorded in ethnography, only the following fall within such a definition:

1) The independent monogamous or nuclear family composed of married parents and their children.

2) The polygamous family (with either polygyny or polyandry), which links the children by two or more spouses to one common parent.

3) The stem family, which links the family of procreation of one married child to his family of orientation in a common household.

4) The lineal family,[2] which links the families of procreation of several married siblings to their common family of orientation but which dissolves with the death of their parents.

Any type of family or household organization which embraces two or more married siblings in its senior generation constitutes an "extended family" and must necessarily be based on a lineal principle—either patrilineal, matrilineal, or ambilineal—rather than exclusively on bilateral filiation. An extended family is essen-

---

[2] Defined in Murdock (1957: 669). The term "lineal," as used here, should now be recognized as inappropriate. A new term is clearly needed.

tially a minimal clan or localized lineage and, as such, should be sharply differentiated from a genuine domestic group.

The kindred should also be recognized as a bilateral kingroup. It is always Ego-oriented, i.e., composed of persons related to a particular individual (or group of siblings) bilaterally (literally "on both sides"). The members of a kindred, other than the core individual and his siblings, need not be, and frequently are not, related to one another. In any society, kindreds necessarily overlap one another endlessly. They are not discrete units; a society can never be divided into separate kindreds as it can be segmented into discrete families, lineages, clans, or communities. From the point of view of the core individual or siblingship, the membership of the kindred can be defined in terms of serial links of filiation produced by the ramifying intersection of families of procreation and orientation. The membership cannot be defined, however, in lineal terms by descent from a common ancestor. A kindred therefore is not, and cannot be, a descent group. There are, to be sure, certain types of descent groups, ancestor-oriented rather than Ego-oriented, which bear a superficial resemblance to kindreds, and they will be analyzed below. At this point it suffices to note that they are invariably ambilineal rather than bilateral.

Because of its lack of discreteness a kindred cannot be a corporate group.[3] The concept of corporateness, as used in the ethnographic literature, is confused and ambiguous, and urgently needs clarification. On the whole, I agree with Leach that it would be desirable to return essentially to Maine's original definition of a corporation as an estate comprising rights over persons and various forms of real, movable, and incorporeal property in whose assets a number of individuals share in accordance with their respective statuses. Thus defined, a corporate group is one whose members share an estate, especially one consisting of land, dwellings, or other material resources which its members have the right to use or exploit according to culturally accepted rules of tenure. As a

---

[3] The so-called "stem kindreds" described by Davenport (1959: 565) may possibly constitute an exception.

practical matter, I would restrict the concept to groups whose rights are regularly rather than sporadically exercised, especially rights to the land (and its improvements) on which the members live and from which they extract their economic livelihood. I would not exclude, of course, incorporeal rights which have genuine significance in the everyday ceremonial, social, or artistic life of a people, such as the crests and associated privileges of Haida lineages. I would, however, prefer to treat as though they were noncorporate all groups whose collective rights and associated responsibilities are seldom exercised and are inconsequential in the total cultural context, e.g., the Sagada descent groups described by Eggan with collective rights in the pine trees planted by a common ancestor or the *alur walis* of the Javanese with its collective responsibility for the intermittent care of ancestral graves.

If the proposed definition is acceptable, kingroups can be conveniently classified in three categories:

1) CORPORATE KINGROUPS: families, lineages, and clans (in the sense of Murdock 1949) are almost universally corporate.

2) OCCASIONAL KINGROUPS: i.e., those which, according to Firth (1959), become operative only on specific occasions, even though they may sometimes be corporate in a technical sense. Firth cites as an example the modern Scottish clan with its periodic reunions.

3) CIRCUMSCRIPTIVE KINGROUPS: i.e., noncorporate groups which never function as units, even on sporadic occasions, but which merely serve to define the limits of certain rights and duties of their members. The sib, for example, is often only a circumscriptive group. Thus in the central Caroline Islands, where sibs are widely dispersed among peoples with differing languages and cultures and only lineages are corporate groups, common sib membership serves only to set limits to the obligation of exogamy and to the right to receive food and overnight hospitality when away from home.

In this classification, kindreds are occasional groups, not only in the five societies under discussion but seemingly in every society where they occur. Sometimes, as in the northern Philippines and in early Europe (Phillpotts 1913), they become operative on occasions for blood vengeance or the distribution of wergild. In most societies, however, they function primarily at crises in the life cycle of the core individual, especially in naming, initiation, wedding, and funeral ceremonies. In unilineal societies, comparable services are often rendered by what Eggan has called "skewed kindreds," i.e., ad hoc groups composed of two or more lineage segments like the Tikopia *kana a paito*.

To return to the case material, all five of the societies under consideration are characterized by the presence of important kingroups of only two types—always the same two—namely, small domestic groups and kindreds. The former are invariably corporate, the latter occasional. Neither, however, is a descent group. Both are bilateral rather than lineal. Davenport, Firth, and Goodenough have already suggested segregating kingroups of the kindred type from other forms of cognatic organization. I accept their suggestion, and propose that the term "bilateral" be reserved for the former. For those who favor the application of such terms to entire societies, rather than rigorously confining them to types of kingroups, it would seem appropriate to speak of a society as bilateral if it has no functionally significant descent groups, either unilineal or cognatic, and possesses only kingroups of the bilateral type such as families and kindreds.

Discussion of the world distribution of bilateral societies will be limited to those with social systems closely resembling the Iban, Javanese, Sagada, Subanun, and Yami, i.e., to societies of the Eskimo type which conform to these eight definitive criteria:

1) Prominence of small domestic units and absence of any form of extended family.
2) Prevailing monogamy with no more than a limited incidence of polygamy.
3) Ambilocal or neolocal residence, i.e., with no invariable unilocal rule.

4) Absence of any functionally important descent groups, unilineal or ambilineal.

5) Presence of bilateral kindreds or at least no specific report of their absence.

6) Absence of distinctions in the marriageability of different kinds of first cousins.

7) Cousin terminology of the Eskimo type.

8) Avuncular terminology of lineal or bifurcate collateral type, i.e., no extension of parental terms to uncles or aunts.

The societies mentioned below include only those for which my own files contain sufficient information for classification, and among these only those which conform to the above eight criteria in every respect. References are cited, however, only for published sources of substantial quality.

Bilateral societies of the Eskimo type are not uncommon in the general region of Southeast Asia. To the five described in this symposium (Murdock 1960) must be added the Bontok (Keesing 1949), Kalinga (Barton 1949), Sugbuhanon, Tagalog, and Tagbanua of the Philippines; the Land Dayak (Geddes 1954) of Borneo; the Andamanese, Nicobarese, and Selung; and the Cambodians. The acculturated Chamorro of Saipan (Spoehr 1954) are the sole representatives in Oceania east of the Philippines. In overwhelmingly unilineal Africa, only the Khoisan hunters have bilateral systems, and among them only the Kung Bushmen (Marshall 1957 and 1959) are adequately described. Except for the Albanians and some Yugoslav groups, all modern European societies and those of European derivation have social systems of the Eskimo type, and my files contain specific reports of kindreds for the Americans, Argentinians, Czechs, Dutch (Keur 1955), English, French, French Canadians, Hutsul, Irish (Arensberg and Kimball 1940), Jamaicans, Lapps (Pehrson 1954; Whitaker 1955), Lithuanians, and Russians. Essentially similar systems prevail in eastern Asia among the Japanese and in parts of the Ryukyu Islands, and in northeastern Asia among the Ainu, Chukchee

(Bogoras 1907), and Koryak (Jochelson 1905-08). The Eskimo, from North Alaska (Spencer 1959) east to Greenland, represent, so to speak, the type specimens. The similar systems of the Catawba and Penobscot in eastern North America possibly reflect acculturative influences, but those of the Tewa and Tiwa pueblos of the Southwest are clearly indigenous. In South America, systems of the Eskimo type are reported for the Carinya of Venezuela, the Cayapa of Ecuador, the Camba of Bolivia, the Abipon of Argentina, and the Ona and Yahgan of Tierra del Fuego, although in the last two instances patrilocal residence may preponderate too strongly to warrent this classification.

The degree of identity in diagnostic characteristics among the peoples mentioned is extraordinary—the more so since they range from simple hunters and gatherers, through intermediate tillers, to European and Asiatic societies of the highest complexity. It seems clear, therefore, that modes of subsistence, technological attainments, elaboration of status distinctions, and levels of political integraton exert little differentiating influence. However great or slight its social and cultural complexity in such respects, if a society for any reason maximizes the small domestic unit and minimizes lineal descent groups it tends automatically to arrive at a single uniform configuration of marriage rules, kin alignments, and kinship nomenclature. The similarities go far beyond the features specifically analyzed. Thus payment of bride-price, the overwhelmingly predominant mode of obtaining a wife throughout the world as a whole, is customary only among the Abipon, Cambodians, Caribou Eskimo, Subanun, and Sugbuhanon of all the societies mentioned or indirectly alluded to in the foregoing discussion.

The social structure of the Sinhalese, though clearly more cognatic than unilineal in its basic organizing principles, contrasts with the bilateral systems analyzed above on practically every essential point. Small domestic units, instead of being prominent and independent, are absorbed in a larger extended family, the *watte* or "coresident compound group." Among the wealthy, these groups tend to be characterized by patrilocal residence and patrilineal succession, and to approximate the structure of patrilineages, although the patrilineal principle is neither fully elaborated nor universally operative. Bilateral kindreds are either absent or too insignificant to seem to Leach deserving of consideration. Cousins are not equally marriageable or non-marriageable. The Sinhalese forbid unions with a parallel cousin but permit then with a cross-cousin; indeed they utilize cross-cousin marriage as a means of reuniting portions of an estate fragmented by bilateral inheritance. In harmony with this, they employ cousin terminology of the Iroquois type, which, unlike Eskimo terminology, distinguishes cross from parallel cousins. In the first ascending generation, instead of lineal terms, they use bifurcate merging terminology, reflecting the patrilocal and patrilineal tendencies in the organization of the extended family.

In all the respects in which the Sinhalese social system differs from cognatic structures of the Eskimo type it approaches norms characteristic of patrilineal systems of the well-known Dakota type (Murdock 1949: 236-238). It might thus be called "quasi-patrilineal." Even the rule of residence—predominantly patrilocal, but matrilocal in *binna* marriages—falls somewhere between the prevailing norms for societies of the Eskimo and Dakota types. Among the societies elsewhere in the world which closely resemble the Sinhalese in structural features are the Bacairi, Camayura, and Wapishana of South America; all are characterized by predominantly patrilocal residence, by extended forms of family organization, by the absence or unimportance of kindreds, by symmetrical cross cousin marriage, by cousin terminology of the Iroquois type, and by bifurcate merging avuncular terms. The same continent also contains a number of "quasi-matrilineal" societies, e.g., the Motilon, Panare, Yabarana, and Yekuana, which are identical to the foregoing in all respects except that the residence rule is predominantly matrilocal. They approach matrilineal societies of the Iroquois type in precisely the same way as the Sinhalese approach the patrilineal Dakota structural type. In the classroom I have used the term "Carib type" to embrace both unilocal variants of cognatic systems with unilineal features, and have distinguished them from the more strictly cognatic "bilateral" and "ambilineal" subtypes.

Social systems of the Carib type are in many instances demonstrably transitional forms in the evolution of unilineal from cognatic structures, or vice versa. Their unusual frequency in aboriginal South America, however, suggests that, at least under certain circumstances, they may achieve a relatively stable equilibrium, which would warrant regarding them as an independent type and not merely as phases in a process of change. The distribution of cognatic systems of the Carib type is by no means confined to South America. Some of those which most closely resemble the Sinhalese in their diagnostic features merit special consideration.

The Aleut and the Nunivak Eskimo (Lantis 1946) of western Alaska retain the bifurcate collateral avuncular terminology of other Eskimo groups but agree with the Sinhalese in adhering to patrilocal residence, in having extended families, in possessing incipient and agamous patrilineages, in permitting cross-cousin marriage, and in using cousin terminology of the Iroquois type. The Polynesians of Rennell Island, whose social system is presumably derived historically from an ambilineal rather than a bilateral form of cognatic organization, have bifurcate merging avuncular terminology as well as extended families, cross-cousin marriage, and Iroquois cousin terms. The Fort Jameson Ngoni (Barnes 1951), who have settled amongst and intermarried with matrilineal peoples in Northern Rhodesia, and have thereby lost all except a few vestiges of their original patrilineal organization, agree with the Sinhalese in having patrilocal residence, cross-cousin marriage, Iroquois cousin terminology, and avuncular terms of bifurcate merging type. Their quasi-patrilineal system is thus in the process of change from a unilineal toward a cognatic structure rather than vice versa.

Because they are so commonly transitional, and thus tend to preserve certain features of their earlier structure, systems of the Carib type show more variability than do those of the Eskimo type. What they all have in common is some degree of dependence, whether vestigial, incipient, or relatively stable, upon a unilineal principle of organization. Thus the Coos and Siuslaw of Oregon, the Maidu and Shasta of California, and the Havasupai (Spier 1922 and 1928) and Pima of the Southwest have patrilocal residence, extended families and sometimes other elements of patrilineal organization, and Iroquois cousin terminology but lack cross-cousin marriage and bifurcate merging avuncular terms. In all cases, however, the unilineal principle of organization remains subordinate to the cognatic principle. Social systems of the Carib type must thus be grouped in the general category of cognatic systems. They nevertheless differ in so many respects from cognatic systems of the bilateral or Eskimo subtype, as well as from the ambilineal systems next to be analyzed, and still reveal so many common features, that it seems advisable to segregate them as a distinctive subtype, for which the descriptive term "quasi-unilineal" is herewith proposed.

In his analysis of Sinhalese society, Leach reaches the conclusion that "social structures are sometimes best regarded as the statistical outcome of multiple individual choices rather than as a direct reflection of jural rules." With this point of view I must register hearty and enthusiastic agreement. Leach amply demonstrates the validity of this approach in analyzing the processes which produce structural continuity and adaptation to underlying economic and technological facts in Sinhalese life. The available evidence on other quasi-unilineal systems seems to me to corroborate his interpretation. I would even go further and assert that social structures are always best regarded in the same light, and that jural rules themselves are the "outcome of multiple individual choices" in situations where one kind of choice is likely to be appreciably more strongly or regularly rewarded than possible alternative choices. This point of view, which seems to me generally shared by American students of social structure, accounts for my own sense of discomfort with the analyses of certain extreme British structuralists who assert the opposite, especially those who reify the concept of structure and speak, for example, of structural principles as exerting pressures upon individuals. Leach's position seems to me to have the enormous advantage of making possible the utilization of psychological principles and of scientific knowledge concerning the dynamics of cultural change in the interpretation of social systems. It has both realism and flexibility, and gives promise of substantial future progress in social structural research.

Of the nine cognatic social systems described in this symposium (Murdock 1960), those of the three Formosan groups treated by Mabuchi—the Atayal, Paiwan, and Puyuma—reveal a series of distinctive structural features which distinguish them alike from the five bilateral societies and from the quasi-unilineal Sinhalese. They are characterized most strikingly by the presence and functional importance of corporate descent groups of the type which Firth has called "ambilineal." Both Firth (1957 and 1959) and Davenport (1959) have subjected this kind of group to penetrating analysis, which requires only minor clarification, especially in regard to terminology, to become fully acceptable.

In a recent article, Fortes (1959) departs from modern usage in two respects in his interpretation of ambilineal descent groups. He confuses the concepts of descent and kinship, referring twice in a single paragraph to "kinship or descent" and once to "descent or kinship" (p. 211). He thus abandons the clarifying contribution of Rivers (1924: 86), who first disentangled the two concepts and proposed applying that of descent "to membership of a social group, and to this only." Secondly, when other students of social structure have long since ceased to use marriage rules, such as exogamy and endogamy, as defining attributes of kingroups, Fortes insists that a "bilateral descent group . . . would have to be strictly endogamous" (p. 211). He thus refuses to class the Maori *hapu* (Firth 1929 and 1957) and "the kind of land-owning groups described by Goodenough" (1955) as descent groups but, curiously enough, regards "the Jews in an East European Ghetto, or a caste, as long as it is coupled with obligatory endogamy" (p. 206) as acceptable examples. He even compounds his confusion by proposing "kindred groups" as an appropriate term for ambilineal structures. In preference to Fortes, the subsequent discussion will follow Goodenough, Firth, Davenport, and the contributors to this symposium.

The Atayal, Paiwan, and Puyuma are characterized, in addition to their ambilineal descent groups, by monogamy, by the extension of marriage prohibitions to all second as well as first cousins, by the application of sibling terms to cousins, by avuncular terminology of the generation type (except among the Atayal), and by ambilocal residence, with matrilocality predominating among the Puyuma and patrilocality in the other two tribes. An individual's membership in a descent group is usually determined by his parents' choice of marital residence, and affiliation is not ordinarily maintained with the natal group of the parent who has shifted residence. In the case of the "ritual groups" of the Puyuma, however, Mabuchi notes certain exceptions—examples both of dual affiliation and of affiliation with a group other than that of residence. Such exceptions do not occur in connection with the comparable groups among the Paiwan. Because of the high incidence of patrilocality among the Atayal, each ritual group consists of a core which resembles a localized patrilineage and of a much smaller fringe affiliated on the basis of matrilocal residence. In all three tribes the descent groups are clearly ambilineal, since affiliation in each successive generation is acquired through either parent and depends, not on filiation links radiating outward from an individual as in the case of a bilateral kindred, but on chains of filiation links converging upon a common ancestor, from whom land rights are derived and in whose name collective rituals are performed.

These Formosan descent groups conform in basic structural respects to the Bellacoola *minmint* (McIlwraith 1948), the Gilbertese *kainga* (Goodenough 1955), the Kwakiutl *numaym* (Boas 1897), the Lozi *mishiku* (Gluckman 1950 and 1951), the Mangaian *kopu* (Buck 1934), the Maori *hapu* (Firth 1929), the Nukuoro *te-haka-sa-aluna,* the Samoan *'ainga sa* (Ember 1959), and the old Scottish clan, the essential features of all of which have been summarized by Davenport (1959) and need not be repeated.

Before citing additional examples from my own files, I should like to propose certain clarifications in respect to terminology.

I have already recommended the adoption of Firth's term "ambilineal" to denote descent groups of this type of contradistinction to "quasi-unilineal" for those of the type found among the Sinhalese and to "bilateral" for the Ego-centered rather than ancestor-centered kindred. The three terms serve adequately to differentiate three distinct variants of cognatic as opposed to unilineal organization. Along with "Eskimo type" and "Carib type" for societies characterized primarily by bilateral or quasi-unilineal structures, respectively, I propose "Polynesian type" for those in which ambilineal structures are emphasized. Such systems are especially prevalent in Polynesia. The alternative, "Hawaiian type," although it has some currency, seems less suitable since the indigenous social system of Hawaii is not yet fully described and may well deviate in important respects from the pattern under discussion.

As a general term for ambilineal descent groups Davenport (1959) uses "sept," borrowed from Boas. Firth (1957: 6), however, proposes a revised definition of the term "ramage," and this seems to me clearly preferable, despite the unquestioned priority of "sept," because of its resemblance to "lineage," the accepted general term for unilineal descent groups. Ramages are the precise functional equivalents of lineages. They are equally consanguineal in composition, and they are equally susceptible to segmentation. Just as the core of a unilocal extended family is called a minimal lineage, so the core of an ambilocal extended family may be termed a minimal ramage. A ramage confined to a ward or similar subdivision of a community may similarly be called a minor ramage, and one coexistent with the community a major ramage. The term "sept" might be retained for a maximal ramage, in parallel to "sib" for a maximal lineage, i.e., for a kingroup substantially exceeding the bounds of a single community. Like lineages, ramages occur in both pure or consanguineal and in compromise or localized forms. If the latter are called clans (patrilocal, matrilocal, or avunculocal) in unilineal societies, it would be appropriate in ambilineal societies to designate them as "ambilocal clans." This would, incidentally, return the word clan to its original meaning.

Two alleged distinctions between lineages and ramages deserve consideration. Davenport (1959: 566) notes that lineages are regularly "exclusive" in the sense that an individual can belong to only one group of the same category at the same time, whereas ramages are often "nonexclusive" with dual or even plural memberships. Firth (1957: 5) points out that affiliation with a lineage is regularly "definitive," i.e., determined by a fixed rule of descent, whereas ramage membership is "optative," i.e., allowing for a choice among alternatives. While both allegations are unquestionably correct, comparative evidence somewhat qualifies their significance. Many ambilineal societies do not permit plural memberships; once the choice of ramage affiliation has been made, it is in an important sense exclusive since the alternative memberships either become latent or lapse entirely. Freeman (1958) calls such a rule of affiliation "utrolateral." I suggest a category of "optative-exclusive" to contrast with "optative-nonexclusive." Although the ramages of the Bellacoola, Kwakiutl, Maori, Puyuma, and Samoans, for example, are essentially optative-nonexclusive, those of the Gilbertese, Lozi, Mangaians, Nukuoro, and Paiwan are optative-exclusive.

Wherever kingroup affiliation is nonexclusive, an individual's plural memberships almost inevitably become segregated into one primary membership, which is strongly activated by residence, and one or more secondary memberships in which participation is only partial or occasional. A similar situation, indeed, often prevails in unilineal societies, where individuals, through what Fortes (1953 and 1959) calls "complementary filiation," commonly acquire and retain certain subsidiary rights and duties of participation in the lineage of the parent through whom descent is not reckoned. Unilineal descent does not even invariably exclude an optative element, since not a few unilineal societies permit full affiliation through complementary filiation under special circumstances. In addition to the widespread practice called "ambil-anak," two specific cases will illustrate the point. The patrilineal and patrilocal Mongo peoples of the Belgian Congo (Hulstaert 1938) accord to a man who has no paired sister whose bride-price can be used to provide him with a wife the right to remove to the village whence his mother came, to affiliate permanently with her patrilineage, and to receive a wife from his maternal uncle. The matrilineal and matrilocal Trukese of Micronesia (Goodenough 1951) encourage a woman with insufficient "mothers" and "sisters" to operate an efficient matrilocal extended family to join the extended family of her husband's mother and sisters; if the situation cannot be rectified within a generation, her offspring become permanently affiliated with their father's matrilineage. As opposed to the usual "definitive-exclusive" mode of kingroup affiliation in unilineal societies, that of the Mongo and Trukese can be regarded as conditionally optative.

The data in my files indicate the probable presence of minor or major ramages in a number of societies not mentioned by Davenport (1959). In Polynesia, they are suggested by the "paternal descent groups" reported by Métraux (1940) for the ambilocal Easter Islanders; by the "exogamous clans" reported by Kennedy (1931) for the ambilocal Ellice Islanders; by the *kutunga* or lineage-like land-owning groups with optative-nonexclusive affiliation described by Burrows (1936) for the Futunans; by the landholding groups reported by Buck (1938) for the ambilocal Mangarevans; by the landowning "families" described by Loeb (1926) for the ambilocal Niueans; by the patrilineal exogamous "joint families" with 10 per cent matrilineal affiliation described by Hogbin (1934) for the Ontong-Javanese; and by the ambilocal longhouse group inhabiting a "district" which Henry (1928) reports for old Tahiti. Although the Palauans of Micronesia tend strongly toward matrilineal descent, Force (1960: 46-48) states specifically that a person "always had membership (or at least membership potential) in both the lineage of his father and the lineage of his mother and . . . he might elect or be forced by circumstances . . . to accept membership in his father's lineage. . . . If a man did follow his paternal lineage he then brought his wife to live with him on land inherited from his father's *keblil* [sib]." In Melanesia, the exogamous *taviti* or "kindred" of Eddystone Island described by Rivers (1926: 71-94) may conceivably be actually a ramage; the *komu* or ambilateral "kindred" which Ivens (1927) reports as inhabiting a Ulawan hamlet is almost certainly such; and Goodenough (1957) specifically compares the *gaabu* and *unuma* of the Bwaidoga to the segmentary ramages of the Maori. Outside of Oceania the incidence of indubitable ramages becomes sporadic. In northwestern North America, Goldman (1940) reports bilateral crest groups with a patrilineal bias among the Alkatcho Carrier, and similar groups are to be inferred from the description by Teit (1906) of the Lillooet. In Africa, bilateral clusters of extended families with a patrilineal bias among the Jukun, which Meek (1931) calls "kindreds," are undoubtedly ramages, and recent information cited by McCulloch (1950) for the Sherbro of Sierra Leone indicates that the *ram,* formerly held to be a matrilineage, is actually a localized ambilateral group with patrilineal as well as matrilineal affiliation.

All thirty of the ambilineal societies thus far considered—three from Mabuchi, twelve discussed by Davenport, and fifteen from my own files—are characterized by Hawaiian cousin terminology and the extension of marriage prohibitions to at least all first cousins, as well as by ambilocal residence and major or minor ramages. A series of agricultural peoples in Mexico, e.g., the Aztec, Mazatec, Mixe, Popoluca, Totonac, Yaqui, and Zapotec, should perhaps be added to this list. All are predominantly patrilocal but definitely nonunilineal. All possess Hawaiian cousin terminology and prohibit marriage with any first cousin. Although strong acculturative influences have obscured the indigenous social organization, early accounts nearly everywhere describe villages as subdivided into "barrios," which may conceivably have been ramages. Only in the case of the Aztec *calpulli* have these been thoroughly analyzed from early records, and Monzon (1949) has demonstrated that the *calpulli* were neither unilineal nor exogamous.

If ambilocal extended families are to be regarded as minimal ramages, the list of ambilineal societies can be extended to include the Hawaiians and Tongarevans of Polynesia; the Ingassana of Sudan; the Chorti and Terena of Central and South America; the

Table 1

Subtypes of Cognatic Social Organization

Structural feature	Bilateral (Eskimo)	Quasi-unilineal (Carib)	Ambilineal (Polynesian)
Small domestic units	Invariably prominent	Rarely prominent	Rarely prominent
Extended families	Invariably absent	Nearly always present	Usually present
Bilateral kindreds	Usually present	Nearly always absent	Occasionally present
Ambilineal ramages	Usually absent	Invariably absent	Nearly always present
Rule of residence	Always neolocal or ambilocal	Usually unilocal	Nearly always ambilocal
Marriage with first cousins	Often allowed	Allowed with cross-cousins	Invariably forbidden
Marriage with second cousins	Usually allowed	Usually allowed	Commonly forbidden
Kinship terms for cousins	Nearly always Eskimo	Nearly always Iroquois	Nearly always Hawaiian
Avuncular terminology	Usually lineal	Usually bifurcate merging	Commonly of generation type

Alsea, Arapaho, Caddo, Cheyenne, Comanche, Hukundika Shoshone, Hupa, Karok, Kiowa Apache, Kutenai, Sinkaietk, Southern Ute, and Yurok of North America. It is noteworthy that these peoples, without exception, also possess Hawaiian cousin terminology and prohibit cousin marriages.

Careful analysis of the data in my files on all nonunilineal societies which do not fall obviously into one or another of the three types already distinguished—the Eskimo or bilateral, the Carib or quasi-unilineal, and the Polynesian or ambilineal—fails to reveal any additional comparable configurations. Many groups differ from a particular type in only one of a half dozen criteria, and the rest share features of two cognatic types. This is, of course, no more surprising than that societies with double descent combine features of both the matrilineal and the patrilineal varieties of unilineal organization. The Ifugao of the Philippines will serve as an example. As Eggan has shown, they possess ambilineal ramages as well as the bilateral kindreds reported by Barton (1919). Their Hawaiian cousin terminology and avuncular terms of the generation type accord with the former; their small domestic units with the latter; their ambilocal rule of residence with both.

By way of conclusion and summary, the principal structural features which differentiate the three basic subtypes of cognatic social organization are categorized in Table 1.

14

This paper was originally published as a chapter in *Miscellanea Paul Rivet* (Universidad Nacional Autónoma de México, 1958, vol. I, 299-315). My interest in the patterning of kinship behavior was stimulated by personal contacts with Fred Eggan and other students of Radcliffe-Brown at the University of Chicago. It found its first expression in an earlier paper—"Kinship and Social Behavior Among the Haida," *American Anthropologist* (36: 355-385, 1934)—which is not reprinted herewith for several reasons, including problems of orthography. The present paper reflects a continuation of the same interest.

Reprinted by permission of the Instituto de Investigaciones Históricas, Universidad Autónoma de México.

Social Organization of the Tenino

THE Tenino, a Sahaptin-speaking tribe of north-central Oregon, reside today on the Warmsprings Reservations, where they were studied by the writer during the summers of 1934 and 1935. Aboriginally they occupied the south bank of the Columbia River from Big Eddy east to Arlington and the lower watersheds of its southern affluents, Eightmile Creek and the Deschutes and John Day rivers. South of them, around modern Tygh Valley and beyond, lived the Molala, a Waiilatpuan tribe, whom the Tenino defeated in war and expelled from their territory in the early nineteenth century, extending their range to meet that of the Lutuamian-speaking Klamath. To the southeast, in central Oregon, lived bands of the Shoshonean-speaking Northern Paiute. To the east, along the Columbia River, resided the Umatilla, a kindred Sahaptin people. North of the river, in Washington, were other villages of Sahaptin speech, presumably affiliated with the Klikitat to the northwest since the Tenino did not acknowledge them as fellow tribesmen. To the west lived two tribes of Chinookan speech—the Wasco on the south bank of the Columbia River near The Dalles and the Wishram on the north bank in Washington.

The Tenino numbered about 1,200 in prereservation days. They were divided into four local groups, all very closely related culturally and linguistically. Each consisted typically of two villages, one occupied during the winter months (November to March) and the other during the warmer part of the year (April to October), though either might be split into two distinct settlements. The four local groups are identified below.

1. *Tinainu.* This group had its principal summer village (name: tinai'nu) on the south bank of the Columbia River about six miles upstream from The Dalles, and its winter village (name: təqa'x-təqax) five miles south thereof on Eightmile Creek. The name of the former, somewhat corrupted, has been adopted for the tribe as a whole, which had no collective name for itself.

2. *Tygh.* This group is an offshoot of the Tinainu which occupied the country of the Molala after the expulsion of the latter. It had a summer village (name: təɫxni') on the site of modern Sherar's Bridge on the Deschutes River, a winter village (name: taix) eight miles to the west at modern Tygh Valley, and a smaller suburb (name: q'wənmi'pa) of the latter a mile and a half to the southeast. During the summer, however, many people of this group continued to frequent the Tinainu fishing village on the Columbia.

3. *Wayam or Deschutes.* The winter village (name: wanwa'wi) of this group was located on the left bank of the Deschutes River just above its junction with the Columbia. Its summer village (name: waya'm) was situated on the Columbia River at Celilo Falls.

4. *John Day.* This group had its principal winter village (name: təkcpə'c) on the right bank of the John Day River about three miles above its junction with the Columbia and a somewhat smaller one (name: maxa'xpa) a mile or two downstream on the

left bank of the same river. The principal summer village (name: ta'wac) was located on the south bank of the Columbia River on the site of modern Quinook, with an offshoot (name: q'ə'məł) about five miles downstream therefrom.

Aboriginally the Tenino practiced no agriculture and possessed no domestic animals except the dog. They subsisted primarily by fishing, with very important supplementary hunting and gathering. The men did all the hunting and most of the fishing. The women dried the meat, smoked the fish, and did most of the gathering, although the men helped in collecting acorns and pine nuts and to some extent in picking berries. Both sexes engaged in trade, but the men confined themselves chiefly to the exchange of horses and to occasional trading expeditions. The seasonal round of economic activities exerted a strong influence on the social organization.

From November to March the Tenino occupied their winter villages, where each extended family had two houses—an oval or elliptical, semisubterranean, earth-covered lodge used for sleeping and a rectangular frame dwelling with mat-covered walls and roof used for cooking and daytime activities. The winter was spent in the manufacture of artifacts, in stream fishing and fuel gathering, and in hunting and trapping.

Late in March the Tenino dismantled their winter dwellings and removed to their summer villages, where each extended family erected a rectangular shed of poles and mats with a flat rather than gabled roof. Half of this structure was used for drying salmon, the other half as living quarters. Special parties ritually gathered roots and caught salmon for an important first-fruits ceremony in early April. Neither salmon nor roots could be eaten until after these rites had been performed.

Following the spring festival, about half the families of a village departed for a series of expeditions into the interior, where the women gathered roots and the men hunted. They lived in temporary camps of mat-covered tipis. The rest of the population remained in the summer village, catching and drying salmon. In July all returned to the villages for another first-fruits ceremony, this one featuring berries and venison ritually obtained by a special party of six men and six women.

After the summer festival the Tenino again divided, part remaining in the villages to continue the salmon fishing and to trade, while the rest visited the mountains to gather berries and nuts, with incidental hunting. In September, at the conclusion of the berry season, parties set out on long hunting expeditions up the Deschutes or John Day River, camping in tipis. The women smoked the meat which the men caught and gathered late-ripening roots and berries. In October a special party collected tule reeds for mats. The drying sheds were now dismantled, and the people moved to their winter villages, reconditioning their semisubterranean dwellings to initiate a new seasonal round.

One major economic preoccupation of the Tenino has not been discussed in the foregoing account of subsistence activities. The region of The Dalles was one of the major foci of trade in aboriginal America. Here the Tenino, with the neighboring Wasco and Wishram, acted as middlemen in a network of trade relations which ramified westward down the Columbia River to the Pacific coast, northward into the heart of the Plateau area, eastward to the edges of the Plains, and southward into northern California. Parties of Tenino men occasionally undertook trading expeditions in all directions, but for the most part the neighboring peoples brought their wares to the summer villages on the Columbia to exchange them for native products and for imports from elsewhere. The trading season lasted from August to October, the period when the run of salmon had somewhat slackened. The visitors went from house to house, bartering with the local women, for there were no shops or markets. Nor was there any true money, although strings of dentalium shells were widely acceptable in exchange for other goods.

To this trade the Tenino contributed chiefly dried salmon, fish oil, and furs. The principal imports were dentalia and other shells from the west; coiled baskets from the north; horses, buffalo hides, and parfleches from the east; and slaves, California baskets and beads, eagle feathers, and Achomawi-Atsugewi bows from the south. The Molala brought tanned elk hides to exchange for fur bedding, and the Paiute, during periods of peace, brought deerskins to trade for horses, of which they had very few. Most of the commerce with the south, however, was mediated by the Klamath, who obtained dried salmon, dentalia, and horses in return for the products brought from California. The Chinookan traders from the lower Columbia exchanged their shells for woven bags, bows, and skins. Trade with the north was mediated by the Wishram, who obtained coiled baskets and some horses in return for slaves, fish, and shells. Furs, hides, dentalia, bows, and dried fish were traded with the Umatilla for products obtained by the latter from tribes farther to the east.

The chief consequence of this extensive trade was widespread intertribal peace. Except for their war with the Molala and one very minor conflict with the Klamath, the Tenino have no memory of warfare with any of their neighbors save the Paiute. This tribe, which significantly had little to trade, was repeatedly raided for slaves. With all other groups, however, the Tenino maintained only the most friendly of relationships. In the case of the Wasco, this amity was even carried so far that each tribe granted to the members of the other free access to its own hunting and gathering territories.

Economic factors were reflected in the composition of the household, which typically included the families of two adult men but occasionally or temporarily also an additional family or two. The two families slept on opposite sides of the winter semisubterranean lodge and shared the adjacent frame living house, where they maintained a single common fire and cooked and ate together. The same household group also maintained a shed dwelling in the summer village, but ordinarily only one family was resident here throughout the season. The other was away from the village most of the time on spring root-gathering trips, summer berry-picking excursions, and the autumn hunt, living in mat tipis at temporary camps, but it shared the shed residence during the two annual festivals and on the brief intervals between trips. Sometimes the two families would alternate on expeditions away from home, but sometimes, especially when one man was much older or less active than the other, his family would remain at the fishing village throughout the summer season. Occasionally the two families would divide equally the salmon, game, roots, and berries which either had obtained, but more commonly the sharing was achieved indirectly through the common table at which both, during the winter months, consumed the products which each had accumulated during the preceding summer.

The owner of the dwelling, usually but not always the eldest male occupant, was the head of the household. The other adult male was usually his married son or younger brother but was occasionally a sister's or daughter's husband or even a remoter relative or unrelated friend. A son, when he married, usually continued to reside with his father, at least for a time. If and when the house became overcrowded, however, he joined with a brother or other relative to build a new dwelling and establish an independent household. Alternatively, if there were room in the house of his wife's father or brother, particularly if the latter were wealthy and personally congenial, he might reside matrilocally with him, but this solution appears to have been somewhat exceptional. On the death of the owner, the dwelling was inherited by his household partner if a near relative, otherwise by his eldest child or next younger sibling living in the community.

Marriages were usually arranged at the instance of the young man but occasionally of his parents, whose permission was always required. In either case, his father selected an old man to act as go-between and to visit the girl's parents and secure their consent to the union. Boys married typically at about twenty years of age, girls at fifteen to eighteen. Local exogamy was preferred and usual, but marriages within the village were not positively prohibited. Unions even occurred fairly frequently with members of neighboring tribes with whom the Tenino maintained friendly trade relations.

Incest taboos, governing sex relations as well as marriage, extended bilaterally to all close consanguineal kinsmen. The exogamous group was the kindred (sta'waxt), which included all persons who could trace descent in any line from a remembered common ancestor. The kindred varied in composition from individual to individual and thus did not form a discrete corporate group, though it performed important functions at all life-crisis ceremonies. Kinship terms were extended throughout the kindred, which in Ego's generation regularly included second cousins and often third cousins as well. Affines, however, were excluded. The Tenino lacked unilinear kin groups of any sort; descent was strictly bilateral. The local community, with its tendency toward exogamy, approached the structure of a patri-deme, but it had none of the characteristics of a true clan.

Weddings ranked with the two annual first-fruits festivals as major ceremonial occasions in Tenino life. They involved an elaborate exchange of presents between the kindreds of the bride and groom, in which the friends and distant relatives of each also participated but in less central roles. The festivities were held shortly after the betrothal at the bride's village, outside of which the groom's party set up a tipi camp. The parties were headed respectively by the groom's father and the bride's mother. If either were dead, his place was taken by the other parent or by some other senior relative of either sex. Each was represented by a spokesman, an old man who was not a close relative. The initial event was a feast at the groom's camp, to which both parties contributed and in which both participated. Then the bride's relatives retired to the village to await the first event in the exchange.

The spokesman for the groom's father went from the camp to the village carrying a bundle of sticks, each representing a horse and blanket contributed by a relative or friend of the groom. He presented these to the bride's mother, describing each horse in detail. She selected one for herself and distributed the rest, the members of the bride's kindred having the prior choice. Each recipient assumed the obligation of returning to the donor a present of comparable value. In this way the two parties became divided into pairs of trading partners, between whom all subsequent exchanges took place. If either party were larger than the other, persons who were related to both the bride and groom shifted sides until everyone was paired off. Before his return, the spokesman received gifts of beads, woven bags, or the like from each recipient.

Next the spokesman for the bride's mother made a series of trips to the groom's camp. On each trip he carried a long stick to which were tied the presents given in return for a particular horse—beads, buckskin clothing, woven bags, etc. He, too, received a gift from each recipient, e.g., a pair of moccasins or a tanned skin.

The groom's mother and another woman, usually an aunt, now paid a visit to the bride's village, wearing ornaments and fine clothes and bringing parfleches filled with furs and skins and a number of wooden combs. The bride awaited them, clad in beads and fine garments, beside two piles of dresses, bags, and ornaments. When they arrived, she removed her finery and added it to the two piles. The visitors dressed her hair and left the combs in it, removed their garments and ornaments and draped her with them, and departed with the piled gifts. Their trading partners stepped forward, removed the combs, clothing, and beads, and carried away the parfleche bundles. The same procedure was followed, in pairs, by the other women of the groom's party. At the conclusion of this exchange the groom, arrayed in fine garments, was escorted by a young male kinsman to the home of the bride, where the couple received a meal and spent the night together, ideally for the first time.

On the next day the mother of the groom with a few other women—usually six in all—visited the bride's camp, where they found spread before them on mats a feast consisting of dishes of root, berries, and other foods produced exclusively by females. They ate a little, and carried the rest, together with the mats and utensils, back to their camp. This time the bride, decked in heirloom finery, accompanied them, the groom remaining behind. On her arrival, the bride was stripped of her clothing and ornaments and was clothed by the groom's mother with comparable garments.

The donors of horses next set out for the bride's village, leading their horses, carrying parfleches filled with furs and skins, and taking the bride with them. A similar but larger feast awaited them, with a separate setting for each. They partook sparingly and returned with the mats, dishes, and remainder of the food. The bride and groom, who had listened to a speech of good advice but had not shared in the feast, stayed behind.

It was now the turn for the bride's entire party to visit the camp of the groom. With them, for their trading partners, they carried large bags filled with roots and berries. They were received with a feast of salmon, venison, bear meat, and other viands obtained exclusively by males, and were seated on valuable skins. They ate heartily, but neither the groom's party nor the bridal couple participated. The visitors returned to their village, carrying with them the skins and the remains of the food but leaving behind the bride and groom, now formally man and wife.

The next morning the groom's party paid another visit to the village, bringing parfleches or skins and receiving a meal of berries and roots. This time everyone ate, including the bride and groom. The bride's party then carried the mats, dishes, and remainder of the food to the groom's camp, where everyone ate a meal of meat and fish. Their departure, leaving the bridal couple and taking the remnants of the meal and the skins upon which they had sat, marked the termination of the festivities.

It will be noted that, throughout the long series of exchanges, the articles contributed by the groom's party, regardless of the sex of the donor, consisted almost exclusively of products produced by men or associated with the male sphere of economic life, whereas those contributed by the bride's party were similarly associated with female activities. The former were, in total, somewhat more valuable than the latter, but the difference was asserted by informants to be due to the inclusion of horses. Before the introduction of these animals from the Plains the exchange may well have been a truly equivalent one.

Polygyny was permitted, and from statements by informants it seems to have occurred with moderate frequency and to have been by no means confined exclusively to chiefs and wealthy men. Five wives was the maximum in any remembered instance. A man might take his wife's younger sister as a secondary spouse, but this was neither preferential nor particularly common. Co-wives lived in the same dwelling and shared household tasks, but the first wife enjoyed a somewhat higher status. The husband slept one night with each in rotation. Both the levirate and the sororate were in vogue. A widow was expected to marry one of the brothers of her deceased husband, and was permitted to choose among them, but she might marry another man if she chose. The sororate was more strongly preferential, and indeed almost obligatory, for the unmarried sister of a deceased wife. The elaborate wedding exchanges were customary only for a first marriage; subsequent unions involved only a few gifts.

Marriages were relatively stable, and divorce was rare. Either spouse, however, could terminate the union on grounds of adultery, childlessness, or incompatibility. Young children went with their mother unless she had deserted her husband, in which case they were cared for by their father's mother. Boys over ten years of age, and sometimes older girls as well, remained with or returned to their father.

The Tenino system of kinship terminology reveals, upon analysis, the following outstanding features: (1) six terms for siblings, extended to both cross- and parallel cousins throughout the kindred, differentiating elder siglings by sex only and younger siblings both by sex and by the sex of the speaker; (2) four grandparental terms, distinguishing the father's from the mother's parents of each sex and used reciprocally for grandchildren; (3) four terms for parents' siblings, distinguishing those of either parent both from the parent and from each other as well as by sex; (4) six terms for nephews and nieces, distinguished by the sex of the speaker and the sex of the connecting relative in all cases and also by the sex of the relative in the case of a female but not of a male speaker; (5) two special terms for the father's sister's husband, differing according to the sex of the speaker and each used reciprocally for the wife's brothers' children; (6) three terms for parents-in-law, used reciprocally for children-in-law, the wife's parents being distinguished from the husband's and also, unlike the latter, by sex; (7) four terms for siblings-in-law, those of opposite sex being differentiated according to whether the connecting relative is alive or dead, those of the same sex being distinguished from each other by the sex of the speaker as well as differentiated from those of opposite sex.

In general, differences in sex and generation are widely recognized, subject in the latter case to the frequent intrusion of reciprocity. Bifurcate collaterality characterizes the terms on all generations except Ego's. Relative age is recognized only in terms for siblings; decedence only in those for siblings-in-law of opposite sex, doubtless reflecting the levirate and sororate. The sex of the speaker is a determining factor in rather more than half of all the terms. A final characteristic is the extensive differentiation of referential and vocative forms. The latter, indicated in parentheses in the list below whenever they differ, reveal distinct roots in about half of all cases. The terms themselves, with their applications, may now be given.

1) pu'ca	Father's father, paternal great-grandfather, father's mother's brother, son's son (m.s.), son's daughter (m.s.), child's son's child (m.s.), sister's son's child (m.s.). Self-reciprocal, as in several other terms below.
2) a'la	Father's mother, paternal great-grandmother, father's mother's sister, son's child (w.s.), child's son's child (w.s.), sister's son's child (w.s.).

3) ti'la — Mother's father, maternal great-grandfather, mother's father's brother, daughter's child (m.s.), child's daughter's child (m.s.), brother's daughter's child (m.s.).

4) ka'ła — Mother's mother, maternal great-grandmother, mother's father's sister, daughter's child (w.s.), child's daughter's child (w.s.), brother's daughter's child (w.s.).

5) pəct (tu'ta) — Father.

6) p°tca' (i'ła) — Mother.

7) ict (t°ta') — Son. Reciprocal with 5 and 6.

8) pəp (ə'ca) — Daughter. Reciprocal with 5 and 6.

9) pi'məx (mə'xa) — Father's brother, father's father's brother, mother's sister's husband, stepfather.

10) paxəya'x (pa'ya) — Brother's child (m.s.), brother's son's child (m.s.), wife's sister's child, stepchild (m.s.). Reciprocal with 9.

11) pi't°x (ka'ka) — Mother's brother, mother's mother's brother.

12) pi't°xp (pi'ti) — Sister's child (m.s.), sister's daughter's child (m.s.). Reciprocal with 11. The referential form was not noted by the author as differing from that for 11 and is cited from Jacobs (1932), who makes the distinction.

13) pici'c (ci'ca) — Father's sister, father's father's sister, mother's brother's wife. Reciprocal with 14 and 15.

14) pamt (pa'mta) — Brother's son (w.s.), brother's son's son (w.s.), husband's sister's son (w.s.).

15) put (pa'wai) — Brother's daughter (w.s.), brother's son's daughter (w.s.), husband's sister's daughter (w.s.).

16) p°xə′x (xa′xa) Mother's sister, mother's mother's sister, father's brother's wife, stepmother. Reciprocal with 17 and 18.

17) i′t°k (i′ti) Sister's son (w.s.), sister's daughter's son (w.s.), husband's brother's son (w.s.), stepson (w.s.).

18) p°si′ts (pi′si) Sister's daughter (w.s.), sister's daughter's daughter (w.s.), husband's brother's daughter (w.s.), stepdaughter (w.s.).

19) psəs Father's sister's husband (m.s.), wife's brother's son.

20) swax Father's sister's husband (w.s.), wife's brother's daughter.

21) p°ca′x Wife's father, daughter's husband (m.s.).

22) cwax Wife's mother, daughter's husband (w.s.).

23) p°na′tc Husband's father, husband's mother, son's wife.

24) pita′p (ya′ya) Elder brother, elder male cross- or parallel cousin. Reciprocal with 25 and 26.

25) °sxə′p (nə′ka) Younger brother (m.s.), younger male cross- or parallel cousin (m.s.).

26) ats (nə′tca) Younger sister (m.s.), younger female cross- or parallel cousin (m.s.).

27) pat (na′na) Elder sister, elder female cross- or parallel cousin. Reciprocal with 28 and 29.

28) patct (nə′pa) Younger brother (w.s.), younger male cross- or parallel cousin (w.s.).

29) °si′p (ni′ya) Younger sister (w.s.), younger female cross- or parallel cousin (w.s.).

30) paminɬa′ Remote cousin of either sex.

31) am (a′m°, mam) Husband. The first vocative form is used only intimately, the second in public.

32) a′cam Wife. Reciprocal with 31.

33) ti′pikət Spouse. Used reciprocally by husband and wife when they have reached old age.

34) t'ła'wi	Co-wife.
35) miyu' (awi't'ał)	Wife's brother, sister's husband (m.s.).
36) pºnu'k	Brother's wife (m.s.), wife's sister, husband's brother, sister's husband (w.s.). Used only if the connecting relative is alive.
37) awi't	Brother's wife (m.s.), wife's sister, husband's brother, sister's husband (w.s.). Used only if the connecting relative is deceased.
38) atc (a'tcº)	Husband's sister, brother's wife (w.s.).
39) xai	Male friend (m.s.), wife's sister's husband. A term of address.
40) t'łaks	Female friend (w.s.), husband's brother's wife. A term of address.

The terms listed above are practically identical with those reported by Jacobs (1932) for the Upper Cowlitz and Klikitat. They are commonly used with pronominal prefixes, but these are omitted since Jacobs records them and since we employ the same orthography. The terms also reveal a striking resemblance with those presented by Morgan (1871) for the Yakima, provided allowance is made for manifest errors in Morgan's list arising for the most part from his failure to distinguish vocative and referential forms.

Patterns of behavior between kinsmen reveal a strong, though by no means perfect, correlation with categories of kinship terminology. The author had expected to find them, both on theoretical grounds and on the basis of his previous field work on the Northwest Coast, and he was inclined to discount assurances by some of his colleagues that significant patterning of kinship behavior does not occur among the bilateral and sibless tribes of the Plateau, Great Basin, and California since earlier field workers, though fully alert to the possibility, had failed to uncover any evidence thereof, even after the most exhaustive research. The first summer in the field, during which intensive research was conducted on the subject of kinship, appeared to confirm this negative assumption, since little evidence of patterning emerged except for obvious differences arising from such factors as age, sex, and family status. It was only during the second summer, when such topics as property, economic cooperation, sex, and childhood training were being investigated, that bits of patterned kinship behavior began to come to light in other contexts. The author can only conclude that the Tenino, unlike many other peoples, do not themselves conceive of kinship as a distinct cultural subsystem and that it exists as such only covertly, being overtly distributed among other subsystems.

One special relationship is that prevailing between a paternal grandfather and his grandchild, especially his grandson. It is the former who is primarily responsible for instilling physical hardihood and military virtues in his grandson. It is customary for him, during the boyhood of the latter, to undress and whip him, to roll him naked in the snow, to make him lie in the bed of an icy stream in the wintertime, and to subject him to comparable hardening ordeals. The motivation is purely educational. No notion of joking is involved, and the boy makes no effort to retaliate, either at the time or in later life.

Despite terminological distinctions, no significant differences in behavior were discoverable between paternal and maternal uncles or aunts and their nephews or nieces through brothers and sisters. Attitudes and conduct toward parents-in-law and children-in-law are modeled on those toward parents and children, and reveal no evidence either of avoidance or of special reserve. The relationship between brothers is affectionate and cooperative, and is particularly close when, as is common, they unite to form a single household. Between brother and sister, however, there prevails a measure of restraint and avoidance. They may never sleep in a house alone, nor walk, ride, or sit together unless someone else is present.

Between brothers-in-law there prevails a friendly and cooperative relationship resembling that between brothers. When a man builds a house, for example, he expects his brothers-in-law to lend assistance without anticipation of payment. A special privilege formerly enjoyed by a sibling-in-law of either sex was that of claiming a valuable possession belonging to any person thus related to him. The claimant was obligated only to give in return a similar object of lesser value. Between siblings-in-law of opposite sex there still prevails a relationship of considerable intimacy, though not of permitted joking. Even sexual intercourse between them is common, and seems almost taken for granted. During one interview, for example, both the informant and the interpreter readily confessed to having had sex relations with the sisters of their wives. This doubtless reflects levirate and sororate usages—as a sort of anticipatory response, as it were.

Perhaps the most striking example of patterned kinship behavior is that prevailing between a father's sister's husband and his wife's brothers' children. These relatives call one another by two special self-reciprocal terms (19 and 20 in the foregoing list), which are not balanced by correspondng special terminology for and by the spouses of other siblings of the parents. The associated behavior is equally distinctive. A boy or young man fetches firewood and does other chores for the husband of his paternal aunt but feels under no obligation to perform similar tasks for the spouses of his other parents' siblings, and a girl or woman similarly regards the tie with her father's sister's husband as especially close. The most characteristic feature of the relationship, however, is the licensed joking which it entails. A person pokes fun and cracks jokes freely at the expense of his father's sister's husband or wife's brother's child, and the relative submits with good nature or retaliates in kind, knowing that no offense is intended. This behavior is carried to greater lengths with a psəs than with a swax. Rough practical jokes are permitted and expected when both relatives are males, but the joking between a man and his wife's niece is largely verbal.

This peculiarly asymmetrical feature of kinship terminology and associated behavior in an otherwise very regular and balanced bilateral social system raises an interesting problem of interpretation. The difficulty is not a functional one, for the Tenino clearly derive a great deal of pleasure and satisfaction from the joking behavior expected in the relationship. The problem is rather one of accounting for its origin. Joking relationships are widely reported in ethnography, but they nearly always appear in contexts where they are readily understandable on structural grounds, notably between grandparents and grandchildren and between potential spouses (see Murdock 1949: 277). Nothing in the Tenino social system, however, seems to provide any such structural basis favorable to the development of a pattern of joking behavior between father's sister's husband and his wife's brothers' children. The writer therefore tentatively concludes that the pattern may have originated under earlier and different conditions of social organization which were conducive to its appearance, and that it has been preserved, through a period of structural change, by the inherently rewarding character of the behavior it prescribes.

Of the various kinds of social systems, that which most commonly presents conditions favorable to the development of this particular pattern is probably a patrilineal organization of Omaha type. In such systems the wife's brother's daughter is often favored as a secondary spouse and thus falls into one of the categories of kinsmen, that of potential spouse, with whom joking behavior is especially common. The Fox and Winnebago of Wisconsin, the Shona and Thonga of Southeast Africa, the Araucanians of Chile, and the Miwok of California are examples of patrilineal societies with Omaha kinship terminology in which the wife's brother's daughter is a potential secondary spouse. Among them, patterns of kinship behavior are fully reported only for the Shona and Thonga, and it may be significant that in both instances the relationship between father's sister's husband and his wife's niece is characterized by joking. It is thus a speculative possibility that the ancestors of the Tenino had a social system with Omaha features as in a number of tribes in north-central California.

We may conclude with a few notes on social stratification and government. The Tenino engaged in the slave trade and practiced slavery to a limited extent. Slaves (acwani'yə) were mainly captured in war, almost exclusively with the Paiute, but were also obtained in trade from the Klamath. Purchased slaves were partly of Modoc but mainly of Achomawi-Atsugewi origin. Most slaves, whatever their provenience, were passed on in trade to the north, through the Wishram, but a few were retained. Informants estimated the number of slaves kept by the Tenino themselves in the immediate precontact period at about twenty-five, three being the largest number held by a single owner. Captured slaves were exclusively women and children, for male war captives were invariably slain. Adult female slaves were neither married nor kept as mistresses. Children were accepted as members of the household. When they grew up, they married Tenino and became free, though they never fully lost the stigma of their slave origin. Debt slavery was not practiced.

Wealth distinctions were recognized, as might be expected in so mercantile a people, but they had not become crystallized into formal social classes as among the coastal tribes. Most marriages, to be sure, occurred between families of comparable means, but unions between rich and poor were neither prohibited nor particularly uncommon.

Each Tenino community had a chief (miu′x), who was usually succeeded by his eldest son. A chief was always a wealthy man and usually had several wives, and he was expected to be generous in giving feasts. In the winter village he occupied a special semisubterranean house larger than those of other men. He was assisted by subchiefs (wapaɫa′mə), usually two in number, who acted as his councillors, messengers, and deputies. A chief was *primus inter pares*, presiding and exercising a guiding influence at popular assemblies where judicial cases, issues of war and peace, and other matters of general concern were argued and decided. His most obtrusive function, however, was that of haranguing his people every morning, noon, and evening on matters of conduct and morals. He advised in the planning of military operations but rarely led or even accompanied a war party. Chiefs enjoyed prestige throughout the tribe and often consulted one another, but the present institution of a single tribal chief is clearly a development of the postcontact period.

15

This paper was written in the field in 1947. It was originally published in the *Southwestern Journal of Anthropology* (3: 331-343, 1947) in co-authorship with Ward H. Goodenough, who collaborated in the field research and wrote the appended corrigenda. For a fuller exposition of Trukese social organization see Goodenough, "Property, Kin, and Community on Truk," *Yale University Publications in Anthropology* (46: 1-192, 1951).

Social Organization of Truk

T HE complex atoll of Truk is located in the east central
Caroline Islands between 7°7′ and 7°41′ north latitude
and between 151°22′ and 152°4′ east longitude. It
consists of a roughly circular atoll reef enclosing a lagoon nearly
forty miles in average diameter. The reef supports a number of low
coral islands of which only one has a permanent population.
Within the lagoon rise sixteen inhabited volcanic islands ranging in
size from a third of a square mile to about nine square miles. The
total land area is about fifty square miles, and supports a native
population of approximately 10,000. The people are Micronesians;
they resemble Polynesians in physical type but are shorter and
slighter and appear to have a somewhat larger Melanesian admix-
ture. The Trukese have a relatively homogeneous culture, which is
shared in considerable measure by 5,000 inhabitants of a dozen
coral atolls and islands extending southeastward to Lukunor

(50°29′ N, 153°58′ E) and westward to Puluwat (7°22′ N, 149°10′ E). The climate, fauna, flora, and basic mode of life are typical of the equatorial islands of the Pacific. Though discovered as early as 1565, Truk experienced no intimate contacts with Europeans until visited by whalers and explorers in the early nineteenth century. The first mission was established in 1879. Though Spanish sovereignty was recognized in 1886, actual administration did not begin until the arrival of the Germans in 1899. Truk passed into the possession of Japan in 1914 and of the United States in 1945. In the face of these acculturative influences the aboriginal culture has shown remarkable vitality, and most of what has disappeared in fact survives in memory.[1]

The people of Truk are divided into about forty matrilineal and strictly exogamous sibs (einang),[2] which also extend to the surrounding atolls from Lukunor to Puluwat. None is confined to a single island, and many are widespread, but no island has representatives of all. Besides the regulation of marriage, sibs possess only a single important function, namely, the channeling of hospitality. A native visiting another island or atoll for trade or any other peaceful purpose resorts to a member of his own sib, from whom he can expect shelter, food, and (formerly) sexual hospitality. True moieties are absent, although tradition divides the sibs into one group which is descended from the coconut palm and another which immigrated from a high island called Achaw, now commonly identified with Kusaie.

Functionally far more important than the sib is the matrilineal lineage (eterenges, or more commonly today faameni), characterized by actual common descent in the female line from a remembered ancestress. On a small island or in a district of a larger island

---

[1] The field work on which this paper is based was done in 1947 as part of the Coordinated Investigation of Micronesian Anthropology sponsored by the Pacific Science Board on the National Research Council. Most of the intensive investigation, e.g., genealogical studies of kinship and land tenure, was done on the island of Romonum.

[2] The spelling of native terms will follow the orthography proposed by S. H. Elbert, *Trukese-English and English-Trukese Dictionary* (United States Naval Military Government, Pearl Harbor, February 1947).

the sibs locally represented are usually divided into two or more lineages, between whom there is no more political or other unity than between lineages of different sibs. A lineage averages thirty or forty members, and if large is often divided into sublineages (tetten). Status within the lineage depends largely upon seniority. The eldest capable male is the lineage chief (sómwonun faameni). He administers the land of the lineage and regulates the economic activities of its members. A female counterpart, the finesómwonun faameni, directs the work of the women. Within a generation the eldest male is called mwääniichi and the eldest female finniichi; both enjoy considerable authority over their juniors.

Each lineage traditionally has its own territory (soópw), common hearth (fanang), men's house (uut), and communal dwelling (imw). The territory consists of a number of named tracts of land, which are divided into plots owned and cultivated by individual members. The common hearth or earth oven is in charge of a senior male in the prime of life, called sómwonun fanang, who may be the lineage chief, a classificatory younger brother of his, or the mwääniichi of the next generation. He manages the food supply and cooking for the lineage. Unmarried males above the age of puberty formerly slept in the men's house, and even today leave the parental roof but sleep in the houses of nontaboo relatives. Married men observing rules of sexual continence before war or ceremonial events also slept in the men's house and often do so even today. There is now often only one men's house in a village, used primarily as a communal meeting place.

Until late in the Japanese regime the house of the lineage—or of a sublineage if the lineage were large and subdivided—formed a hamlet at some distance from other dwellings, oftentimes located in the interior of the island. Today these hamlets have been abandoned, and the natives have moved into larger villages at convenient locations along the coast. Even within the present villages, however, the houses of a lineage, or at least of a sublineage, tend to be clustered together. The dwellings themselves are smaller than formerly, and a modified Japanese house type is supplanting the older thatched houses.

The prevailing rule of residence has always been, and still is, matrilocal. Hamlets thus tended strongly to be inhabited by the women and unmarried children of a lineage, together with the husbands of the women. The men of the lineage resided in other hamlets with their wives. Rarely, however, did they live at any great distance, so that they were able to spend considerable time with their own matrilineal kinsmen. They worked on their own lands as well as on those of their wives, contributed food to the common hearths of both lineages, and were always welcome to eat with their sisters or to spend a night in the men's house of their own lineage.

Essentially the hamlet or subhamlet was a large matrilocal extended family. The nuclear family of father, mother, and children, though socially recognized, was overshadowed by the extended family group, and even today is only rarely the residential unit. Although lineage and sublineage dwellings have disappeared, the matrilocal extended family is still apparent in clusters of adjacent houses inhabited by a group of matrilineally related women with their husbands and children. Today as formerly, most economic activities are carried on in common within the extended family, which collectively takes care of all dependents.

Marriage is both lax and brittle. Adultery, though theoretically prohibited and punishable, is exceedingly common, and divorce and remarriage are so frequent as to constitute the rule rather than the exception. Monogamy prevails overwhelmingly; complete genealogies for the island of Romonum, going back six or more generations, revealed only a single case of polyandry and only three instances of polygyny. Levirate and sororate unions, though permissible, are neither preferred nor common. Incest taboos and exogamy extend not only to the entire matrilineal sib but also to all members of the father's lineage, with the result that cross-cousin marriage does not occur.

From a purely descriptive or synchronic point of view Trukese social organization appears to be a typical matrilocal system, with minor exceptions which might readily be attributed to acculturation. When, however, its internal dynamics is examined by genealogical methods, noteworthy patrilineal and patrilocal features emerge, and the seeming acculturative exceptions are found to conform to ancient patterns. The patrilineal alternative in the inheritance of real property will be described below under land tenure. Patrilocal residence occurs regularly, in former times as well as today, whenever the number of women closely akin matrilineally is too few to maintain an efficient extended family organization. Thus when a lineage approaches extinction, with only one or two surviving women, they go to reside with their husbands in the hamlets or households of the latter. Patrilocal residence is also a common alternative in interisland marriages; the woman in such cases has no lineage mates in her husband's district and consequently usually goes to live with his matrilineal relatives, or at least in a house built on his land. Since houses are built by men for their wives rather than for their sisters, a man with considerable land may build a house for his wife and her sister on his own property. This may result in a shift in the location of the entire hamlet of his wife's lineage, or in a split in the lineage. In the latter case it is likely that in time a new fanang (hearth) will be organized and a new uut (men's house) built, and that in this way a new lineage will emerge.

Even more interesting, perhaps, is the possibility of shifting from one matrilineal lineage to another by way of a patrilineal connection. Several instances are attested in the genealogies. After a patrilocal marriage, either of an immigrant woman or in the case of a decadent lineage, if the woman has several daughters they will establish a matrilocal extended family in the next generation, and a new lineage will be founded or a decadent one reestablished. If, however, there are only one or two daughters for a couple of generations, they will either continue to marry patrilocally or, if they marry matrilocally, they and their children will become assimilated to the lineage with which they reside, i.e., that of the father or grandfather who married patrilocally. In this latter case they observe an additional rule of exogamy, avoiding marriage not only with members of their own sib and of their father's lineage but also with members of the lineage with which they reside and ultimately with any member of the sib to which this lineage belongs. After a few generations the matrilineal descendants will forget their original sib membership and be considered full members of the sib to which their adopted lineage belongs.

Political structure in Micronesia is in general characterized by a striking degree of complexity. Truk and the surrounding coral atolls constitute the outstanding exception. Above the localized lineage with its chief there was aboriginally only a single level of political integration, the district. The district consisted, and still consists, of an area over which one lineage has gained ascendancy. A small island usually forms a single district, whereas a large one will be divided into three or four. The dominant lineage may in some instances be the one which first colonized the island, but in most cases it has attained its position through war. The other lineages are usually graded in rank order, their relative position being closely correlated with the extent of their land holdings.

The chief of the dominant lineage is recognized as district chief (sômwonun fönü). The basis of his power is his ultimate right, a sort of eminent domain, over all the cultivable land of the district, the other lineages holding their lands theoretically at his pleasure. He collects tribute from the other lineages in the form of periodic gifts and first fruits. He officially opens and closes the all-important breadfruit season, sets the dates for ceremonies in the annual cycle, and exercises overall direction of the economic activities of his subjects. He is also the traditional war leader. Although the German and subsequent administrations have accorded him judicial powers, he did not originally possess them. Disputes and crimes were discussed and disposed of at an assembly of the adult men of the district in the man's house of the chief's lineage.

It was considered appropriate for a district chief to have a knowledge of oratory, warfare, cosmology, mythology, the history of the district with special reference to land rights, and a variety of magical skills. A man with such qualifications was known as an itang, and if the district chief was not himself an itang he was usually assisted by one. An itang was greatly respected, and was feared for his magical powers, but he was not a priest nor was he primarily concerned with divination, sorcery, or therapy.

The Germans created, and the Japanese continued, a third level of political integration, the area (finäik or "flag"), under which were consolidated the districts of a large island or of a group of adjacent smaller islands. Under the recent American administration several additional levels of chiefs have been added, forming an unwieldy political hierarchy. Since the area and higher chiefs have been vested with judicial and administrative powers for which the local culture has as yet developed no adequate system of controls, the new complexity in political structure has created potentialities for corruption and despotism which constitute the principal threat to the success of the present administration.

The system of property and inheritance exerts a significant if not a determining influence on Trukese social organization. Movables are individually owned. Property rights in them are based primarily upon manufacture or appropriation. A person may dispose, by gift or by sale, of any artifact which he has made himself. If, however, he makes an object to give to some one else, whether at his own initiative or upon request, he must first secure the permission of his own children, who may appropriate it if he does not do so. Permission is not required to sell the object, but if he does so he must give his children a portion of the proceeds of the sale. The recipient of a gift may not alienate the article by gift during the lifetime of the maker without first securing the permission of the latter, who may reclaim it if he has not been consulted. He may, however, sell the article without permission, but if he does so he must give the maker a share of the proceeds. Sale by the maker or by a recipient from him with his permission constitutes a definitive alienation of the property title.

The owner of a pig which produces a litter may keep the shoats himself, sell them, or give them to a child or a lineage mate to raise. In the last case, the recipient must give him a share of the pork when the animal is slaughtered or the owner may claim the price of the pig in goods. The recipient, however, has full title to the offspring of the pig given to him. A pig may not be given to a member of another lineage without permission of the donor's children. Property in chickens parallels that in pigs except that the right of the donor is to share in the eggs, not in the meat.

Property rights in artifacts, domesticated animals, and other movables are transmitted by inheritance from parent to child. Both sexes participate in inheritance unless the property is appropriate to one sex alone, in which case sons inherit from the father and daughters from their mother. The rule of inheritance is not strictly patrilineal, however, for if a man has no children his sisters' children take precedence over brothers' children and other patrilineal heirs.

The transmission of incorporeal property rights is almost equally matrilineal and patrilineal. The most important of these rights, technological skills and the magical rites (rong) associated with them, are taught by women to their children and by men to both their own and their sisters' children. Transmission to a spouse, insofar as is appropriate, is also permissible. A man may not teach specialized skills and rong to any one else without first securing the permission of both his own and his sisters' children. If his brother has died, he may impart some but not all of his knowledge to that brother's children. The lore of the itang constitutes a partial exception to the general rule respecting incorporeal property. An itang may teach his son a part of what he knows but never all; only his sisters' children may receive his entire stock of knowledge.

The inheritance of real property is exclusively matrilineal in principle, although even under aboriginal conditions men not infrequently gave plots of land to their sons during their own lifetime and the legitimacy of such patrilineal transmission was fully recognized. The German administration attempted by law to substitute patrilineal inheritance of land for matrilineal inheritance, and the Japanese administration followed the same policy. The natives resented this violation of their aboriginal custom and found a means of evading the law, namely, by transmitting the bulk of their real property by gift to their matrilineal heirs before death. Despite such evasions, nearly fifty years of administrative pressure introduced certain changes. Patrilineal inheritance did take place in many cases, and it acquired a certain legitimacy in the minds of the natives. With the advent of the American administration native custom with respect to land was again recognized, and the insistence on patrilineal inheritance rescinded. Today, matrilineal inheritance is alone recognized for any land of which a man is possessed at the time of his death. It has become customary, however, for most land rights to be transmitted by gift before the owner reaches old age, the latter retaining rights of use until his death. Owners may dispose of land in this way as they wish, either to matrilineal or to patrilineal heirs or to both. It is considered proper, however, for an owner to divide his land approximately equally between matrilineal and patrilineal heirs, giving some preference to that group which is relatively poorer in land.

The cultivable land of Truk is divided into named tracts (eif), each of which is associated with a particular lineage. Tracts vary greatly in size, averaging slightly larger than an acre. The territory (soòpw) of a lineage includes a number of tracts, often though not necessarily adjacent to each other. Tracts are for the most part divided into plots (äpär), about three to a tract on the average, each of which is associated with an individual land owner. Offshore waters suitable for fishing, especially fringing reefs, are also divided into named tracts which are similarly owned.

The native system of land tenure is relatively complex. A distinction is made between rights to the land itself (pwün, soil) and usufruct rights to the land and what grows upon it, which are defined as rights to trees (irä). Titles differ in seniority as well as in type, and any plot is subject to a graded series of rights somewhat reminiscent of subinfeudation in European feudal land law. The system may best be illuminated by describing the various types of tenure in the order of their seniority.

1. *Eminent domain of the district chief.* Under aboriginal conditions the district chief had a paramount claim to all the lands held by the lineages subject to him. This was acquired by conquest and could be extinguished only by conquest. It was manifested in the right to receive tribute in the form of first fruits and periodic gifts of produce from the lands of the subject lineages. If any lineage failed in its tribute obligation, the district chief had the power to confiscate the land and award it to another lineage. This type of tenure has lapsed today, or rather it has been transferred to the colonial administration, whose right to levy taxes and to appropriate property for administrative use is justified thereby.

2. *Lineage fee simple.* The members of a lineage collectively enjoy a basic claim to all the lands which constitute its traditional territory (sòòpw). This title, which is administered by the chief of the lineage, may be acquired by settlement, by conquest, by purchase or gift from another lineage, or by patrilineal inheritance from a lineage which has become extinct, and may be extinguished by conquest, sale, gift, extinction of the lineage, or abdicating or forgetting of its claim. Lands secured by a lineage are distributed in tracts and plots to members of the lineage, who thereby acquire intra-lineage usufruct titles (see below). As long as these lands are held by members of the lineage, the lineage chief has the right to receive tribute from them in the form of first fruits and periodic gifts, and he may re-allot abandoned or unused plots. With his permission, however, a usufruct title may be transferred to a member of another lineage, but even after this has occurred any member of the lineage may plant upon any unused portion of the land and enjoy for life the produce from what he has planted.

3. *Intra-lineage usufruct tenure.* Any member of the lineage which holds the fee simple may secure title to a tract or plot by allocation from the lineage chief or by gift or matrilineal inheritance from another member of the lineage. In contradistinction to the two previous types of land tenure, however, this right is one of

usufruct only and does not include any title to the land itself. A usufruct owner may transmit his property to another member of the lineage by gift or bequest, but he may not transfer it to a member of another lineage, e.g., a son, without the permission of his own lineage chief, and if he does so he can alienate only a portion of his rights, the remainder being residual and transmissible only in the female line. The alienable rights include the right to plant trees or crops on the land, title to the trees which he has planted himself, and the right to the product of all the trees on the land whether planted by himself or his predecessors. What he cannot transmit is the title to the trees planted by his predecessors. For the right to use the produce from these trees the new owner and his heirs must continue to pay first fruits and periodic gifts to the alienator and his matrilineal heirs as long as any of the trees survive, after which this residual right is extinguished. The lineage chief's permission is required because by such a transaction he resigns his claim to first fruits in favor of the alienator.

4. *Extra-lineage usufruct tenure.* Tenure of this type may be acquired by purchase, gift, or patrilineal inheritance from another usufruct owner, whether the latter is or is not a member of the lineage which holds the fee simple. As in the case of an intra-lineage usufruct title the rights involved are partly alienable and partly residual and hereditary in the female line. The alienable rights are those of planting on the land and of using the product of all trees and crops growing upon it as well as the title to the trees which the alienator has planted himself. Title to all trees planted by previous usufruct owners is retained by the matrilineal heirs of the persons who have inherited or received the trees from them, and hence cannot be alienated. An extra-lineage usufruct owner owes the usual periodic gifts to the matrilineal heirs of all previous usufruct owners who have title to any trees still growing on the land. If this obligation is not fulfilled, the claimants of residual rights have the power of regaining the usufruct to the trees which they own as well as the other alienable rights of the usufruct owner, who retains only the title to and use of the trees which he himself or

his immediate predecessor has planted. As an additional inalienable right each successive extra-lineage usufruct owner acquires for his lineage a potential fee simple claim to the land itself. Of several such claims the prior one becomes converted into a full lineage fee simple title upon the extinction of the lineage previously possessing this title or when time has extinguished the memory of the previous fee simple title. Prior to the advent of the Germans usufruct titles of the extra-lineage type, though known, were relatively few in comparison to those of the intra-lineage type. As a result of German and Japanese administrative pressure in favor of patrilineal inheritance, however, the relative proportions of the two types have been reversed, and today most of the plots to which a lineage holds fee simple are the private usufruct property of members of other lineages. The actual system of land tenure, nevertheless, has not changed.

5. *Life usufruct tenure.* The final type of land title results from the fact that any member of the lineage holding the fee simple and any member of the lineage of the full usufruct title holder can, with the latter's permission, plant trees or other crops on the land and can enjoy their product as long as he lives. At his death, however, his rights revert to the full usufruct owner. Members of the lineage with the fee simple, if refused permission by the usufruct owner, can claim all the alienable rights to the land. If they do, the case comes to trial and, depending upon the determination of facts, they may be awarded or refused their claim or allowed it for a portion of the plot involved.

To secure a clear fee simple title to any plot of land in Truk today is a complicated matter. The purchaser must buy up the claims of any life tenants, pay the usufruct owner for his alienable rights, pay the latter's matrilineal heirs for their claim to residual rights, compensate the matrilineal heirs of all prior usufruct owners for their residual rights, and finally pay the chief of the lineage with the fee simple a sum larger than the total of all other payments to obtain title to the land itself. This has contributed to the fact that very little of the land of Truk has thus far been alienated in fee simple to foreign planters or business men, missions, or wealthy native and half-caste individuals.

An outstanding feature of Trukese social organization is the special relationship which prevails between the members of a matri-lineal lineage and the children of the men of that lineage, who are collectively called the öfökür of the former. This is correlated with the patrilineal features of the property system—the patrilineal in-heritance of movables and to a lesser extent of incorporeal and real property, the control which a man's children exercise over his disposition of personal property, and especially the obligations of a patrilineal inheritor of land toward the matrilineal heirs of the donor, who is usually his father, with respect to their residual rights. The relationship ranks next in importance to that between members of the same lineage, and is similarly characterized by exogamy. It is noteworthy that fee simple rights to land pass, when a lineage becomes extinct, to the öfökür of that lineage and not to another lineage of the same sib, even if it is possible to trace actual genealogical connections with the latter. The relationship is also reflected in the kinship terminology; all members of the father's lineage are terminologically classed with the father and his sister, irrespective of generation, and all öfökür, including the children of a mother's brother or mother's mother's brother, are called "child." The result is a kinship system of the Crow type, despite the characteristic Malayo-Polynesian paucity of distinct denotative terms.

A list of the Trukese kinship terms is given below, with the extensions of each. All terms are given in the first person singular possessive form.

1) semei   Father, father's brother, husband of a maternal or paternal aunt, grandfather, spouse's father, male lineage mate of an ascending generation (alternative to 3 for a male speaker), any other male relative of an ascending generation except sons of male lineages mates, father's sister's son, father's sister's daughter's husband,

father's sister's daughter's son, any male of the father's lineage, husband of any female of the father's lineage.

2) inei   Mother, mother's sister, father's sister, wife of a maternal or paternal uncle, grandmother, spouse's mother, any female relative of an ascending generation except daughters of male lineage mates, father's sister's daughter, father's sister's son's wife, any female of the father's lineage, wife of any male of the father's lineage.

3) ääi mwään   Elder sibling to the same sex as Ego (alternative to 4), any older person of Ego's sex, generation, and lineage (alternative to 4), mother's brother (male speaking only, alternative to 1), any male lineage mate of an ascending generation (male speaking only, alternative to 1).

4) pwii   Sibling of Ego's sex (alternative to 3 for an elder sibling), mother's sister's child of Ego's sex (alternative to 3 for an elder cousin), father's brother's child of Ego's sex, any sibmate of Ego's sex and generation (alternative to 3 within Ego's lineage for a person older than Ego), father's sister's son's child of Ego's sex, child of any man of the father's lineage if of Ego's sex, wife's sister's husband, husband's brother's wife, any person who has married a person of the sex, generation, and lineage of Ego's spouse, a special friend of the same sex with whom one has formally agreed reciprocally to adopt the term and accept the associated privileges and responsibilities.

5) feefinei   Sister (male speaking), any female of Ego's sib and generation (male speaking), father's brother's daughter (male speaking), daughter

	of any man of the father's lineage irrespective of generation (male speaking).
6) mwääni	Brother (female speaking), any male of Ego's sib and generation (female speaking), father's brother's son (female speaking), son of any man of the father's lineage (female speaking).
7) nei	Son, daughter, brother's or sister's child, grandchild, spouse of a son or daughter, any relative of a descending generation unless the connection is traced through a member of the father's lineage, child of any man of Ego's lineage irrespective of generation.
8) pwünüwei	Husband, wife, sibling-in-law of opposite sex, spouse of any one whom Ego calls pwii (see 4), any one whom Ego's spouse calls pwii.
9) öösei	Sibling-in-law of Ego's sex, spouse of any one whom Ego calls feefinei or mwääni (see 5 and 6), any one whom Ego's spouse calls feefinei or mwääni.

Whenever ambiguity arises in the use of any of the above denotative terms, all of which are highly classificatory, the Trukese resort freely to compound descriptive terms. Thus among a person's various nei (7) a grandchild may be referred to as nöwün nei (my child's child), the child of a man of one's own lineage may be called nei öfökür, and sex and age distinctions may be made as needed, e.g., nei äät (my immature son), nei mwään (my adult son), nei nengngin (my immature daughter), nei feefin (my adult daughter). The terms listed are used primarily in reference. In address, personal names are strongly preferred, although paapa (father) and maama (mother), presumably derived from English, are occasionally heard.

Patterns of behavior between kinsmen correspond rather closely to terminological categories. Sexual intercourse and marriage are prohibited as incestuous, not only with a person of one's own sib or of one's father's lineage, but also with any consanguineal relative to whom one of the above kinship terms is applied. If the relationship is purely affinal, however, as in the case of wife's mother or son's wife, sex relations are mildly tolerated as with nonrelatives. Between persons who call one another pwünüwei (8), indeed, sexual intercourse is fully privileged, as between husband and wife.

The responsibility and authority of parents for the education and socialization of their children is shared by other relatives whom the children call "father" (1) and "mother" (2), especially by those within the extended family. A father's authority over his children and others whom he calls nei (7) ceases, however, when they reach puberty; thereafter it is improper for him to speak sharply to them. A man's elder brother, maternal uncle, and others whom he calls ääi mwään (3) exercise authority over him and can reprimand him not only during his childhood but after he becomes adult, and while he is a child one of them acts as custodian of any property which he may have inherited. In general, a person may freely borrow a tool or other artifact from any primary or secondary relative, merely notifying the latter subsequently that he has done so; in the case of an ääi mwään, however, permission to do so must be secured beforehand.

A married man exercises authority over his wife. He contributes labor and food to her extended family and to his own lineage, and divides his time between the two. When widowed or divorced, a man formerly returned to his own lineage and lived in its men's house but took his meals largely with his classificatory "fathers" (1). Today it is more common for him to go to live with a classificatory "father" (1), e.g., a father's sister's son.

The relationship between brother (6) and sister (5), own and classificatory, is marked by a considerable degree of avoidance. After both have reached puberty they cannot sleep in the same house or use unchaste language in each other's presence, and a brother will not allow others to use obscenity when both he and his sister are present. It is considered tantamount to incest if a man sees the breasts of any woman whom he calls "sister" (5); hence

women, who commonly go unclad above the waist in the vicinity of
the home, rush to cover their breasts if an own or classificatory
brother approaches, and always wear an upper garment when they
go out in public. It is likewise considered indecent for a man to
view the breasts of the adult daughter of a brother or sister.

A man may joke freely, engage in horseplay, and exchange ribald
remarks in public with any woman other than his own wife whom
he calls pwünüwei (8). He may also joke and use obscenity with
men whom he calls "father" (1), "brother" (4), and "son" (7).
He is much less free with his ääi mwään (3), and as an exception to
the class of "fathers" he must observe great restraint with his wife's
father. Refraining from obscenity as a token of respect is also
required in the presence of a person called öösei (9), and ribaldry
is prohibited between a man and any woman whom he calls
"mother" (2), "sister" (5), or "daughter" (7).

Respectful behavior reaches its apogee in the phenomenon of
"crawling," which has become obsolete on Truk in the memory of
living informants but still occurs in some of the atolls to the west,
e.g., Puluwat. In the presence of a district chief or an itang
ordinary people were permitted to stand up or walk erect only if the
chief or itang were standing; if he were sitting, squatting, or kneel-
ing they could move in his presence only by crawling on all fours.
Identical behavior was observed in two kin relationships, namely,
by a woman toward any man whom she called mwääni (6) and by a
man toward any woman whom he called nei (7). It was initiated
only after both persons had reached puberty, i.e., after the
woman had emerged from her first menstrual isolation and after the
man had assumed the loin cloth of an adult male. If a woman
approached within approximately fifty feet of an own or classificatory brother, or a man of an own or classificatory adult daughter,
the former would call out "Wüütäämo!" ("Please stand up"). The
latter would then either rise and allow the former to approach erect,
or answer curtly "Ȯpwȯrooto!" ("Crawl hither"), in which case the
former could proceed only by assuming the crawling position.

The relatives who are expected to participate in the ceremonies which attend the major crises in the life of an individual are the members of his own and his father's lineages, their spouses, and the öfökür (children of the men) of both lineages. Among these, the ones who play the most prominent roles are the women of the father's lineage, who are classificatory "mothers" (2), and own and classificatory "children" (7) of both sexes. All relatives in these two categories, for example, are expected to bring gifts when a child is born, when a girl first menstruates, when a man or a woman is married, and when a person dies.

Corrigenda by the junior author based on two months of additional field work: Research on other islands than Romonum revealed the existence of subsibs (called by the same terms as lineages) comprising lineages of several districts which share a tradition of common ancestry. Sexual hospitality is associated with the subsib, not the sib. Except on Romonum, and for the dominant sib of a district, there is usually only a single lineage of a sib in any district. Commonly, too, only one or two lineages of a district have a men's house, and only a few of them a hearth, members of other lineages frequenting those of their fathers' lineage. Both levirate and sororate proved to be preferential in theory, though accounting for only a moderate proportion of remarriages. Revision of Romonum genealogies revealed three additional cases of polygyny, resulting from levirate usage. The eminent domain of the district chief derives from the theory that all other lineages hold their lands through patrilineal inheritance from his, the founding lineage. His first fruits and confiscatory rights are interpreted as those of a father who has given land to a child. The term ääi mwään (3) refers primarily to an elder sibling of the same sex, and is applied to maternal uncles only in connection with inheritance or other matters when it is important to distinguish between "fathers" (1) of one's own and one's father's lineage. Like a father, but unlike an elder sibling of the same sex, a maternal uncle ceases to exercise authority over a sister's son who has passed puberty, except in regard to marriage and matters of lineage concern.

16

This paper was presented before the Section of Anthropology of The New York Academy of Sciences on October 25, 1948, and was published in *Transactions of The New York Academy of Sciences* (ser. 2, 11: 9-16, 1948). Its conclusions require modest modifications on the basis of subsequent published sources, especially by Barnett and Force on Palau, Schneider on Yap, and Goodenough and Lambert on the Gilberts.

Anthropology in Micronesia

MICRONESIA consists of a series of archipelagoes in the mid-Pacific which stretch east and west for about 3,000 miles on and just north of the equator. The Gilberts and Nauru Island in the southeast are British. The rest of the area is administered by the United States—Guam as an American possession, the remainder of the Marianas Islands and all of the Caroline and Marshall Islands as a Trust Territory under the United Nations.

The United States Navy has for some years taken a special interest in these islands since it has been charged, first with the military task of wresting them from the Japanese and subsequently with the administrative task of governing their native inhabitants. Anthropologists have long been curious about the area because its ethnography has been little known, though suspected of containing clues essential to an understanding of culture history in the farther

Pacific. During the past five years, these two interests have been joined in a series of common enterprises, which have resulted in the accumulation of a wealth of new information useful alike in the improvement of administration and in the solution of scientific and historical problems. Previous to that, the ethnography of Micronesia was for the most part known only from a German expedition 40 years ago.

This cooperation began in 1943 when, with several of my anthropological colleagues at Yale, I was called into the Navy to assemble all the known information on the area and to summarize it in a series of Civil Affairs Handbooks. It was continued after the war when the Navy asked Felix M. Keesing of Stanford University to assist in planning and operating a School of Naval Administration for the training of officers sent out to administrative posts in the Trust Territory. In 1946 another anthropologist, Douglas L. Oliver, was called upon to organize an Economic Survey of the area; four anthropologists, along with other specialists, spent several months in the major islands and produced a series of valuable, though largely unpublished, reports. The CIMA program—the Coordinated Investigation of Micronesian Anthropology—is the latest in this succession of cooperative ventures.

CIMA was made possible by a substantial appropriation from the Office of Naval Research to the Pacific Science Board of the National Research Council, supplemented by a generous grant from the Viking Fund, Inc., and by contributions from a number of participating institutions. With these funds, and with transportation, supplies, and local facilities also provided by the Navy, the Pacific Science Board has been able to send into Micronesia during 1947 and 1948 some 40 scientists from 22 different institutions—human geographers, linguists, physical anthropologists, and specialists in culture and personality, though the largest group have been general ethnologists or cultural anthropologists.

Since scientists will naturally be more interested in the results of the expedition than in the details of its organization and operations,

I shall attempt a preliminary synthesis. It should be recognized that this will be in the highest degree tentative since, in addition to the findings of the Yale team on Truk, I have thus far seen only the final reports of Chave and Spoehr on the Marshalls, of Murphy on Mokil, and of Buck and Elbert on Kapingamarangi. These I have supplemented from my knowledge of the previous literature, from brief personal visits to Ponape and Palau, from a couple of days of intensive field work on Truk with natives from Puluwat, and from correspondence and brief conversations with some of those who have worked in Kusaie, Ponape, the Mortlocks, Ifaluk, Yap, and Palau.

The main cultural divisions or subareas of Micronesia are by now fairly clear. Proceeding roughly from east to west, they are as follows:

1. The Gilbert Islands.
2. Nauru.
3. The Marshall Islands.
4. Kusaie, the easternmost of the Caroline chain.
5. Mokil and Pingelap.
6. Ponape and the adjacent atolls.
7. The Polynesian outliers of Nukuoro and Kapingamarangi.
8. The Nomoi or Mortlock group and nearby atolls.
9. Truk and the Hall Islands.
10. Puluwat, Pulusuk, and Pulap.
11. The so-called Central Carolines, *i.e.,* Ifaluk, Woleai, and other atolls east of Yap and south of Guam.
12. The Marianas Islands, including Guam.
13. Yap, in the West Central Carolines.
14. Palau, including Angaur.
15. The Southwestern Islands, *i.e.,* Sonsorol, Pul, Merir, and Tobi, which stretch from Palau toward West New Guinea.

Kusaie, Ponape, Truk, Yap, Palau, and all of the Marianas are so-called "high islands," being mainly volcanic in structure. The rest of Micronesia, consists exclusively of "low islands"—78 atolls and 17 single coral islands. The total land area, inclusive of the

British possessions, comprises about 1,250 square miles, inhabited by approximately 100,000 people of Micronesian stock.

The linguistic situation is beginning to emerge with some clarity. There are no Papuan or other non-Malayo-Polynesian languages in the area. The dialects of Yap, Palau, and the Marianas are sharply differentiated from all others, and are apparently affiliated more closely with the languages of the Philippines and Indonesia than with those farther out in the Pacific. Nukuoro and Kapingama-rangi are specifically Polynesian. The languages of the rest of Micronesia, including apparently the four islands southwest of Palau as well as all those east of Yap, appear to be fairly closely related and probably deserve collectively the name "Micronesian." Though definitely distinct from Polynesian, their affiliations appear tentatively to point in this direction rather than toward Indonesia and the Philippines.

Since space is lacking to present an analysis of Micronesian culture in all its aspects, I shall confine myself to the field of social organization, and shall attempt some historical reconstructions in connection with a presentation of the distributional evidence. The principles applied are those described in my volume, *Social Structure,* and hence need not be explained in detail here.

All the evidence points strongly to the presence of a bilateral social structure of Hawaiian type, coupled of course with the usual Southeast Asiatic tendency toward local endogamy, among the Malayo-Polynesian peoples prior to their wide dispersion. This type of organization predominates in Indonesia and in Polynesia, despite special local developments. In Melanesia, bilateral organization or traces thereof appear precisely among the populations most likely to have been intrusive, the more complex forms of social structure elsewhere being presumably derived from the aboriginal inhabitants prior to the eastward migration of Malayo-Polynesian speakers.

In Micronesia, Kapingamarangi and Nukuoro reveal a bilateral organization of characteristic Polynesian type, as might be expected from their linguistic affiliations. A similar situation prevails in the

Gilbert Islands. Everywhere else, except possibly in the Southwestern Islands, social structure is strongly matrilineal. How can we reconcile the prevalence of the matrilineate in Micronesia with our hypothesis of an earlier bilateral organization among all Malayo-Polynesians?

Strong support comes from an analysis of the kinship terminology. Any full-fledged unilinear structure, whether matrilineal or patrilineal, requires a fairly rich kinship vocabulary. There is a need, for example, to differentiate cross from parallel cousins, paternal from maternal aunts and uncles, sororal from fraternal nephews and nieces. Matrilineal societies comparable to those of Micronesia exhibit such differentiation practically everywhere else in the world, whether in North or South America, in Asia, or in Africa. Micronesian kinship systems, by contrast, are marked by an extraordinary paucity of distinct terms. The Trukese, for example, get along with only eight elementary terms—father, mother, child, brother (woman speaking), sister (man speaking), sibling of the speaker's sex, spouse, and sibling-in-law of the speaker's sex. This paucity of terms, however, is specifically characteristic of bilateral structures of the Hawaiian or "generation" type, in which sibling terms are extended to all cousins, parental terms to all uncles and aunts, and terms for children to all nephews and nieces. To be sure, examples are not lacking in Micronesia of new terms developed for new categories of kinsmen, e.g., cross-cousins, but the general impression is distinctly one of unilinear structures in a relatively early phase of adapting a limited vocabulary of traditional kinship terms to a new set of social complexities.

In a few places, this adaptive process seems scarcely to have begun. This is the case, for example, in Ifaluk, according to information from E. G. Burrows. Elsewhere, however, the development has proceeded along one of the two lines followed by matrilineal societies all over the world, i.e., toward terminology of the Iroquois or of the Crow type. Both Nauru and the Marshalls have taken the former path, retaining sibling terminology for parallel cousins but developing new words to designate cross-cousins.

Ponape, the Mortlocks, Truk, Puluwat, and Yap have followed the other path, developing terminology of the Crow type by classifying the father's sisters' children with relatives of the parental generation and the mother's brothers' children with one's own or one's siblings' children.

Most of us would doubtless assume that, starting with a Hawaiian or "generation" system, the transition to an Iroquois system would require fewer internal readjustments than that to a Crow system. The Micronesian evidence belies this. Spoehr's excellent report on Majuro shows that the Marshallese, in converting the earlier Hawaiian into an Iroquois system, have found it necessary to develop at least three new terms—for maternal uncle, for sister's child (man speaking), and for cross-cousin of opposite sex. The Trukese, on the other hand, have been able to achieve a Crow system without inventing any new terms. They have simply taken the terms for "father" and "mother," which with typical Hawaiian economy were already used to designate uncles and aunts, grandparents, and parents-in-law as well as the actual parents, and have extended them to one additional category of relatives, namely, to all members of the father's matrilineal lineage irrespective of age, including of course the children of the father's sister. Reciprocal usage results in applying the term for "child" to the children of all the men of one's own lineage, including of course one's mother's brothers' children. Even today, Trukese kinship terminology conforms completely to the generation type in every respect except this reciprocal use of parent and child terms between the members of a matrilineage and the children of the men of that lineage. This suffices, however, to convert the whole system into the characteristic Crow pattern.

The kinship structure of Micronesia thus yields clear internal evidence of derivation from the Hawaiian pattern which still survives nearly everywhere in Indonesia and Polynesia, and which comparative data demonstrate to be functionally associated with bilateral descent. The inference is inescapable that the matrilineate in Micronesia is a fairly recent development. Differentiation of kinship terminology would certainly have developed further if the ancestral Micronesians had already been matrilineal at the time of the original Malayo-Polynesian dispersion.

The problem thus arises of how the Micronesians acquired the matrilineate. My own cross-cultural researches abundantly support Lowie's hypothesis that unilineal descent normally springs from a unilocal rule of residence in marriage, either matrilocal or patrilocal. Such a residence rule assembles in one place—a village, a hamlet, or a ward—a group of males or females who are in fact unilinearly related, together with their inmarrying spouses. In time, proximity tends to emphasize the kinship of this central core of the local group and gradually to convert bilateral into unilinear descent. What may have happened in Micronesia is suggested by the situation in Borneo. On this island, matrilocal residence is the rule nearly everywhere. Descent, however, is still bilateral except in one isolated area. Here, in the Siong branch of the Maanyan tribe, actual exogamous matrilineal sibs have developed out of the groups aggregated by matrilocal residence. In Micronesia, presumably, a similar process started much earlier and has gone much farther, though not quite as far as in full-fledged matrilineal societies elsewhere in the world.

Although kinship adjustments to the matrilineate are only incipient, it should be emphasized that matrilineal descent itself is full-fledged everywhere in Micronesia (excepting, of course, the Gilberts and the Polynesian outliers). In addition to lineages, there are exogamous matrilineal sibs in every subarea, and sometimes these are very widely diffused. The identical sibs, for example, are found in the Mortlocks, Truk, and the Puluwat-Pulusuk group, and are strictly exogamous over the whole territory.

Not only is matrilineal descent fully elaborated throughout Micronesia, but in many places its original matrilocal basis has for some time been disintegrating. In Guam and the other Marianas, of course, the whole matrilocal-matrilineal system has long disappeared as a result of three centuries of intensive acculturation. Preliminary reports indicate that patrilocal residence is general in both Palau and Yap. For Majuro in the Marshalls, Spoehr reports that patrilocal is at least as common as matrilocal residence. Murphy's data reveal not only that residence in Mokil is exclusively patrilocal today, but also that a true patrilocal extended family organization has come into being. German reports indicate that patrilocal residence is also common or usual in Kusaie, Ponape, the Central Carolines, and the Southwestern Islands. Only in Nauru, the Mortlocks, Truk, and the Puluwat-Pulusuk area, apparently, is the earlier rule of matrilocal residence still intact.

The last three of these subareas seem to preserve approximately the type of organization that must once have prevailed throughout Micronesia, and in addition they reveal clearly the factors which have led to modifications elsewhere. The most basic structure is the exogamous matrilineage, localized in a hamlet or section of a village with its eldest competent male as lineage chief. Next in importance is the matrilocal extended family, consisting of a group of married sisters, mothers and daughters, or maternal aunts and nieces, with their husbands and children. Third in order of significance is the exogamous matrilineal sib, which clearly represents the end product of fission and migration which have scattered the descendants of an original lineage. Spoehr's analysis of Marshallese social structure also emphasizes the primacy of the lineage and strongly corroborates the reconstruction here presented.

On Truk, we discovered two facts of the utmost importance for an understanding of the social history elsewhere in Micronesia subsequent to the acquisition of matrilineal sibs. The first of these is that patrilocal residence is an alternative of long standing in even this strongly matrilocal society. Genealogies extending back to 1800 or earlier demonstrate clearly that patrilocal residence has always occurred in circumstances under which a functioning matrilocal extended family did not exist or could not be established. For example, whenever a matrilineage is reduced to only one or two adult women, too few to maintain an efficient extended family, these women go to live with their husbands and participate in the latters' family and lineage organization. Obviously, this provides a precedent for an increasing frequency of patrilocal residence, such as is found widely elsewhere, whenever local conditions for any reason favor such a change.

Our second significant discovery on Truk was the germinal form out of which a feudal type of political organization and a complex system of social classes could easily evolve. Small feudal states with an elaborate class structure are found everywhere in Micronesia except in the central part of the Caroline chain—in the Puluwat-Pulusuk group, in Truk, in the Mortlocks, and of course in the Polynesian outliers of Nukuoro and Kapingamarangi. Petty warring states and stratification into noble and common classes of several levels characterize both the Marshalls and the Gilberts, and a similar class structure reappears in Nauru. In Kusaie and Ponape, paramount chiefs succeeded in achieving greater stability for their realms, and the former island was actually unified under a single petty king. Social stratification is pronounced in both instances. Skipping the stateless and classless areas in the middle Carolines, we encounter a strictly parallel elaboration of political and status institutions in western Micronesia. For the ancient Marianas, Thompson reports three social classes—nobles, commoners, and slaves—and a complex political structure based on land tenure, with local chiefs in rural districts and superior chiefs in the larger towns. Palau has a number of paramount chiefs, among whom two stand out above the rest, dividing the island into two complex and rivaling political systems. Yap has not achieved quite so high a degree of political integration, for the island is divided into a number of petty feudal states, but some of these have succeeded in extending their sovereignty over the atolls of the Central Carolines for hundreds of miles to the east. With respect to social stratification, however, Yap has gone farther than any other subarea, for the local culture recognizes no fewer than nine sharply differentiated social classes.

In Truk and the neighboring subareas, political integration has not gone beyond the level of the local community, which consists of a small island or a restricted district of a larger island, within which all the residents maintain daily face-to-face relations. Each such local community consists of a number of matrilineages belonging for the most part to different sibs. Each has its own land and is localized in a hamlet or a section of a village, where the married women of the lineage live with their husbands and children and where a men's house is maintained for the occupancy of the unmarried boys above the age of puberty and of the older men of the lineage when visiting their relatives for social or ceremonial reasons. Political authority in the community is vested in a local chief, who is the head of one of the constituent lineages, typically the one which, according to local tradition, first settled the district. He enjoys theoretically a right of eminent domain over all the land in the community, the other lineages being deemed to have received their holdings from his, and in recognition of his primacy he receives a sort of rental from them in the form of periodic gifts and first fruits from the produce of the land. Lineage chiefs receive similar tribute from their own subjects. Local and lineage chiefs exercise considerable authority and enjoy a large measure of prestige, but they do not constitute a special social class. The influence they exercise is in essence that of the oldest brother over his younger siblings. Their status is official and personal, and does not have the effect, for example, of elevating their families above the general run of the population.

From these facts, it is easy to see how a feudal political structure and an elaborate system of social classes could evolve. All that was necessary to initiate the complexities found in eastern and western Micronesia was military conquest. War between local districts or communities was endemic in Truk and the neighboring atolls, but it rarely eventuated in conquest. It occasionally resulted in transferring the chiefship from one lineage to another within the local community, but victory in war almost never led to the seizure of the lands of the loser by the winner, their incorporation with his own holdings, and the imposition of tribute or feudal dues upon the conquered group, and when it threatened to do so, shifting alliances among communities usually rectified the situation in a new war.

In a situation like this, however, genuine conquest and the expropriation of land are always a strong likelihood. Once accomplished by an energetic chief, and maintained successfully over a period of time, this would automatically create a petty state uniting two or more local districts. Its organization would necessarily be feudal because based on land tenure and because the conqueror would inevitably demand tribute in accordance with the precedent of periodic gifts of produce from the land to lineage and local chiefs. The enhancement in power and wealth of the new paramount chiefs would greatly accentuate differences in status and encourage confining the succession within a particular family line. This would differentiate the families of rulers, and not alone the chief himself, from the general population. Moreover, defeated lineages whose lands had been expropriated would tend to sink into a condition of dependence and serfdom. In this way, social class distinctions would arise through the very same process that produced political integration.

Western Micronesia, and Ponape and Kusaie in the east, appear to represent the completion of this process with the achievement of relative political stability. In the Marshall Islands, and apparently also the Gilberts, stability has not yet been attained. Petty feudal states and a complex class structure have developed, to be sure, but conflict among paramount chiefs still continued bitter during the Discoveries Period, and their territories never became precisely defined and traditional as, for example, in Ponape and Yap. The Trukese and their immediate neighbors, with all the elements for such a transition already implicit in their own social structure and with examples of its achievement both to the east and to the west, would almost certainly have initiated a parallel change within a very few generations if Europeans had not arrived to interfere with the process. In Micronesia, consequently, we have been able to catch "on the hoof," so to speak, a process of state development and class formation which has occurred in strikingly similar fashion in other parts of the world, e.g., in Japan, in medieval Europe, and in parts of native Africa.

By way of conclusion, we may summarize the reconstructed sociopolitical history of Micronesia in the following probable stages:

1. Autonomous and endogamous local communities with a bilateral social organization of Hawaiian type, i.e., the original Malayo-Polynesian social structure which still survives in various localities in both the near and the far Pacific.

2. A similar bilateral organization in which the rule of residence has become normally matrilocal, as in Borneo.

3. A matrilineal organization consisting of exogamous matrilineages localized in hamlets, arising on the basis of matrilocal residence, with several such hamlets within the still autonomous and endogamous community.

4. A full-fledged matrilineate consisting not only of lineages but also of exogamous sibs developed in consequence of fission and migration, but with as yet no adaptive modification of the original Hawaiian kinship terminology. Ifaluk and the nearby atolls in the Central Carolines are still apparently at this level.

5. A matrilineal organization of the same type in which adaptive changes in kinship terminology have produced Iroquois systems in some regions and Crow systems in others. The Mortlock, Truk, and Puluwat-Pulusuk subareas are still at this level.

6. A matrilineal social organization characterized by a marked increase in the prevalence of patrilocal residence, accompanied by a feudal political organization of unstable petty states and by stratification into several differentiated social classes. The Marshall Islands are typical of this level.

7. A social structure with matrilineal sibs and exogamy but with patrilocal residence, patrilineal inheritance, and at least a tendency toward patrilineal succession, accompanied by a stable political organization of petty feudal states with traditionally recognized territories and by a highly elaborate system of social classes. Yap clearly typifies this final level of development, which is also at least approached with various degrees of closeness in Kusaie, Ponape, Palau, and the pre-Spanish Marianas.

RELIGION, CEREMONIAL, AND
RECREATION

V

17

This paper, originally prepared in May, 1959, for a seminar on religion at the Center for Advanced Study in the Behavioral Sciences at Stanford University, was published in *Ethnology* (4: 165-171, 1965).

Reprinted by permission.

Tenino Shamanism

THE Tenino are a Sahaptin-speaking tribe who formerly lived on and near the Columbia River in north central Oregon. They subsisted primarily by fishing, augmented substantially by hunting, gathering, and trade. Their annual round of economic activities and their social organization have been described elsewhere (Murdock 1958).

During field work on the Warmsprings Reservation in the summers of 1934 and 1935, I established a somewhat unusual relationship with one informant, John Quinn, the oldest and most respected shaman of the tribe. When we came to discuss the treatment of illness, I encouraged him to unburden himself of his knowledge by trading him, item by item, comparable information from other primitive societies. It soon came to pass, to my surprise, that he assumed that I, too, was a knowledgeable shaman, and thereafter our discussions, though conducted through an intepreter, took the form of extended "shop talk" between two interested professional specialists. The data on shamanism in this paper derive almost exclusively from his revelations.

Since the second half of the nineteenth century the Tenino have subscribed concurrently to two religious systems. One, a form of the widespread Prophet Dance (see Spier 1935) of the Plateau, fused elements derived from Christianity and from the preachings of historical prophets from a number of neighboring tribes with a substantial core of indigenous beliefs and practices. At the time of observation it was organized as a church, whose communicants included all but a few families of the tribe. It recognized a High God and a fairly elaborate cosmology and cosmogony. Before the world was populated by men, it was inhabited by animals. Later the High God created a number of demiurges of both sexes, each representing an activity appropriate to one sex, e.g., hunting, basketmaking, berry gathering. The demiurges mated in pairs, producing the first human beings, to whom they transmitted their cultural knowledge.

With the Prophet Dance were integrated the two major indigenous annual ceremonies—a first-fruits festival in April concerned with salmon and roots, and a subsequent first-fruits ceremony in July centering on venison and berries. It also incorporated the aboriginal eschatology and a conception of sin and a moral order of the universe derived in part from Christianity but largely from the preachings of a series of native Salishan and Sahaptin prophets.

The specifically Christian elements were relatively few in number and oddly assorted. The High God was not named but was referred to by an expression translatable as "Our Father in Heaven." Grace was said before meals, tossing bits of food over the shoulder, and Sunday was observed as a day of rest and religious observances. There was also a conception of a last judgment and the resurrection of the dead, when the bones of the righteous will rise from their graves with a vast clanking noise to be reborn for eternity. There were, however, no traces of a divine Savior, no conception of a Trinity, no rituals resembling Communion or the

Mass. These absences would be incredible if the borrowing had occurred through direct contact with Christian missionaries, and Spier (1935) is probably correct in assuming that they were acquired at third or fourth hand through intermediaries of other tribes.

The second religious system—the one with which we shall hereafter be exclusively concerned—centered on the concept of supernatural power derived from animal guardian spirits. It embraced shamanistic therapy, sorcery, magical tricks, and the impersonation of spirits at winter dance ceremonies. This shamanistic religion was essentially amoral, albeit with unmistakable judicial overtones, and it had no church organization. The two systems overlapped only slightly, but were not inherently inconsistent, and most Tenino as late as the 1930's found no more difficulty in subscribing to both than have the Chinese in concurrently accepting Confucianism, Taoism, and Buddhism.

At the age of six or a little older, every child, male or female, was sent out alone at night into the wilderness in search of a guardian spirit, and this procedure was repeated from time to time until the child had accumulated five such spirits as lifelong helpers. For the most part these tutelary beings were animals or birds, but occasionally a plant, an inert object, or a natural phenomenon would reveal itself to the seeker as a supernatural guardian. The child did not go out unprepared. He was instructed by an experienced old man or woman where to go, how to behave (e.g., to keep awake by erecting piles of rocks), and what to expect. Moreover, through attendance at the winter dances he had become familiar with the distinctive cries, movements, and songs of most of the spirits he was likely to encounter.

Nevertheless, one need only project oneself backward to the aboriginal situation to imagine how anxiety-provoking a spirit quest must have been. Alone at night, remote from his family and his village, the child was fully aware of the danger of encountering an actual wolf, bear, cougar, or rattlesnake. With no light except from the moon or stars, his heightened sensory perceptions could easily magnify dim shadows and rustlings in the bush into the imagined form and movements of any animal, and he had to tense himself for any eventuality. When the dimly sensed shapes and sounds appeared to crystallize into a human figure speaking the Tenino language—for it was always thus that a spirit addressed a seeker—the child must have felt immensely relieved, and his imagination could readily structure the actual, presumed, or visionary encounter in terms of cultural expectations.

Upon revealing itself to the child in human form, the spirit uttered its characteristic animal cry, sang its special spirit song, explained the specific power it was conferring and how to evoke it, and finally resumed its animal form and disappeared. The power bestowed could be that of invulnerability in war, prowess in hunting, ability to cure sickness or control the weather, clairvoyance, fire walking, or a variety of other skills or immunities. A power offered could not be rejected or revealed to others, on penalty of punishment or its loss, but the successful seeker was expected to sing his spirit song and dance his spirit dance at the next winter ceremony. In this manner people became aware of the spirit helpers of their neighbors, but only in a general way of the powers they controlled.

A person became a shaman by discovering after puberty, and hence after the completion of the normal spirit quests, that other spirits were attracted to him. These were the guardians of deceased people, especially of dead shamans, who were conceived to be "hungry" and eager to attach themselves to a new master who would "feed" them. Unlike ordinary people, who were limited to five supernatural helpers, shamans acquired a large number of guardian spirits. John Quinn claimed to control fifty-five, and considered this only slightly more than the average.

The additional spirits accumulated by a shaman were for the most part those of animals. The powers conferred by different animal spirits were sharply differentiated, and were scaled with reference to one another, largely in terms of projections from the innate or traditional characteristics or propensities of the natural animals themselves. Among the strongest animal spirits were the grizzly bear, the rattlesnake, and the eagle. The grizzly bear had ascendancy over most other animal spirits, but not over the rattlesnake, which in turn yielded ascendancy to certain bird spirits, including the eagle. In accordance with the prevailing theory of disease, that of spirit possession, a shaman could employ his spirit helpers either to injure or to cure. He could cause a victim to fall ill or die by projecting one of his spirits into his victim's body, or he could cure a patient thus afflicted by injecting a stronger spirit into the body to eject the intrusive one.

In addition to a variety of spirits which he could use for purposes of therapy or sorcery, a shaman normally had one or more spirits of two special categories. One was a diagnostic spirit—characteristically a curious animal like a magpie—whom he could inject into the body of a prospective patient to ascertain the identity of the intrusive spirit and thereby learn which of his own spirits he might employ to extract it. The second type was not an animal spirit at all, but a human ghost, e.g., that of a dead baby whom the shaman had attached to himself. Control over such a ghost-spirit enabled the shaman to treat illnesses explained by a rarer secondary theory, that of soul loss. Occasionally, when a person was particularly distraught over the death of a beloved parent, spouse, or child, his soul would leave the body and follow that of the dear one to the afterworld in the west. The body would then waste away, and a shaman would be called in to effect a cure. When his diagnostic spirit discovered that the cause of the illness was not an intrusive spirit but the absence of the patient's own soul, the shaman summoned his ghost-spirit, dispatched it to the afterworld to fetch back the lost soul, and restored the latter to the body.

To practice, it was not sufficient merely to have accumulated the requisite number and variety of spirit helpers. The prospective shaman also had to pass the equivalent of a state medical board examination conducted by the shamans who had already been admitted to practice. These experienced practitioners led the neophyte to the edge of a high "rim rock," where he was required to demonstrate his control over his spirits. Only shamans, it was believed, could see and hear the guardian spirits of other people, and the theory was that they could judge the expertise of the neophyte in controlling his spirits on the test errands on which he was directed to dispatch them.

As scientists, of course, we must assume that there were no spirits for the neophyte to direct or his elders to observe—or rather, perhaps, that they were figments of an hallucinatory imagination. What, then, was the function of the examination? At the very least, the older shamans could determine the genuineness of the neophyte's conviction regarding his own powers; a faker would scarcely have dared subject himself to the ordeal. Moreover, as became clear in my discussions with John Quinn, the older shamans took advantage of the occasion to review carefully the entire life of the candidate. They had known him, of course, since childhood and were thoroughly familiar with his strengths and defects of character, his honesty and moral fiber, his judgment, the degree of his control over his aggressive impulses, etc. Actually, though not ostensibly, their decision as to whether or not to admit him to practice seems clearly to have rested on their collective estimate of his personal characteristics, of his fitness to be entrusted with the exercise of great power. The personality of John Quinn himself, as well as all that I could learn from him, convinces me that Tenino shamans, far from being dishonest, exploitive, or hysterical individuals, were people of unusual decency, upright character, judgment, and responsibility. Those who proved seriously defective in these respects were eliminated through sorcery.

Once he was accepted by his seniors, the young shaman could begin to practice. For his first five cases, however, he could accept no fees. Thereafter he was generously rewarded with gifts, but he received these only if his cures were effective. Women as well as men could become shamans, and they were not considered inferior in power, but they were appreciably fewer in number. When operating in a professional capacity, shamans commonly wore insignia appropriate to their guardian spirits, e.g., bear claws, eagle feathers, or a rattlesnake's rattles. Shamans sometimes assisted one another, and they acted in concert in the examination of neophytes, but otherwise they lacked any collective organization.

By far the principal function of Tenino shamans was the practice of magical therapy. When a person fell ill and did not respond to lay treatment, his family summoned a shaman, who immediately proceeded to his bedside. In the house were assembled the relatives and friends of the patient, lending him social support and enhancing his faith in the therapeutic procedures and his will to recover. On hand were the necessary accessories, including especially a coiled basket full of water. During the performance the audience sang and beat time on a dry log with short sticks, and the shaman accentuated the drama of the occasion by singing his spirit songs, uttering explosive sounds, making biting motions, and pantomiming the struggle of the spirits.

The necessary first step in the cure was diagnosis. After washing his hands, smoking, blowing on the basket of water, and sprinkling the patient, the shaman summoned his diagnostic spirit and projected it into the patient's body, usually through a tube. After an interval of time for its exploration of the interior of the body, the spirit returned to the mouth of the shaman and informed him of the identity of the intrusive spirit (or, alternatively, of the absence of the soul). If the shaman had no guardian spirit with ascendancy over the intrusive one—if, for example, the latter was the grizzly bear and he did not control a rattlesnake spirit—he resigned immediately from the case and recommended another shaman to take over. Otherwise he would have lost his life when his spirit was overcome by the intrusive one in the ensuing struggle.

If, however, the shaman's roster of supernatural helpers included one with ascendancy over the intrusive spirit, he summoned it and meanwhile called upon two strong men to assist him. They stood of either side of him, grasping his arms, while be blew his spirit helper into the patient's body. When the latter encountered the intrusive spirit, a violent conflict ensued between them, during which the patient writhed helplessly. When a moment of calm intervened, the shaman sucked the intrusive spirit into his mouth. Then began a titanic and dramatic struggle—this time between the vanquished spirit and the shaman—in which the shaman's body tensed, was thrown into contortions, and then became inert as he lost consciousness. His two assistants exerted themselves valiantly to keep him erect, for had he fallen he would have lost his life. Ultimately the convulsions subsided, and the shaman spat the intrusive spirit into his cupped hands, thereby initiating a new struggle in which the shaman, with the help of his assistants, with great effort gradually lowered his hands into the basket of water. This finally subdued the spirit.

The shaman then withdrew his hands from the water and exhibited the vanquished spirit to the audience on the palm of his hand. Only the shamans present, of course, could actually see it, but perhaps the reader may be interested in a shaman's description of an extracted spirit. According to John Quinn, such a spirit, regardless of the animal it represented, was approximately the size and shape of a cigarette butt, was grayish in color, and had a colloidal or mucus-like substance. After the viewing, the shaman, with a puff of breath, sent the spirit back to its proper place in nature. He then retrieved and similarly dispatched his own guardian spirit.

John Quinn readily admitted that shamanistic therapy was not invariably successful. Failure was explicable on such grounds as that the shaman had been summoned too late or that no spirit was available with ascendancy over the intrusive one. There is no reason to doubt, however, that genuine cures were often effected, at least in cases of "functional" ailments. Social support, a faith unshaken by skepticism, confidence in the integrity of the shaman, and the dramatic quality of the curing performance must all have contributed to a favorable result, as most modern psychiatrists are prepared to agree.

Next in importance among a shaman's activities was the sponsorship or direction of the winter dances in which guardian spirits were impersonated. Much less frequent, but socially very significant, was the practice of sorcery. This was usually, though not exclusively, directed toward tribal enemies, in times of peace as well as of war. The Tenino community credited John Quinn with having killed three fellow tribesmen by sorcery during his lifetime, and this was corroborated by colleagues of mine trained in psychoanalysis, who analzyed a collection of his dreams which I had gathered.

Special interest attaches to one of these cases, since the death was inadvertently caused, and the deep sense of guilt which John Quinn felt as a result ran like a thread through many of his dreams. A Tenino shaman was expected to keep tight rein over his thoughts as well as his actions. In the case in question, John Quinn had had a momentary hostile thought about another man. Though he himself was scarcely aware of it, it was noticed by one of his guardian spirits, who was present and who immediately dashed out of the house to do what he understood to be his master's bidding by possessing the body of the presumed enemy. As it happened, however, an innocent girl was just then passing the door, and the spirit accidentally collided with her and entered her body instead of that of its intended victim. She sickened and died before John Quinn became aware of her predicament or another shaman could be summoned to cure her.

From the other two cases and other evidence, admittedly inconclusive, I strongly suspect that in-group sorcery served primarily a judicial purpose among the Tenino. Under aboriginal conditions they lacked any political organization transcending the village, and the local headman had functions that were more advisory and hortative than authoritarian. No legal mechanism existed for coping with serious and repeated criminals—murderers, rapists, perennial troublemakers, or the like. I believe that this void was filled by the shamans through the practice of sorcery. It was clear that John Quinn felt that two of his own in–group–sorcery murders were socially justified. It was also clear that a person who engaged in shamanistic practices without permission, or who, as a shaman, used his power unduly for maleficent purposes, laid himself open to sorcery from the respected shamans. If the latter refused to come to his aid when he fell ill, he was helpless, for no one shaman by himself controlled the entire range of therapeutic powers.

It therefore seems highly probable that a Tenino shaman was expected to keep close track of malefactors within the community. When the transgressions of one of the latter exceeded the limits of toleration, in the shaman's opinion and that of his neighbors as he sensed it, he presumably assumed the responsibility, possibly after consultation with his fellow shamans, for dispatching one of his guardian spirits to possess the evildoer as an act of justified social vengeance. In other words, he acted in an emergency as judge, jury, and executioner combined. The fact that shamans were known to be capable of sorcery, and the presumption that they were prepared to use it for judicial purposes, doubtless operated to reduce the rate of serious crime and thereby to limit sharply the incidence of sorcery within the community.

If the above interpretation is correct, it would account for the high premium placed by the Tenino on personal character, responsibility, and judgment in their shamans. After all, these are the same qualities that we ourselves expect in our judges. Whatever the situation may be in other societies, the shaman's role among the Tenino certainly did not provide a social niche for the accommodation of deviant, abnormal, and neurotic personalities.

The foregoing account includes a number of specific features which the author has not encountered elsewhere in the literature on American Indian shamanism. Among them are the examining board of shamans, the specialized diagnostic and human-ghost spirits, and the emphasis placed on judicial qualities in the selection of shamans. To the extent that such facts may be novel and theoretically illuminating, the author hopes that much of the credit will be accorded to the interest and generosity of his respected former friend and "professional colleague," John Quinn.

18

In the course of writing a chapter on the Haida Indians for *Our Primitive Contemporaries* (1934) I felt extremely dissatisfied with accounts of the "potlatch" in the existing ethnographic literature. As described, this institution seemed bizarre and inconsistent with known facts about human nature. Convinced that any major element of culture must make reasonable sense in its ethnographic context, I sought enlightenment from Edward Sapir, whose interpretation of the system of rank and privileges among the neighboring Nootka impressed me as extremely suggestive. He was, however, unable to give me much help in regard to the Haida situation and persuaded me, quite properly, to conduct a firsthand investigation in the field. As a consequence, I spent four months among the Haida in the summer of 1932. This article incorporates my findings. It was originally published in *Yale University Publications in Anthropology* (no. 13, 1936, pp. 1-20).

Reprinted by permission of the Department of Anthropology, Yale University.

Rank and Potlatch
Among the Haida

THE potlatch of the Northwest Coast, though extensively treated in the literature, has always remained something of an ethnological curiosity. Whether viewed in psychological terms as an exaggerated and institutionalized expression of vanity or narcissism, or in economic terms as a disguised form of investment, insurance, or exchange, or even in sociological terms as the conventional road to social recognition and prestige, the seemingly reckless distribution or destruction of property has appeared, at best, only partially understandable. To call the potlatch the product of historical accident under unique circumstances does not, of course, dispose of the question; it merely begs it. The field research of the author among the Haida has disclosed what seems to be, for this tribe at least, a reasonably adequate sociological interpretation of the potlatch. It has made the practice appear no longer as an arbitrary or accidental excrescence on the culture, but rather as an integral part thereof, an element deeply enmeshed in and inextricable from the whole social fabric. In particular, the potlatch is discovered to be the dynamic factor in the most vital of all native institutions—the system of rank and status.

The author conducted his researches principally among the northern Haida of the Queen Charlotte Islands, now resident at Massett, although he made comparatively short visits to the other two surviving groups; the central branch, now gathered at Skidegate, and the Alaskan or Kaigani branch at Hydaburg. The data and terms cited below, unless otherwise labeled, refer particularly to Massett usage. The historical present is used throughout, although the folkways in question have long since fallen into disuse.

The potlatch (gä"ᵼsau)[1] is known to the Haida in five principal forms, which may be conveniently designated as the housebuilding, totem pole, funeral, vengeance, and face-saving types. All of them conform to a single basic pattern, namely, the ceremonial distribution of property to invited members of the opposite moiety, and all have some reference to rank, which they either confer, validate, or uphold. An explanation of the precise manner in which the potlatch is integrated with the system of rank should properly follow a detailed description of the several types of potlatches themselves.

The housebuilding potlatch (Massett and Hydaburg: 'wa'ɬal; Skidegate: wa'ɬgal), given to build or repair a house, is by far the most important type. For years in advance a man accumulates the products of his industry, the profits of trade, and the plunder of war, to which his wife adds all the property she can assemble through gift, inheritance, or her own labor, often amounting to as much as that amassed by her husband. Both spouses pool their contributions in a common fund. Occasionally a man, anxious to give a

---

[1] The phonetic orthography follows that of Edward Sapir in "The Phonetics of Haida," *International Journal of American Linguistics*, 2, nos. 3, 4: 143-158, 1923, with the following exceptions: an inverted breve is here placed beneath anterior palatal k and x, and above anterior palatal g.

potlatch but still somewhat short of the requisite amount of property, will borrow the balance from his father, brother, or maternal
uncle. He must do so secretly and at night, however, for if detected
he will be discredited and his potlatch will be considered as without
effect.

One year before the actual ceremony, when the goal of the accumulation is clearly in sight, comes "lending day" (stɫaˑntedja'ŋ),
the first act in the potlatch. From the common store of property—
consisting principally of trade blankets, in former times probably of
sea otter furs—the wife, not the husband, lends to the various members of her clan and moiety from one to ten or more blankets each.
The recipients may use the blankets to repay a debt, to give a funeral
potlatch, or for any other purpose, but they assume the obligation to
return one year hence double the number borrowed, i.e., to repay
the loan with 100 per cent interest.

A year later, shortly after the winter season begins, a canoe is
sent to friendly villages, often at a considerable distance, to issue
invitations to the potlatch.[2] Invitations are extended to both sexes
but only to members of the host's moiety, i.e., the opposite
moiety from the standpoint of his wife, who, as we shall see, is to be
regarded as the real donor of the potlatch. The guests bring their
spouses and often their children, so that those foregathering for a
housebuilding potlatch commonly number several hundred. At
one potlatch, witnessed some fifty years ago by two reliable informants, nearly the entire population of the four surviving villages in
the northern Queen Charlotte Islands was brought together for the
festivities. The visitors remain for a considerable part of the
winter, living in the various houses of the village and being fed and
entertained by the hostess and her clansmen.

The first day of the potlatch is called tcɑ'naŋ. The visitors from
each outlying village, as they arrive, lash all their canoes together
off the shore and perform a special dance on them before they land
and are ceremoniously received. The same evening the members of

[2] On the mode of extending a potlatch invitation, see Swanton (1905:
167-168).

the home village assemble at a large house belonging to a clansman of the host. The invited guests with their spouses paint their faces, don festive or ceremonial attire, and enter the house in couples. Each man and wife, as they enter, dance to the beat of the drum during the singing of four songs by the audience, and then take their seats. In this dance, called sɑ'ada'l (Swanton: sq!ā'dal), the men, but not the women, carry rattles. When all the visitors have danced and taken their places, the local men of the hostess's moiety retire with their wives, adorn themselves, return, and dance in similar fashion, couple by couple. The adolescent and adult but unmarried members of the hostess's moiety in the home village perform a dance by themselves on this occasion, although the visiting youths do not dance. It should perhaps be noted that, in the sɑ'ada', dance, the visiting performers include both men and women of each moiety, whereas among the local dancers the men are all of one moiety and the women of the other. A feast is now served on ceremonial dishes to the invited guests, i.e., to members of the host's moiety alone. Those present who belong to the other moiety also eat, but from ordinary utensils. During the feast one or two daughters of the host and hostess dance the ĝɪta·'sa·χeɬ, an energetic and sprightly dance expressive of their pride in and gratitude toward their parents. Following the feast come several informal dances, in which hosts and visitors mingle.

On the next day the people abstain from food. In the evening they all assemble in a large house to smoke—in former days to chew—tobacco. On this occasion the host appoints five of the more prominent guests, invariably men of his own moiety, to act as foremen in securing the timbers for the new house. One is made responsible for obtaining a sound cedar log, sixty to seventy feet in length, for the totem pole, and each of the others for getting the timbers for one section or quarter of the house. Each foreman selects a crew from the men of his own moiety to do the actual work under his supervision. On the following day the crews leave by canoe in search of timber, accompanied by a few women to cook for them and by some men of the other moiety who labor with them

without expectation of material reward. Five days or more, punctuated by feasts and dances at the "logging camps" in the evenings,
are required to select, fell and strip the timbers, launch them, and
fasten them to the canoes. The crews then return to the village,
singing towing songs as they paddle, and are welcomed with a feast
and a dance. At another smoking session, the host assigns to
individual guests specific tasks in the preparation of the timbers,
e.g., to one the carving of a section of the totem pole, to another
the hewing of particular wall planks, and so on (cf. Swanton
1905: 163). He appoints women as well as men, provided, of
course, that they belong to his own moiety. A woman thus chosen
lets her husband do the work in her stead, but it is she who will
receive the payment. The work thus proceeds, with one or two
more smoking sessions to assign further tasks, until the new house is
completed and its totem pole is carved and ready to be raised.

The labor is punctuated and enlivened every few days by a
dance, and more rarely by spirit performances of longer duration.
The dances are held in the evenings. The performers, wearing
ceremonial costumes and carrying rattles, dance to the beat of a
wooden drum and to the accompaniment of songs, usually four in
number. The dances are regularly given in pairs—sometimes, as in
the sɑ'adaʹl, first by the guests and then by the hosts, sometimes by
the members of the hostess's moiety followed by those of the
opposite moiety. Two of the dances deserve special mention. The
sɑ'aʹgɑ (the term is the same as that for "shaman") is danced by
one or two men or women during the singing of four songs. The
performers wear elaborate headdresses consisting of a tall cylinder
of beautifully carved and inlaid wood with a tail of ermine skins
behind and a circle of sea lion whiskers around the top. The crown
is filled with the down of eagles which, in the slow movements of the
dance, is dislodged by nods of the head and scattered through the
air like snow. One night is alway devoted to the q'ɛʹnxɘ or "spring
dance." About ten young men from the moiety of the hostess,
sometimes joined by one or two young women, dance first, and are
followed by a similar group from the moiety of the host. Each

group has a leader and, as it dances, sings four songs which he, after taking the appropriate medicines and salt water emetics, has composed especially for the occasion. The leader stands in one place, his body quivering or trembling all over, while his followers dance energetically.

The spirit performances associated with the housebuilding potlatch have been adequately described by Swanton (1905: 155-181), whose account tallies closely with such facts as the present author was able to obtain thirty years later. These performances are expressly stated to have been borrowed in the main from the Bellabella through the medium of slaves captured from that tribe. Swanton, perhaps too strongly influenced by the findings of Boas (1895: 311-738) among the Kwakiutl, associates the spirit performances with "secret societies" and speaks of "novices" and "initiates." Whatever may be the situation at Skidegate, whereof the present author, because of his very brief visit there, cannot speak with authority, secret societies neither do nor did exist at Massett and the other northern villages. The performers have no other organization or common bond than their membership in the clan of the potlatch hostess or in a closely allied clan of the same moiety. Their actual behavior, however, appears to have differed very little from that reported by Swanton for Skidegate, and it seems necessary here to record only a few supplementary remarks.

The 'wi·'lala (Swanton: ū'lala) performance can apparently be given in connection with a house-building potlatch by any one who can afford the additional expense, about fifty blankets. In corroborating Swanton's account my informants pointed out that the possessed persons or "novices" are the sons of the donors of the potlatch, that they are careful to bite only persons of high rank, and that whenever they bite a person in the arm or destroy a canoe or do any other damage, the host makes restitution in blankets to the injured party on the spot—not at the final distribution. According to Swanton (1905: 180), La·'teł had the sole right to perform 'wi·'lala in the northern villages. My informants admitted that

La·'teɫ acted 'wi·'lala at the housebuilding potlatch given by his parents, but recalled, in addition, that Si'gai had enacted the performance at 'At'ai'wa's (Massett) and Ga''u at Qaŋ, both at their parents' potlatches. An eye-witness of Si'gai's performance stated that the 'wi·'lala was a privilege of the Skɪda·'q'au 'la'nas clan of Ravens at Massett, which had acquired it from a captive Bellabella, but another informant, in general more reliable, denied that any clan enjoyed an exclusive right to the ceremony.

The 'wi·'ɫam or dog-eating performance is also an importation; even the words of the songs are said to be in Bellabella. It occurs near the end of the potlatch festivities and is enacted, not by any "secret society," but by the persons who are shortly to be tattooed, all of whom are clansmen of the hostess or members of allied clans of the same moiety. Early in the morning of the day of the performance, before the first raven has cawed, the participants climb to the top of a roof and sing a song there. For the actual ceremony, a number of poles, painted red, are set up in a wide circle around the fireplace in the dance-house, and are connected by a rope of cedar bark. The performers enter the house in single file and march around the fire within the circle, beating time with their feet, singing, and holding their arms outstretched in front of them. The leader carries in his arms the carcass of a slaughtered dog. He sings a song by himself and then, while his followers join in the refrain, buries his teeth in the flesh, sometimes eating it but more often merely pretending to do so. For the next song he passes the dog to the person next in line, who repeats the performance, as does each in turn to the end of the line. Afterwards, the actors contribute two blankets each, tear them into strips, and distribute the strips among the spectators belonging to the opposite moiety.

The gɑgi·'t (Swanton: gāgī'd) performance commonly takes place on the same day as the dog-eating ceremony. A clansman of the hostess, presumably possessed by a spirit-monster with a spiny face and hairy body, runs wildly about the village clad only in a scanty breechclout, trying to frighten everybody. Kwʋns, of the Tʋɫk'a' git'ɑne clan of Eagles, acted gɑgi·'t at the potlatch given at

Yan by his mother's sister's daughter, Xʋ'tɫkɪŋau, and her husband, Skɪ·'lkɪŋa·ns, of the 'Au' st'ɫaŋ 'la'nas Raven subclan. Whether or not Stɫa·'kɪŋaŋ also acted gɑgi·'t, as Swanton (1905: 181) states, my informant could not say.

The raising of the totem pole comes as the final act and climax in the actual construction of the new house.[3] Everybody participates—hosts as well as guests, women as well as men. A hole, six feet or more in depth, is dug close to the house in the center of the façade, and the finished pole is laid on the ground with its base beside the hole and its top pointing away from the building. The men grasp the ends of stout pieces of wood placed laterally under the pole, and lift in unison bit by bit to the accompaniment of shouts. When the pole is raised sufficiently, two X-shaped braces or supports of heavy timbers are thrust beneath it—a short one near the center and a tall one near the end—and these are advanced as the pole rises. When the men can no longer lift, they seize staves, place the ends against the pole, and push upwards, while the women stand in line behind the house and tug at a long rope fastened to the top of the pole. When the pole approaches the perpendicular, its base slips into the hole, and it is held upright until earth is filled in and tamped down. The Haida of Alaska in former times often placed a slave in the hole to be crushed to death when the pole was raised, thus enhancing the prestige of the builder, but this form of "foundation sacrifice" seems not to have prevailed on the Queen Charlotte Islands proper.

The day following the raising of the totem pole is devoted to the tattooing of the children of the host and hostess and of others who pay for the privilege. The intervening evening, however, is made the occasion for an important dance, called 'aɫa'gandaŋ, at which the performers are all those who are to be honored on the morrow. Even little children dance, and babies are carried in the arms of older dancers. The participants paint their faces, carry rattles, and wear ceremonial garments decorated with their clan crests. They

[3] At Skidgate, however, according to Swanton (1905: 162, 167), the totem pole was erected before the house itself was built.

form a continuous circle around the wall of the house, keep time with their feet to the beat of the drum and sway in unison from side to side. During the dance the host and hostess, and they alone, sing privileged songs belonging to the clan of the hostess.

All those who are tattooed belong to the clan of the hostess or to closely affiliated clans of the same moiety. They include: (1) the own and adopted children of the donors of the potlatch, (2) the children of the host's brothers, of the hostess's sisters, and of the donor's daughters, all of whom are tattooed gratuitously, (3) other children of the same moiety whose parents pay the hostess from five to ten blankets per child for the privilege, and (4) adult men, but not women, of the same moiety in return for a similar payment. Children under ten years of age and persons already fully tattooed merely have the appropriate crests marked with charcoal on their skins, but this counts in every way as an actual tattooing, and is paid for as such. The persons appointed to do the work are, in so far as possible, the 'la'na'laŋ (male cross-cousins) and sq'a·'na'laŋ (father's clanswomen) of the subjects. If they are not sufficiently skilled, however, and nearly always if they are women, they delegate the task to others, with whom they divide the fee of five or ten blankets which they receive at the final distribution. As a rule, four artisans operate on each son of the host and hostess, two on each daughter, and but one on each other person tattooed, but each subject has, in addition, a sq'a·n (father's clanswoman) to prepare the charcoal and wipe the blood from the wounds. A complete tattoo covers the back of the hands, the upper and lower arms, the chest, the thighs and lower legs, the upper surface of the feet, and even the dorsal side of the fingers and toes; also sometimes the back and the cheeks beneath the eyes. Only a portion is done at a single potlatch; a Skidegate informant, for example, acquired his nearly complete tattoo bit by bit at six potlatches. Many persons, consequently, are only partially decorated. Tattooing is a mark of rank, and the amount exhibited by a person furnishes a very rough indication of his social status.

The day following the tattooing, the last day and climax of the potlatch festivities, is called 'wa'ɫal ha'stɫa. Early in the morning, before the people have arisen, the donor of the potlatch goes forth and sings four "property songs" (gida·'ksalaɳe) of a type sung only on such occasions. These songs are privileges, not of his own clan, but of a clan of the opposite moiety—his father's clan according to my informant, but possibly the clan of his wife and children, since the two are frequently the same and were confused by my informants in other instances. After breakfast, the young clansmen of the hostess, the "children" (ĝɪ'ta'laɳ) of the host, visit in turn the various houses of the village and ceremoniously invite all the members of the host's moiety to the new house for the potlatch proper, i.e., the actual distribution of property. The following account is a description, with a few general comments, of a potlatch given at the village of Yan near Massett some fifty years ago by Kɑɳigwa'u, a Raven of the 'Au' st'ɫaɳ 'la'nas subclan, and his wife, Statɫq'a'was, of the Tci'tc git'ɑne clan of the Eagle moiety. On this particular potlatch the author has especially full information, since it was witnessed and described by his two best informants, one of them the son of the donors.

As the guests arrived at the new house, a slave, stationed outside the door, called out the ceremonial name of each. Just inside the door stood Kwʋns, a member of the Tʋɫk'a' git'ɑne, a local Eagle clan closely associated with that of the hostess. He carried a staff, and in a loud voice announced each incoming guest by his ceremonial name. Two young men, Na'kɑdjut and Djɑgi'ɑs, sons respectively of an older and of a younger sister of the hostess, ushered the guests to their seats. The posts of honor—to the right and left just inside the door—were assigned to clan chiefs from neighboring villages: Xe·'djɪgwe, chief of the Kwʋn 'la'nas clan of Ravens at O'aiya'ɳ, and Si'gai, chief of the Sḵɪda·'q'au 'la'nas clan of Ravens at Massett. The members of other visiting Raven clans sat on the left of the house (as viewed from the door); the local Ravens sat on the right. The seating was by clans; within a clan the individuals of highest rank sat in back next to the walls, while those of lesser rank sat in front on the lower tiers of the excavated floor. The local and visiting Eagles were gathered in the rear of the house, i.e., furthest from the entrance and just in front of a curtain of sails which concealed the pile of blankets and other property from the audience. This seating arrangement prevailed only at potlatches.

Behind the curtain stood the host and hostess, dressed in ceremonial blankets. Kɪŋigwa'u, the host, had his hair tied in a knot with cedar withes and his face painted with a single diagonal stripe. His wife, Statłq'a'was, wore a large spruce-root hat and a broad belt woven from cedar bark, and had her upper lip painted in token of her high social status. When the house was filled, the curtain was dramatically thrown open, exposing the pile of property, before which the host and hostess strutted proudly back and forth, while the Eagles, but not the Ravens, clapped loudly in applause. Statłq'a'was, who was carrying a basket of the berry-picking type on her back and was holding an iron agricultural implement in her hand, explained to the assembled people that these were symbolic of the occupations—picking berries and raising potatoes—by which she had accumulated her share of the property to be distributed. Kɪŋigwa'u, who was carrying an adze, spoke in praise of his father, a famous canoe-builder, and told how he himself had amassed his property at the same occupation.

It was at this point in the proceedings, apparently, that Kɪŋigwa'u assumed his "potlatch name," 'Iłag̑ɪtq'altłasta'ns. When a house chief dies, his potlatch name descends to his heir and successor; the latter assumes this honorific title, however, not at the funeral potlatch (although one informant so stated) when he comes into the position and property, but only when he subsequently gives a housebuilding potlatch. "After that," says Swanton (1905: 118), "he could add a new one every time he made a potlatch." According to my own information, however, a chief assumes a potlatch name only once—at his first housebuilding potlatch—although he may inherit and transmit the right to other names, holding them in trust, as it were, and conferring them at funeral potlatches but not using them himself. Potlatch names may originate in various ways. Skɪdkɪŋa·'ns, a Raven house chief at

Yan, at his housebuilding potlatch assumed the title of Skaxwe·'t, the name of a Tsimshian chief who had failed to pay him a debt. A former chief of the Tci'tc git'ane clan of Eagles at Yan obtained the potlatch name Naska'itɫ by gift from a Tlingit chief with whom he established a formal st'a'gʋɫ (guest-friendship) relation (see Murdock 1934: 355-385). With this explanatory digression, we may return to Kʌŋigw'au's potlatch.

After the dramatic exposure of the accumulated property and the speeches by the hostess and the host, all the local Eagles, i.e., the members of the moiety of the hostess, filed out of the house by the front door and dispersed to their homes, where they painted their faces and donned ceremonial attire. Returning to the potlatch house, they brought with them the blankets they had borrowed from the hostess the year before, an equal number representing the interest at 100 per cent on their loans, and additional blankets in payment for all the children and others who had been tattooed on the previous day. They marched in single file, each with a load of blankets thrown over his shoulder, and entered the door slowly, one by one. As each appeared, two or three of his sq'a·'na'laŋ (paternal aunts and female cross-cousins) spoke up to compliment him on his appearance, oratory, or the like, and whoever did so then and there received a blanket as a gift. The rest of the blankets were piled high on top of those collected by the donors of the potlatch, and the curtain was closed.

The hostess, standing in front of the curtain, summoned to her by name each of her children, in order of age, and then, accompanied by two of her sisters, Xʋtɫkʌŋa'u and Djat'a'tɫias, sang two low lullabies (ĝʋ'tq'agan) in their honor. This ceremony, involving a public announcement of the names of the children, had an important social function. The name of a newborn child is selected, shortly after its birth, by the mother in consultation with the father and grandparents, and is bestowed at a small feast a few days later. Advice is usually sought from a wise old woman or seeress, for a child is believed to be a reincarnation of the ancestor or deceased relative whose name it bears. The choice is invariably made either from the fund of names belonging to the maternal clan or from the list belonging to the clan of the child's paternal grandfather. When the parents later give a housebuilding potlatch, the childhood names are publicly announced and confirmed, and thereby invested with an honorary or ceremonial significance, or else a new name of an honorary character is conferred. In the particular potlatch under discussion the childhood names of the daughters received public confirmation in the rite just described, while the only son was given a new name, that of his paternal grandfather, in the following ceremony.

When the children had returned to their places, the hostess called back her son, as well as two of her husband's nephews, and they all retired behind the curtain. Here her husband made his son sit on a large "copper" (t'au), which his nephews lifted upon their shoulders. The curtain was then thrown open, and all the Eagles applauded while the nephews marched back and forth with their burden, followed by the proud parents. When the applause ceased, the procession stopped, and the host explained to the assembled people that he was bestowing upon his son the name of his father, who had been cradled in a "copper" the day after his birth. He also announced that his father, St'ast, the chief and last survivor of the Do' git'ane clan of Eagles, had said that his grandson and namesake should inherit from him, when he died, his privileges and his property rights on Nasto' or Hippa Island.

The actual distribution of the property followed. The hostess supervised the distribution, aided by her husband, who stood by her side and called her attention to any mistakes. Na'kadjut, the son of her elder sister, stood beside the pile, took each time the number of blankets she indicated, threw them upon the floor, and called aloud the ceremonial or potlatch name of the recipient, who answered: "Xade!" Four Eagle boys acted as pages, picking up the blankets, carrying them on their shoulders, and depositing them in front of the proper persons. The first three recipients were, in order: Xe·'djιgwe of Q'aiya'ŋ, Si'gai of Massett, and Na·łaŋ of Yan, chiefs of Kwυn 'la'nas, Skιda·'q'au 'la'nas, and St'łaŋ 'la'nas clans respectively. After the outstanding chiefs had been provided for, donations were made to other guests for their various services, beginning with those responsible for carving the totem pole.[4] Persons who had themselves given housebuilding potlatches received larger gifts than did others who had rendered similar services—on the principle, so often reiterated by my informants, of "making it even." Additional blankets were also given to the women who had assisted the hostess as midwives at the birth of her children. A number of blankets still remained, reserved for a special distribution called ĝä'djuksau. The hostess presented one or two of them to each Raven guest who had distinguished himself by exceptionally hard work or good dancing, and then asked any one whom she had overlooked to speak up. If a volunteer had really done well, she gave him a blanket; but if he were bluffing, she gave him only a strip of sail, and the crowd jeered at him. She added another touch of comedy by presenting the last ragged blanket with mock solemnity to her husband, who belonged, of course, to the moiety of the recipients; his "reward" was precisely equal to that received by the tiniest Raven boy who had done his bit by fetching water. In all, approximately nine hundred blankets were distributed, although a scant hundred had sufficed at another remembered potlatch given a generation earlier, at a time when two blankets constituted an adequate reward to a young man for a whole season's work.

After the presentation of the blankets, the host gave away two "coppers," one to Xc·'djɪgwe and the other to Si'gai. Contrary to Swanton (1905: 156), "coppers" are not "sold" at a potlatch, but are given away—usually to a man, or the heir of a man, who on some previous occasion has given a "copper" to the chief whom the donor has succeeded. Following the presentation of the "coppers," the hostess, aided by a female relative and four girls as assistants, distributed a great quantity of clothing, dishes, horn spoons, mats, and other feminine articles in much the same manner as the blan-

[4] The order of distribution seems to have been different at Skidegate; cf. Swanton (1905: 169-170).

kets had been given away. Any chief who wanted one of the boxes in which the blankets and other property had been stored, asked for it, and it was given him. The guests then departed, to carry their gifts to the houses at which they were staying, but they shortly returned to participate in a dance, which lasted well into the evening. On the following day, all who had come from other villages returned to their homes, and the people of Yan celebrated the end of the potlatch festivities with an informal picnic (q'a'igwʊdaŋ) in the new house.

Numerous facts suggest that, although a man is commonly spoken of as having given a housebuilding potlatch, the actual donor is not he but his wife. It is she who makes the loan the previous year, and she who superintends the actual distribution. To be sure, he presents the "coppers," but he merely stands by while she gives away the blankets, dishes, and other articles. In Skidegate and Hydaburg, the husband presides over the distribution of blankets, but in the latter place it is specifically stated that the wife alone has the power to decide how many each recipient is to get and to correct her spouse if he makes a mistake. In Hydaburg, moreover, it is the wife, not the husband, who distributes the slaves and "copppers." The songs, dances, and ceremonies performed at the potlatch, in so far as they are privileges, belong to the wife's clan or related clans, not to the husband's. The participants in the spirit performances and the assistants at the final distribution are her kinsmen and kinswomen. The comic presentation of the last bedraggled blanket by the hostess to her husband is another eloquent piece of testimony. Finally, this interpretation alone squares with the native theory, often explicitly expressed by my informants, that all potlatches are given to the opposite moiety. Swanton (1905: 155), therefore, would seem to have interpreted the situation incorrectly when he states that a housebuilding potlatch "was given by a chief to the members of his own clan" and that he "borrowed from the opposite clan through his wife, and paid back to the heads of his own clan."

The second major type of potlatch is one which may be called the totem pole potlatch. At Massett, it is called cₐ na′gₐt, a name derived, according to one informant, from caŋ na′gat (air house). The more usual name at Hydaburg is kwei na′gat. This ceremony requires the distribution of only about half as much property as the housebuilding potlatch, and confers rather less than half as much prestige and status. It is usually undertaken by a man and wife who have not accumulated sufficient property to build a house, but who are forced to take immediate action either to give their children enough status to marry well or else to counteract some derogatory remark made in public about the low status of one of their sons or daughters. A totem pole alone is erected, the building of the house being postponed until further property has been amassed. With the exceptions noted, the cₐ na′gₐt follows precisely the pattern of the housebuilding potlatch, for which it is a substitute, and includes the same ceremonial elements. Another alternative is the gut′ɩ′n'wa (Hydaburg name), which is a housebuilding potlatch given, not by a single couple, but by two brothers and their wives, who pool their resources for the purpose. The elder brother becomes the house chief, and the younger inherits from him. Na·′łaŋ and Gɩndlɩga·′s of the 'Au st'łaŋ 'la′nas Raven subclan at Yan gave such a potlatch. It differs from an ordinary housebuilding potlatch only in that the children of both brothers acquire status thereby and that their enhancement in status is only about as much as if their parents had given totem pole potlatches. Neither the cₐ na′gₐt nor the gut′ɩ′n'wa is permitted at Skidegate, and it is probable that both represent comparatively recent innovations.

The third major type of potlatch, the cₐ k'a′ (Swanton: sî′k!a) or funeral potlatch, involves the expenditure of scarcely one-tenth as much property as does the 'wa′łal, and is correspondingly less important. It is given to erect a mortuary column for a deceased house chief or other important person of either sex, but never for a child or a person of inferior social status. The donor is always a male and is normally the next of kin in the maternal line, i.e., the eldest surviving brother of the deceased or, in default of brothers, the eldest sororal nephew. The potlatch is usually held during the winter season following the completion of the funeral ceremonies and feasts, but it may be postponed a year if insufficient property is available. The donor may use the property he has inherited from the deceased, but must make up any deficit with his own possessions, supplemented by donations from his clansmen. The guests invariably belong to the moiety opposite to that of the deceased and his heir. They include all local residents of the opposite moiety and perhaps one clan from a neighboring village, to whom a formal invitation is extended.

The first day, as in the case of the housebuilding potlatch, is marked by dancing (especially the sɑ'ada'l) and a feast. On the second day, tasks are assigned and the guests depart to select, fell, and bring back a cedar suitable for the mortuary column. Shaping the pole, carving it with crests pertaining to the clan of the deceased, and erecting it consume perhaps ten days, which are interspersed with feasts and dances. If the donor can afford the additional expense, a spirit performance may be held, but this is somewhat exceptional. Tattooing does not occur in conjunction with the funeral potlatch. In its stead, the classificatory grandchildren (t'ak'ɑ'nɑ'laŋ) of the deceased have their ears and nasal septum pierced and, in the case of girls, also the lower lip for the reception of the labret. Contrary to Swanton (1905: 162, 169), these mutilations are not performed, save very exceptionally, at a housebuilding potlatch. The children operated upon belong exclusively to the moiety of the deceased, although not necessarily to his clan. Those who perform the mutilations are the sq'a·'nɑ'laŋ (paternal aunts and female cross-cousins) of the donor of the potlatch. They receive a few blankets each for their services, which they never delegate to others.

The actual distribution of property comes on the final day of the potlatch. It is preceded, however, by a name-giving ceremony (q'auɬi'da). When the guests are assembled in the house, the donor of the potlatch makes his appearance from behind the curtain which conceals the pile of blankets. He is not accompanied by his wife as in the housebuilding potlatch. The children who have had their ears, noses, and lips pierced sit in a line before him. To each of them he gives a name, preferably an eminent one, from his clan fund of names. These names do not supersede the ordinary ones in everyday life but, like those bestowed upon children at a 'wa'tal, are used at potlatches and similar important occasions. Though honorary, they are not to be confused with the far more important "potlatch names" assumed by a man giving a housebuilding potlatch. In one funeral potlatch upon which the information was pariculary full, the names were bestowed, not by the donor of the potlatch, but by his clan chief and the chief of a closely associated clan of the same moiety residing in the same village. The author suspects that this may have been the usual procedure. After the name-giving, the donor directs the distribution of the property, mainly blankets, which are carried to the recipients by his younger classificatory siblings. The carver of the crests on the mortuary column receives about ten blankets, the other guests two or more, in proportion to their services. The festivities terminate with a dance given by the guests.

The fourth type of potlatch, the gada'ŋ or vengeance potlatch, is given by a man or woman of high rank who has been insulted, or whose honor has been injured in any way, by a person of similar rank belonging to the opposite moiety or to another clan of the same moiety. No one gives a vengeance potlatch against a fellow clansman or against a person of low social status, an insult from whom is ignored as though from a dog. The donor issues invitations to members of the opposite moiety in all the villages for miles around. His own relatives also gather at his house to watch the proceedings with pride. When the guests are assembled, the host brings out some valuable property and destroys it in the presence of his antagonist, who must then make a similar sacrifice or suffer irreparable loss of prestige. The host may kill a slave, or hack a valuable canoe to pieces, or crumple a "copper" and throw it into the sea. In some of the villages on the west coast, poles are said to have been erected at vengeance potlatches. The commonest procedure, however, is to tear a number of blankets into strips and distribute the pieces to the invited guests, who belong necessarily to the opposite moiety. In a typical case—a potlatch given by Kɐŋigwa′u, a Yan chief, against ′A′niłas, a chief at Massett, who had accused him of taking a piece of driftwood from a strip of beach belonging to himself—the donor had his sororal nephews tear twenty blankets into shreds, hack a valuable "copper" into narrow strips, and distribute the pieces of both. Every one present who belonged to the opposite moiety, regardless of rank, received a strip of blanket and a piece of the "copper." The antagonist, who chanced to be of the other moiety received a whole blanket. He then, in turn, had a similar number of blankets and a "copper" cut into strips and distributed, and gave a whole blanket to Kɐŋigwa′u. (Had the two opponents belonged to different clans of the same moiety, the opposite moiety would have been the recipients from both.) This reciprocal destruction of property satisfied the honor of the donor, left his opponent undamaged in prestige, and restored peace between them.

The vengeance potlatch is occasionally used to ruin an opponent who is too poor to make an equivalent sacrifice of property, even by calling upon his relatives for assistance. For a similar reason, a person rarely gives a gɐda′ŋ against a wealthier opponent, lest the latter destroy more property in return than the donor can raise. In Skidegate, where the vengeance potlatch seems to be a more serious matter than in Massett, a poor man is said to make no attempt to meet the challenge of his opponent, lest the latter thereupon give a gɐda′ŋ quite beyond his ability to return. As a rule, however, a vengeance potlatch takes place between equals, and ends in a draw. Indeed, in Massett, the ceremony is usually marked, not by hostility anf bitterness, but by mutual good will and even joviality. It is a festive occasion rather than a grim contest. The aforementioned potlatch between Kɐŋigwa′u and ′A′niłas is a case in point. When the donor bade his nephews destroy his two "coppers," his opponent, who had but a single "copper," called out: "Brother-in-law, take one of them back; I can't make it even." Kɐŋigwa′u then good-naturedly withdrew one of his "coppers," and the ceremony went on. The object of the potlatch seems, consequently, not so much to take vengeance against an opponent as to wipe out a slight and uphold the prestige of the donor—"to restore the integrity of the individual," as Pareto (2: 736 ff., 1935) would say.

Somewhat resembling the fourth type of potlatch is the fifth principal type, the 'a·'nsɩŋada or cɩŋa'da, which may be called the face-saving potlatch. Whenever a person of high social status suffers in public a mishap which makes him appear ridiculous or causes him to be laughed at, e.g., tripping and falling at a feast or potlatch where members of other clans are present, he can "save face" and prevent all future reference to the mishap by giving a small potlatch. On the evening of the following day he invites all the villagers belonging to the opposite moiety to his house for a feast, after which he tears ten or more blankets into strips and distributes the pieces among the guests. The higher he is in rank, the more careful he must be to wipe out thus even the slightest injury to his dignity, e.g., merely stumbling in public. A face-saving potlatch is also given by the parents of a child of high social status if the latter trips and falls on a path and is helped up by a member of another clan, or tumbles from a canoe into the water and is rescued by an outsider, or suffers any comparable public mishap. The father invites the members of his own moiety, i.e., the opposite moiety from the point of view of the child, and the mother tears up ten or more blankets and distributes the pieces to the guests. No one thereafter may allude to the accident. Ridicule is effectively stopped.

Despite their differences, all the five types of potlatch bear some relation to rank. In Haida society, however, rank is not a simple phenomenon. There are really operative two independent but interrelated systems of rank, namely, political rank or *position* and sociological rank or *status*. The former relates to chiefship alone; the latter to membership in what has often been loosely called a "social class." The potlatch operates as the decisive factor in both systems, but in different ways.

As regards *position*, the Haida distinguish two grades of chief:

house chiefs and clan chiefs. Any one who owns a dwelling is a
house chief ('na 'le·'). Such a position can be acquired only by
giving a potlatch—either a housebuilding potlatch to get a new
dwelling erected and thereby establish oneself as its chief, or a
funeral potlatch to validate the inheritance of a house and its
chiefship. A house chief exercises a mild paternal authority over
the members of his household, who normally include his wife or
wives, his unmarried daughters, his sons under ten years of age, his
married daughters with their husbands and children, his younger
brothers with their wives and children, a sister's adolescent son or
two, one or more married nephews (who may or may not be sons-
in-law as well) with their families, and perhaps some other poor
relative and a slave or two. He directs the economic activities of
the household, protects and cares for its members, and is treated
with respect and a measure of reserve. His nephews (including his
sons-in-law) are his right-hand men, obeying his orders, assisting
him in his economic activities, and manning his canoe on military
and trading expeditions.

The clan chief is always also a house chief, usually the richest
and most influential in the village. He exercises authority over all
the house chiefs of his own clan who reside in the village. He can
normally count on their support in war and other enterprises, even
though he has no recognized power to force obedience or punish
insubordination. His authority, therefore, resides mainly in the
prestige of his position and in his wealth and personal qualities. He
acts as trustee of the lands and prerogatives of the clan. He is
treated with marked deference, is greeted with the special expression "naŋ 'i'tɬadas," and receives from his clansmen small presents
of fish and the like from time to time. He is known by the title
either of "village master" (Massett: 'la'na 'le·; Hydaburg: 'la'na
lɑ'ai'; Skidegate: 'la'na ǀgai'ga) or of "village mother" (Massett:
'la'na 'a"we; Hydaburg: 'la'na a'we; Skidegate: 'la'na 'au'ga). The
latter title, in Massett at least, is also applied to the wife of the chief,
who is always consulted by the women of the clan before they plan
a communal picnic or the like. As to why the chief of a clan,

though a male, is called the "mother" of the village, three informants gave as many different explanations, obviously rational-
izations. According to one, the clansmen always consult their chief
before they do anything, as a child asks permission of its mother;
according to the second, the chief gives feasts just as one's mother
provides one with food; according to the third, the chief issues
orders to his clan, "which is like a big household," just as a mother
gives orders to her children. The authority of a clan chief does not
extend beyond the limits either of the clan or of the village.
Aboriginally, the clan and the village seem to have been cotermi-
nous (cf. Swanton 1905: 66). A clan was merely a localized
segment of a moiety, a group of Ravens or Eagles settled in one
village. Sometimes a discontented house chief, if influential
enough, would desert the village with a band of followers and
establish another settlement, with himself as its chief. In this way a
number of Haida clans have become divided into subclans resident
in different towns. In all such cases, the chiefs of each subclan are
entirely independent, and each has the titles and prerogatives of a
clan chief. With time, of course, such subclans would develop into
distinct clans, with no mark of their former union save a common
fund of privileges. The evidence seems clear that this process has
actually taken place in a fair number of cases.

Under aboriginal conditions it was apparently quite exceptional
for a village to be inhabited by more than one clan. Even since
white contact, which has resulted in a marked decrease in the
number of settlements, the several clans of a village have been quite
independent. The chief of one clan may, through superior wealth
or status or because his group is larger or possesses more privileges,
come to enjoy greater prestige than the others, but he wields no
actual authority outside of his own clan. This is definitely true of
the northern or Massett and of the Alaskan or Kaigani branches of
the Haida. The sole exception is found at Skidegate, where the
chief of the Gᴧtᴜ'ns clan of Eagles, the original inhabitants of the
village, acquired a measure of authority over the chiefs of the clans
which moved in later. This development seems to have been recent

as well as localized, and to have been influenced by contact with the whites. The "town chief" mentioned by Swanton (1905: 68) cannot, therefore, be distinguished from the clan chief as an aboriginal functionary.

Chiefship, in both the household and the clan, is hereditary in the female line. The old chief's property, his widow, and his position with its prerogatives and authority, descend in a body to the heir, who must validate his inheritance by giving a funeral potlatch. Normally, the succession falls to the eldest surviving brother of the deceased chief; in default of brothers, to the eldest son of the eldest sister (in Skidegate, the eldest nephew by any sister). If there are no male heirs, a woman may succeed—a sister, niece, or granddaughter. An incumbent has the power during his lifetime to set aside the next of kin in favor of a junior heir, but he seldom does so unless the senior already holds an equally high position, or is disqualified by some physical, mental, or moral defect, or—most important of all—does not enjoy a high social status. If a house chief fails to name his successor, the clan chief appoints him. If a clan chief dies without selecting his heir, a council of the clan meets to do so. All the men and women of the clan resident in the village, provided they do not lack social status, assemble to smoke—formerly to chew—tobacco and to discuss and vote upon the available candidates. They usually select the next of kin unless he is disqualified by reason of poverty, laziness, incapacity, low status, or nonresidence in the village. Their decision is announced to the hier, if he is not present, by the widow of the deceased. A clan council also has the power to set aside the nominee of the old chief, if he is obviously unfit. Once chosen, however, a clan chief cannot be deposed for any reason.

As regards sociological rank or *status,* the literature on the tribes of the Northwest Coast commonly distinguishes three "social classes"—nobles, commoners, and slaves—and treats them as hereditary although also founded very largely on wealth. This view, falsely suggesting a parallel in type with the social classes prevalent in Europe and other parts of the world, is definitely misleading, at least in so far as the Haida are concerned. To be sure, the slaves (xa'ldaŋ; plural: xa'ldansɪda) of the Haida do represent a fairly typical servile class. Recruited by war or purchase, they are objects of property and labor for their masters at the more unpleasant tasks. Their status is hereditary, although they are not allowed to marry and rarely have children. Utterly despised, they lack all rights and are generally neglected and ill treated. Their numbers seem never to have been large; most households had no slaves, and the largest number recorded for a single household was three. The so-called classes of "nobles" and "commoners," on the other hand, are not, among the Haida, hereditary at all. Nor are they, strictly speaking, based upon wealth. They are dependent, rather, on the distribution of property, on potlatches. What gives a person status, moreover, is not his own potlatches but those given by his parents. A Haida cannot inherit status; he cannot acquire it by his own liberality; he can possess it only if his parents have potlatched.

Fundamentally, therefore, the so-called "nobles" and "commoners" of the Haida are, respectively, merely those who possess status and those who lack it, those whose parents have potlatched and those whose parents have not. There are, however, numerous gradations of status, depending in every case upon the number and type of the potlatches given by the parents. A person whose parents have given a housebuilding potlatch is known as 'ya'ɛ́t (pl.: 'ya"ɛduk), and enjoys what may be regarded as the norm of full social status. He is definitely outranked, however, by a person whose parents have given two housebuilding potlatches, and even by one whose father has given a funeral potlatch in addition to a 'wa'lal. Those whose parents have given only a totem pole potlatch or a gut'ɪ'n'wa (a housebuilding potlatch given jointly by two brothers and their wives) are classed with 'ya"ɛduk, and associated freely with the latter, but enjoy a considerably lower status—one rather less than half as high. No difference in rank obtains between two children whose parents have given equivalent potlatches, even though the parents of one outrank the parents of the other. A child born subsequent to his parents' potlatch, moreover, enjoys a status precisely equal to that of his elder sibling born prior to the event, even though he does not bear the outward symbol of his rank in an extensive tattoo. Status depends, therefore, not upon the rank of one's parents, the date of one's birth, or the quantity of one's tattoo, but solely upon the number and quality of the potlatches given by one's parents. Persons whose parents have given a housebuilding or totem pole potlatch enjoy preferred seats at feasts, have the right to speak first at all public gatherings, are alone eligible to inherit a chiefship, associate little with those of lower status, and can insult the latter with impunity. They feel called upon to defend their exalted status and prestige against any infringement, and they do so through the instrumentality of face-saving and vengeance pot- latches. Psychologically, they typically resemble those individuals in our own society who are said to "carry a chip on the shoulder," i.e., who are quick to lash out with fist or tongue at the slightest invasion, real or fancied, of their personal prestige, their vanity, or their "rights."

A person who lacks status entirely, whose parents have never given a potlatch, is known as 'isa'ngᵢda. He is universally scorned and may not resent any affront from his superiors. He lives in the rear corner of the dwelling of some maternal relative and at feasts occupies an inferior seat near the door. He cannot inherit a chiefship; even is he is the next of kin, he will be passed over in favor of a junior heir who possesses the requisite status. Though greatly superior socially to a slave, his status is as permanent, and he is as helpless to improve it. If he is capable and industrious he may acquire wealth and give liberal potlatches. He may thereby secure a measure of respect for himself, and even become a self- made house chief, but he can never escape the stigma of his low status. His case is paralleled by that of the *nouveau riche* in our own society, to which, however, it is at best somewhat inferior. Nevertheless, by his potlatches he can advance his children to the status of 'ya"ɛduk and make them in every way the social equals of the offspring of more exalted parents. Conversely, a man who enjoys a high social standing through the liberality of his parents, but who is too lazy or shiftless to accumulate property and give a potlatch of his own, loses the respect of the community but does not forfeit his status. He is called 'isa'nia, a term of reproach for a poor man. His situation resembles that of the "black sheep" of a respectable European family, but it is his children who suffer in status, not himself. One's own potlatches count for little in comparison with those given by one's parents.

A person is not utterly without status, even if his parents have not potlatched, providing either his father's own brother or his mother's own sister has given a housebuilding or a totem pole potlatch. He basks, as it were, in the reflected glory and acquires a measure of status—enough to raise him a bit above his fellows who are less fortunate in their aunts and uncles, but not enough to remove the stigma of the term 'isa'ngᵢda. This does not hold true in Skidegate, where, however, the potlatch of a maternal grandfather has much the same effect. Slightly better off is the person whose father, though he has given no housebuilding or totem pole potlatches, has nevertheless held a funeral potlatch. Such a person may not be called 'isa'ngᵢda nor may he be insulted with complete freedom, but his status is far inferior to that of the 'ya''ɛduk and he may associate only with those who have little or no status.

From the foregoing account, as from the available literature, it might be inferred that "commoners" constitute a majority and "nobles" a small minority in Haida society, as is the case in most stratified societies. Such an inference, however, is quite erroneous. Informants at both Massett and Hydaburg insisted strongly that persons lacking in status never constituted more than ten per cent of the total adult population. "Nobles" have always greatly outnumbered "commoners." The explanation of this fact lies in the widespread practice of adoption. Orphans and the children of shiftless parents are commonly adopted by a paternal uncle and his wife. Adoption regularly involves giving a housebuilding potlatch; indeed, it is invalid without one. The donors of a wa'ɫal customarily take advantage of the occasion to adopt any children of the host's brothers whose prospects of acquiring status otherwise are slim. An adopted child is called ĝɩtqʻaid. By virtue of the potlatch he becomes the legal child of his foster parents and acquires the same high status as their own offspring. In general, therefore, a person fails to acquire status only if his father is deceased or incapable and he also has no paternal uncle able to adopt him with a potlatch.

Illegitimate children present a special case. They fall into two categories: (1) qʻaigwaʻɫdiɑ or the offspring of an unmarried mother, and (2) ʼa·ʻŋĝɩda or the progeny of an endogamous union. Even under aboriginal conditions, it is said, unions between a man and a woman of the same moiety, though rare, sometimes occurred. An endogamous union, however, has never been regarded as a valid marriage, nor its offspring as legitimate. Illegitimate children possess no status and can acquire none, for they have no legal father and their mother cannot give them a potlatch by herself.

Distinctions in rank are clearly reflected in the native system of composition for murder. When a clan has lost a member through murder or sorcery it seeks vengeance by slaying a clansman of the murderer, unless prevented by the mediation of the chiefs of neutral clans. In the latter case, the clan of the aggressor either surrenders the culprit to be killed or, as happens much more frequently, renders compensation in property. The compensation, which is used to give a funeral potlatch to the deceased, is always graded in amount strictly according to the status of the victim. Even if vengeance has been taken, however, the case is not necessarily closed. The blood feud, to be sure, is terminated, but a balance remains to be settled one way or the other by a transfer of property unless the two victims happen to be identical in rank. If, for example, the murdered man is a ʼyaʼɛʼt, while the person slain in retaliation enjoys only the partial status conferred by a totem pole potlatch, the death of the latter extinguishes only approximately half of the "wergild." Even the slaughter of three ʼisaʼnĝɩda in a feud does not quite compensate for the loss of one ʼyaʼɛʼt.

The system of rank and its integration with the potlatch, as they have been described above, prevail among all branches of the Haida tribe with only minor variations. Whether or not a comparable situation exists among the mainland tribes is uncertain. The evidence in the published literature on the Tsimshian and Tlingit is not so much negative as inconclusive. That among some of the Tlingit, at least, the situation may approximate that among the Haida becomes not improbable in view of information given by one Hydaburg informant. This informant, the son of a Tlingit father and a Haida mother, had himself married a Tlingit woman and had lived for twelve years with her people near Sitka, where he had personally witnessed several potlatches. According to him, the potlatch-status complex in essentially the Haida form prevails among the Tlingit of the islands as far north as Sitka, and was borrowed he believed, from the Haida. The Tlingit, he said, have both the housebuilding and the funeral potlatches, which they call ya'datiye and ko'i'k respectively, but they lack the totem pole potlatch since they do not ordinarily erect totem poles. He was unable to recall any significant differences between the Tlingit and Haida potlatches that he had seen. Among the Tlingit of the islands as among the Haida, he insisted, status depends upon the potlatches given by one's parents, a person whose parents have given a housebuilding potlatch outranking one whose father has given only a funeral potlatch and being outranked by one whose parents have celebrated two ya'datiye. Among the Tlingit, too, the real donor of the potlatch is the wife, who is said to have, as among the Haida, the final word as to the distribution of the property. Whether the pattern in question has a wide or a restricted distribution among the Tlingit can probably be determined only by further field work.

19

This article was written for a popular audience and was originally published in *Newsweek* (32, no. 9: 69-70, 1948). It is reprinted herewith because the data seem to me to have implications of some theoretical interest.

Waging Baseball on Truk

TO the natives of Truk, war was always a favorite pastime.
Until they were subdued and disarmed by the Germans
about 1900, district fought district or island fought island
at the drop of a hat. Ambush and trickery alternated with wily
diplomacy. War parties were led by renowned magicians, who
brought to bear all their supernatural skills. The most potent
"medicine" was to capture an enemy by stealth, kill him, cut off his
lips, and prop up his body with its mouth open on the beach facing
the enemy country. This was supposed to induce the voracious god
of war to go over and eat up the foe.

Traders encouraged these habits. On the little island of
Romonum, only a mile long, an American set up shop at one end of
the island in the 1890's and a Japanese at the other. Each sold
firewater to the natives in his district to inflame them against the
other, and firearms with which to express their hostility. Although

the Germans stopped this slaughter, it was the Japanese after 1914 who first gave the Trukese a satisfactory substitute for war. They introduced American baseball.

The new game caught on like wildfire. Regulation balls, bats, mitts, gloves, masks, and uniforms were imported, and teams were organized in every district. Today every male is a player. The island of Romonum, with a total population of only 230, boasts three regular teams and a large squad of substitutes. Women don't play because baseball, like war, is men's business.

All the Trukese know baseball lingo, and it is about the only English they speak. The Japanese introduced the American vocabulary with their own peculiar mispronunciations, and the Trukese have given it some further twists. The positions are called "peecha," "catch," "fasto" (first base), "secundo," "sorto" (short-stop), "sato" (third base), "righto," "senta," and "refto." Umpires call out "Seerike wan!" (strike one) and "Faw bworr!" (foul ball). Spectators encourage their teams with "Wan way!" (one away) and "Caman bebby!" (come on, baby).

The Trukese know all the rules, even those about balks and infield flies, but they ignore two of them: The hitter does not run when a third strike is dropped, nor is a caught foul fly considered an out. Pitchers try to get away with murder, e.g., tossing a quick one when a batter hitches up his pants. Arguments with the umpire are taboo—probably as a result of Japanese-instilled respect for authority—but spectators don't hesitate to miscall balls, strikes, and outs in the effort to confuse him.

The natives don't play baseball, they wage it. An interisland game is serious business. The players practice almost daily and observe all the sexual and other taboos which used to precede war. For several days before a game, for example, they sleep apart from their wives in the men's clubhouse. The women and children form groups around the playing field, singing songs and executing magical dances designed to discommode the foe. Special baseball songs constitute one of the principal forms of native music.

A particularly popular one, with mixed Japanese and English

words, is set to the tune of "Someone's in the kitchen with Dinah." It ends with the refrain: "Maybe you go benjo." Since the last word is Japanese for "latrine," the song is a way of telling the opposing team where they can head in, with overtones of conjuring up a touch of dysentery.

All work stops when teams arrive from another island. The entire day is devoted to sport. Such an occasion happened on Romonum shortly after the arrival of an American scientist (the author). He was invited to umpire, and when a second game immediately followed the first, he discovered what he was in for. After arbitrating five full games in a row under the tropical sun, he acquired an unexpected sympathy for Magerkurth and his ilk. He managed to gain a little respite by admitting that he had seen in action the great "Babe Root," about whom everyone had heard.

In the summer of 1947 a confident Navy team, composed of men from the land station and the ships in the harbor, issued a challenge to the all-Truk team. The first two games were close and divided, when word came to the governor that the natives out of respect were holding their punches. He assured them that it was quite all right to try their hardest. So in the third and deciding game the Truk pitcher, a man by the name of Pwinipwinin with a wicked fast ball and a wide-sweeping curve, "poured on the coal." The startled Navy boys went down by a score of 14 to 3. Some of them were heard to mutter afterward that the big-league teams ought to send their scouts out a little farther.

CROSS-CULTURAL COMPARISON

VI

20

This paper was read at the tenth anniversary of the Department of Social Relations at Harvard University and was published in *Behavioral Science* (2: 249-254, 1957). The survey from which the comparative data were drawn appeared under the title of "World Ethnographic Sample" in the *American Anthropologist* (59: 664-687, 1957).

Anthropology as a
Comparative Science

ANTHROPOLOGY, in common with its sister disciplines in the behavioral sciences, has at least three major objectives. The first of these, which is pursued principally by archeology and is shared especially with history, is to reconstruct the record of the origin, spread, differentiation, and evolution of culture from its simplest beginnings to the manifold forms that occur throughout the world in modern times. A second major objective, which anthropological students of primitive art, music, folklore, religion, and philosophy share with the various fields of the humanities, is to attain an understanding and appreciation of the diverse manifestations of the human spirit. The third ultimate goal is to create a science of human behavior by developing a systematic body of verified knowledge about the principles governing the interaction of men in society, the formation of groups and of social norms of behavior, and the transmission and differentiation

297

of culture. It is with this third objective, shared by anthropology especially with sociology and psychology, that this paper is concerned.

There are many approaches to the achievement of a science of human behavior, but attention shall be confined here to one of them, the comparative or cross-cultural approach. This approach is not uniquely anthropological, for it has also been diligently pursued by sociologists and has been employed to a more limited extent by psychologists, historians, and others.

The first point to be made is that there can never be any generally valid science of man which is not specifically adapted to, and tested with reference to, the diverse manifestations of human behavior encountered in the thousands of human societies differing from our own that are known to history and ethnography. Whatever other methods of investigation may be employed—and they are numerous—the comparative method is indispensable. Without it, no combination of other methods can achieve scientific results of universal application. At the most they can only produce culture-bound generalizations, approximately valid for a particular group of related societies during a particular segment of their history, but incapable of generalization to other societies except as highly tentative working hypotheses, and equally incapable of predicting future developments in periods of rapid social change or even of comprehending them after they have occurred.

The admirable body of principles worked out in our sister science of economics provides an excellent illustration. Originally adapted to a group of European societies which had passed through the Industrial Revolution and were characterized by individual enterprise, a money economy, and mechanisms of exchange and distribution relatively unfettered by governmental intervention, they have had to be revised radically to fit even approximately the systems of distribution and price determination found in some of the same societies after they had adopted fascist, communist, and socialist governments with rigorous state controls. Even thus modified, the principles of economics still provide the anthropologist with remarkably little guidance for the understanding of economic behavior in a host of simpler societies.

Political science is also culture bound, though its limits are somewhat less restricted, extending back in time well before the Industrial Revolution to the period of Plato and Aristotle and stretching in space to include the major societies of Asia as well as of Europe. Historical research normally encompasses very much narrower ranges of time and space. Its conclusions are so invariably specific to a single culture at a particular period of time that, of course, in this sense "history never repeats itself." The great body of research in sociology, being conducted in our own society or in closely related ones in the European tradition, is also culture bound, and even its best validated conclusions cannot be accepted as universally valid until they have been cross-culturally tested and verified. Unlike economists, political scientists, and historians, however, the leading sociologists of every generation have been aware of this fact and have deliberately acquired substantial conversance with ethnography with the aim of achieving universality for their generalizations. It is necessary only to cite such names as Herbert Spencer, Emile Durkheim, William Graham Sumner, W. I. Thomas, A. G. Keller, and Talcott Parsons.

From at least the time of Wundt an occasional psychologist has manifested an interest in the cross-cultural approach, and this awareness appears to be currently on the increase, as witness the recent research activities of Irvin Child and Leonard Doob at Yale on socialization and cultural change respectively. On the whole, however, psychologists have tended to concentrate upon unraveling the basic mechanisms of behavior, whether of perception, learning, or personality development, and when they have attempted to explain cultural phenomena have usually applied their principles directly without reference to the highly diverse conditions under which these operate in different societies. From Freud's *Totem and Taboo* to the present, consequently, most psychological interpretations of cultural phenomena have erred in seeking to explain too much, in contrast to sociological interpretations, which typically explain much too little.

Merely to assert the importance and the indispensability of a comparative approach to the study of human behavior is, of course, not enough. Allegations should be buttressed by at least some measure of empirical support. This is now presented in the form of a simple quantitative demonstration based on a survey of representative cultures from all regions of the world and from different periods of history compiled independently for quite another purpose.

In this survey, each society was classified with respect to thirty distinct cultural categories, mainly in the areas of productive economy, division of labor, settlement patterns, government, social stratification, marriage, and kinship. This classification was examined to determine the extent to which cultures of European derivation resemble, or differ from, both one another and cultures of other regions. Therefore a purely random selection was made of ten societies each from Asia, Africa, Oceania, and native North and South America. Ten European societies also were selected—not at random, for this might have led to the inclusion of closely related peoples, but in a manner consciously intended to obtain the widest possible range in regard to time, space, language, and cultural diversity. These European societies were the following: the Athenians of the Periclean Age, about 450 B.C.; the Boers of the Transvaal after the Great Trek, about 1850 A.D.; the Brazilians of Bahia about 1650 A.D.; the English of the Elizabethan period, about 1600 A.D.; the Hungarians immediately prior to World War II; the Icelanders of about 1100 A.D.; the Lithuanians prior to their absorption by Soviet Russia; the Romans of the Imperial period, about 100 A.D.; the Russians of the Soviet Union today; the Spaniards of modern Andalusia.

When the classification of our thirty cultural items for the contemporary United States was compared with those for these diverse European societies, 61 per cent of all items were discovered to be

identical and only 39 per cent variant. But when they were compared with those for other regions of the world, the identities fell to
26 per cent, ranging from 30 per cent for Asia to 22 per cent for
Africa. Other tests confirmed the probability that any two distantly
related European cultures will share about six out of ten classificatory elements, whereas only about one in four will be similar when
any European culture is compared with any non-European culture. This suggests how unsafe it is for a sociologist, psychologist,
or historian to generalize his knowledge of Euro-American societies, however profound, to mankind in general.

Moreover, almost 50 per cent of the items listed for the 50
randomly selected non-European societies fell into categories which
were completely unrepresented in any of the European cultures,
suggesting that a complete analysis of all European societies would
reveal only about half of the major classificatory categories under
which anthropologists customarily analyze the cultures of the
world. Note that the reference here is to purely classificatory
categories, not to specific items of cultural content. For these the
differences between European and non-European cultures would be
infinitely more numerous.

Customs of other peoples for which there is no precedent in
European cultures, and which even lie quite beyond the range of
human behavioral variation conceivable to most Europeans, are a
stock-in-trade of anthropologists, and constitute one of the reasons
why this profession is such a detestable bunch of bubble-prickers.
Two examples selected from personal field experience on the island
of Truk in the central Pacific are presented.

The normal, routine posture assumed by the Trukese in copulation is one that is not even mentioned in Kinsey or, to my knowledge, in any other occidental work on sexology or pornography. It
probably has never even been approximated by any native-born
American couple, however experimental. The curious may be
referred to Malinowski, who describes a similar posture for the
Trobrianders.

If the Trukese fall outside the range of European expectations in an aspect of behavior so closely linked to instinctive reflexes, comparable divergences in purely ideational behavior are certainly to be expected. Thus the people of Truk have a concept and expression, "kinisou," which expresses a sense of personal indebtedness, and corresponds to the English phrase, "Thank you," for which it is, indeed, the customary term. In addition to expressing obligation for a gift or favor received, however, "kinisou" is used to verbalize the attitude of a victim of sorcery toward the person who has employed the black arts to his detriment. To us, these two situations appear to have nothing in common, but to the Trukese they seem nearly identical. The recipient of a gift or favor has incurred an obligation which he is bound to repay. Sorcery, to the Trukese, is inconceivable except as a reaction to some unfulfilled social obligation. Hence the victim of sorcery, by saying "kinisou," acknowledges his obligation, his gratitude for having it brought to his attention, and his intention of fulfilling it. When he does this, the sorcerizing ceases and social equilibrium is restored.

Perhaps I have dwelt over-long on the indispensability of a cross-cultural approach to the social scientist if he is to comprehend the range of variation actually exhibited in human social behavior and arrive at generalizations valid throughout this range. Some of the methods and problems of comparative research also deserve attention.

Throughout the nineteenth century, and in some instances well into the twentieth, the comparative method, whether used by anthropologists, sociologists, psychologists, or jurisprudes, consisted essentially in surveying a wide range of ethnographic sources and extracting masses of cases in support of some hypothesis, evolutionary or otherwise, which had been formulated beforehand on other grounds. In the hands of scrupulous scholars this often brought considerable illumination, but the procedure had two serious defects. First, it lent itself too readily to perversion, for the treasure-house of ethnography is so rich and varied that it is relatively easy to support almost any hypothesis by a conscious or unconscious selection of cases. Second, the cases themselves were torn from their context, obliterating their relationships with other aspects of the cultures in which they were embedded. It was Tylor (1889) who first recognized that these intracultural relationships, or "adhesions" as he called them, may be considerably more significant than the isolated elements of culture themselves. In recent decades all users of the comparative method accept Tylor's position, refrain from the mere amassing of isolated case material, and adopt some form of what Eggan (1954: 743-763) has called "the method of controlled comparison."

One kind of controlled comparison is to utilize ethnography as the equivalent of a laboratory—as an array, so to speak, of nature-made experiments. A scientific problem is subjected to test by close examination of some society where the relevant variables happen to be assembled in precisely the combination one would bring together if one were able to construct an experimental situation. This particular technique has been employed with success by Mead (1928), using Samoa as a crucial case for the study of adolescent problems, and by Holmberg (1950), using the Siriono of Bolivia to test his hypothesis regarding the relationship of drive deprivation to the content of dreams and other manifestations of the unconscious.

When a scientific hypothesis relates to items of cultural behavior that are of relatively rare occurrence but are nevertheless historically independent, one may attempt to assemble all the known ethnographic examples and test the hypothesis by analyzing the "adhesions" or cultural associations in which they are embedded. This has recently been done, for example, by Homans and Schneider (1955) in an effort to account for the two different types of preferential asymmetrical cross-cousin marriage.

A danger of this procedure is that the discovered associations may occur and have other correlates in the societies rejected because they do not exhibit the phenomenon under examination, thereby possibly invalidating the presumed causal relationship. Tylor's remedy was to examine a large number of cultures drawn from the entire range of ethnography, regardless of the presence or absence of the particular phenomenon under investigation, and to determine its degree of correlation with the presumably associated variables by statistical means. He has been followed by many subsequent users of the comparative method, e.g., Hobhouse, Wheeler, and Ginsberg (1915), Murdock (1949), Simmons (1937: 495-517), Horton (1943: 199-320), Beatrice Whiting (1950), and Whiting and Child (1953).

The great problem in worldwide statistical comparisons is the selection of the sample. It would be improper to include the entire universe of known cultures, even if this were feasible, for cultures are not discrete and completely independent units. Complete coverage would result in the heavy overrepresentation of areas with many small and independent societies of similar culture, such as the Basin Shoshoneans, and in the underrepresentation of large and integrated societies, like those of China and Western Europe, and of small and isolated societies with distinctive ways of life, like the Tasmanians, the Vedda of Ceylon, and the Guanche of the Canary Islands.

Nor can the cultures compared be chosen by any method of random sampling. Not only would this result equally in the disproportionate representation of small, large, and unique cultures, but in addition it would mean the selection of many cultures that are inadequately described and the rejection of many of those for which the literature offers the fullest and most pertinent information.

Nor can we be content merely with choosing a large number of cases for which good descriptive information is available. Hobhouse, Wheeler, and Ginsberg did this, with the result that a substantial majority of their hunting and gathering cultures were selected from aboriginal Australia. Consequently all their correlations of other traits with hunting and gathering were meaningless except perhaps as crude reflections of native Australian culture.

In my *Social Structure,* I made what now seems to me a half-hearted attempt to combine the requirements of good descriptive coverage, wide geographical distribution, and restriction of the number of cases selected from any particular culture area. Errors were made in including some cases that were essentially duplicates of one another, and in not striving hard enough to secure cases from areas like eastern Indonesia, Indochina, Central Asia, Europe, North Africa, and Middle and South America where the sources were relatively inaccessible to me for linguistic or other reasons. This was demonstrated two years ago in a graduate class where we assembled two worldwide samples of 300 societies each, one completely unselected and the other very carefully compiled to give equal representation to all the culture areas of the world. The major statistical correlations of the *Social Structure* volume were recalculated for these two samples. While there were no serious upsets, the results from the selected and unselected samples were sufficiently divergent in enough instances to convince me of the imperative need of far more careful representative sampling.

I have been engaged in working out a world sample of some 550 cultures, with tabulated data on basic economy and social and political organization. This will cover the complex civilizations of Europe and Asia, and those recorded from antiquity, on exactly the same basis as preliterate cultures. It will give, as nearly as possible, equal numerical representation to all the major variants in man's way of life, and will include, for each culture area, a number of cases closely proportionate to its diversity within the entire range of known cultures and carefully distributed by subareas.

The historical relatedness of different cultures through diffusion does not cause me the concern that others seem to exhibit. The evidence is now fairly clear that societies borrow from one another, much as they invent for themselves, elements for which they feel a need and which are reasonably congruent with existing usages, and that borrowed like invented and preexisting traits undergo a process of integrative modification. However, a world sample must not include cultures so similar as to constitute genuine duplication. Provided care is taken to guard against this, as by avoiding the inclusion of geographically contiguous societies unless they differ significantly in language, economy, or social organization, similarities in culture, whether due to diffusion or to parallel adaptation, can be assumed to have undergone integration with their respective cultural contexts and can therefore usually be safely treated as essentially independent.

Though this paper is entitled "Anthropology as a Comparative Science," sociologists have been at least as prolific in comparative studies as have anthropologists, and there is no reason why the method cannot be used equally well by psychologists or any other group of scientific students of human behavior. The only block is the lack of familiarity with, and accessibility to, the ethnographic sources. And this the Human Relations Area Files is specifically designed to overcome.

In conclusion, I may perhaps be forgiven for recounting a true story as a sort of parable of the need of a cross-cultural orientation. When a ruling Arab sheikh recently visited a certain American city, the matron who was the leader of local society gave a ceremonial dinner in his honor. When he arrived with his retinue, they were offered cocktails. Being a Moslem, the sheikh felt compelled to observe his religion's taboo on alcoholic beverages, at least on so public an occasion, and intimated that he would accept a Coca Cola instead. There happened to be none in the house, so the butler was dispatched to the neighborhood store. While he was away, the others present courteously but uncomfortably refrained from drinking out of respect to the guest of honor. Later at the dinner table, when the entree was brought on, it was, of all things, a roast suckling pig with an apple in its mouth. When the Arabs politely refused servings of this abomination, the embarrassed hostess had nothing to offer as a substitute except cold cuts. And it was soon discovered that the only cold cuts in the house were ham.

21

This modest paper was originally published in *Social Forces* (15: 551-553, 1937).

Comparative Data on the Division of Labor by Sex

C ERTAIN data on the distribution of economic activities between the sexes, secured by the author and his students
as a by-product of a research project in a graduate class in
ethnology, are presented herewith as possibly of general interest.
They were obtained in the course of abstracting material from the
outstanding ethnographical monographs on 224 tribes selected
from all parts of the world with due regard to geographical distribution. A few higher civilizations were included in order to yield
results representative of all types of culture.

The material is presented below in tabular form. The first
column gives the number of tribes in which the particular activity is
confined exclusively to males. The second enumerates those in
which women engage in the occupation only relatively infrequently
or in a subordinate capacity. The third column embraces the tribes
in which the occupation is carried on indifferently by either sex or

Table 2

Division of Labor by Sex

	M	M−	=	F−	F	Per Cent
Metal working....................	78	0	0	0	0	100.0
Weapon making.................	121	1	0	0	0	99.8
Pursuit of sea mammals..........	34	1	0	0	0	99.3
Hunting........................	166	13	0	0	0	98.2
Manufacture of musical instruments	45	2	0	0	1	96.9
Boatbuilding....................	91	4	4	0	1	96.0
Mining and quarrying............	35	1	1	0	1	95.4
Work in wood and bark..........	113	9	5	1	1	95.0
Work in stone..................	68	3	2	0	2	95.0
Trapping or catching of small animals.........................	128	13	4	1	2	94.9
Work in bone, horn and shell......	67	4	3	0	3	93.0
Lumbering.....................	104	4	3	1	6	92.2
Fishing........................	98	34	19	3	4	85.6
Manufacture of ceremonial objects.	37	1	13	0	1	85.1
Herding........................	38	8	4	0	5	83.6
Housebuilding..................	86	32	25	3	14	77.0
Clearing of land for agriculture...	73	22	17	5	13	76.3
Netmaking.....................	44	6	4	2	11	74.1
Trade.........................	51	28	20	8	7	73.7
Dairy operations................	17	4	3	1	13	57.1
Manufacture of ornaments.......	24	3	40	6	18	52.5
Agriculture—soil preparation and planting....................	31	23	33	20	37	48.4
Manufacture of leather products...	29	3	9	3	32	48.0
Body mutilation, e.g., tattooing....	16	14	44	22	20	46.6
Erection and dismantling of shelter	14	2	5	6	22	39.8
Hide preparation..............	31	2	4	4	49	39.4
Tending of fowls and small animals .	21	4	8	1	39	38.7
Agriculture—crop tending and harvesting......................	10	15	35	39	44	33.9
Gathering of shellfish............	9	4	8	7	25	33.5
Manufacture of nontextile fabrics..	14	0	9	2	32	33.3
Fire making and tending.........	18	6	25	22	62	30.5
Burden bearing.................	12	6	33	20	57	29.9
Preparation of drinks and narcotics	20	1	13	8	57	29.5
Manufacture of thread and cordage	23	2	11	10	73	27.3
Basketmaking..................	25	3	10	6	82	24.4
Matmaking....................	16	2	6	4	61	24.2
Weaving......................	19	2	2	6	67	23.9
Gathering of fruits, berries, and nuts	12	3	15	13	63	23.6
Fuel gathering.................	22	1	10	19	89	23.0
Pottery making.................	13	2	6	8	77	18.4
Preservation of meat and fish.....	8	2	10	14	74	16.7
Manufacture and repair of clothing	12	3	8	9	95	16.1
Gathering of herbs, roots, and seeds	8	1	11	7	74	15.8
Cooking.......................	5	1	9	28	158	8.6
Water carrying.................	7	0	5	7	119	8.2
Grain grinding.................	2	4	5	13	114	7.8

cooperatively by both. The fourth and fifth columns list the tribes in which the activity is, respectively, predominantly and exclusively feminine. The sixth column gives a rough index of the degree of masculinity of the occupation in general; the percentages were obtained by scoring tribes in the first five columns 100, 75, 50, 25, and 0 respectively and striking the average. Although errors have doubtless crept into the tabulation, the general result is probably not seriously distorted.

Complexes of activities have in many cases been split up. Thus agriculture is subdivided into the clearing of land, soil preparation and planting, and crop tending and harvesting; pastoral activities into the herding of large animals, the tending of fowls and small animals, and dairy operations; housebuilding into the construction of permanent dwellings and the erection and dismantling of transportable shelters such as tents; the textile arts into weaving proper, the manufacture of nontextile fabrics such as barkcloth, etc. Other occupations might appropriately have been similarly subdivided. That fire making, for example, is often a masculine activity, whereas fire tending is feminine, is not revealed by the table.

The tendency among primitives to segregate economic activities according to sex is even stronger than the tabulation indicates, for in perhaps the majority of cases listed in the intermediate columns certain specific activities are regarded as masculine and others as feminine. For example, in a tribe where housebuilding is listed as mutually pursued, the men may confine themselves to setting up the timbers and the women to preparing and affixing the roofing material. Of the various conclusions deducible from the table one of the most interesting is that, while a number of occupations are universally masculine, none is everywhere feminine; men have, here and there, taken to themselves even such predominantly feminine activities as cooking, the making of clothing, water carrying, and grain grinding.

22

This paper was orginally published in *The Annals of the American Academy of Political and Social Science* (22: 195-201, 1950). It was undertaken as a specific test of the efficiency of the Human Relations Area Files as an aid in comparative research. From the initial planning of the article, through the assembly of the material from the Files and its analysis, to the completion of the writing and typing of the paper, the total elapsed time was only twenty-nine hours—as compared with at least as many days consumed in the preparation of earlier comparable studies conducted by the ordinary laborious processes of library research.

Family Stability in
Non-European Cultures

THIS paper presents the conclusions of a special study of the
stability of marriage in forty selected non-European societies undertaken in an attempt to place the family situation
in the contemporary United States in cross-cultural perspective.
Eight societies were chosen from each of the world's major ethnographic regions—Asia, Africa, Oceania, and native North and
South America. Within each region the samples were carefully
selected from widely scattered geographical locations, from different culture areas, and from levels of civilization ranging from the
simplest to the most complex. The data were obtained from the
collections in the Human Relations Area Files, formerly the Cross-
Cultural Survey. The selection was made in as random a manner
as possible except that it was confined to cultures for which the
descriptive literature is full and reliable. Once chosen, a particular
society was rejected and another substituted only in a few instances

where the sources failed to provide (1) information on the relative rights of the two sexes in divorce, or (2) evidence permitting a solid judgment as to the degree of family stability relative to that in our own society.

The method, it is believed, comes as close to that of purely random sampling as is feasible today in comparative social science. The results, it must be admitted, contain a number of surprises—even to the writer, who has been steeped for years in the literature of world ethnography. The forty selected societies are listed and located below.

1. *Asia:* the Chukchi of northeastern Siberia, the Japanese, the Kazak of Turkestan, the Kurd of Iraq, the Lakher of Assam, the Mongols of Outer Mongolia, the Semang Negritos of Malaya, and the Toda of southern India.

2. *Africa:* the Dahomeans of coastal West Africa, the Ganda of Uganda, the Hottentot of South-West Africa, the Jukun of Northern Nigeria, the Lamba of Northern Rhodesia, the Lango of Kenya, the Siwans of the oasis of Siwa in Egypt, and the Wolof of Senegal.

3. *Oceania:* the Atayal aborigines of interior Formosa, the Balinese of Indonesia, the Kalinga of the northern Philippines, the Kurtatchi of the Solomon Islands in Melanesia, the Kwoma of New Guinea, the Murngin of northern Australia, the Samoans of Polynesia, and the Trukese of Micronesia.

4. *North America:* the Aztecs of ancient Mexico, the Creek of Alabama, the Crow of the high plains in Montana, the Haida of northern British Columbia and southern Alaska, the Hopi pueblo dwellers of Arizona, the Iroquois of northern New York, the Klamath of interior Oregon, and the Yurok of coastal California.

5. *South America:* the Cuna of southern Panama, the Guaycuru or Mbaya of the Gran Chaco, the Incas of ancient Peru, the Kaingang of southern Brazil, the Macusi of Guiana, the Ona of Tierra del Fuego, the Siroino of lowland Bolivia, and the Witoto of the northwest Amazonian jungle.

From these cases it emerges, as a first conclusion, that practically all societies make some cultural provision for the termination of marriage through divorce. The Incas stand isolated as the solitary exception; among them a marriage, once contracted in the presence of a high official representing the emperor, could not subsequently be dissolved for any reason. None of the other thirty-nine societies in our sample compels a couple to maintain their matrimonial relationship where there are reasons for separation that would impress most contemporary Americans as genuinely cogent.

Perhaps the most striking conclusion from the study is the extraordinary extent to which human societies accord to both sexes an approximately equal right to initiate divorce. In thirty of the forty cultures surveyed it was impossible to detect any substantial difference in the rights of men and women to terminate an unsatisfactory alliance. The stereotype of the oppressed aboriginal woman proved to be a complete myth.

The author expected, in line with general thought on the subject, that males would be found to enjoy superior, though perhaps not exclusive, rights in a substantial minority of the cultures surveyed, if not in a majority. They were discovered to possess such prerogatives, however, in only six societies—a bare 15 per cent of the total. In two of the Moslem societies, the Kurd and the Siwans, a husband can dismiss his wife with the greatest of ease, even for a momentary whim. He needs only to pick up three stones and drop them, uttering to his spouse a routine formula of divorce. She has no comparable right; she can only run away and hope that her male relatives will support her. Among the Japanese, divorce is very easy for the husband or by mutual consent, but can be obtained by a woman against the will of her spouse only for serious cause and with considerable legal difficulty. A Ganda man, too, is free to dismiss his wife for any cause, whereas she has no right to initiate a permanent separation. If severely mistreated she can only run away to her male relatives, to whom the husband must justify himself and make amends in order to get her back. For the Siriono it is reported that only men, never women, initiate divorce. A Guaycuru man who wants to terminate his marriage for any reason merely removes for a few days to another hut in the same village, until his wife takes the hint and returns to her family. Women rarely seek a divorce directly, but not infrequently they deliberately act in such a manner as to provoke their husbands into leaving them.

In four societies, or 10 per cent of the total sample, women actually possess superior privileges as regards divorce. Among the Kwoma a wife is relatively free to abandon her husband, but he has no right to dismiss her. His only recourse is to make life so miserable for her that she will leave of her own accord. In the stable form of Dahomean marriage, i.e., that characterized by patrilocal residence and the payment of a bride price, a woman can readily desert her husband for cause, but he cannot initiate divorce proceedings directly; he can only neglect his wife, insult her relatives, and subject her to petty annoyances until she takes matters into her own hands and departs. A Yurok marriage can be terminated at the initiative of either partner, but it involves the return of a substantial bride price. A wife is in a much better position to persuade her male relatives of the justice of her cause than is her husband. His claims are scrutinized with great skepticism, and are often rejected. While in theory he could still agree to an uncompensated separation, no male in his right mind in this highly pecuniary culture would think of incurring voluntarily such a financial loss. A Witoto woman can secure a divorce by merely running away. In such a case the husband is always blamed, because people assume that no woman would leave her male protector unless cruelly mistreated. A man can dismiss his wife for cause, but this makes him a target of damaging ridicule and gossip, and unless he is able to justify his action to the complete satisfaction of the local council of adult men, he becomes a virtual social outcast.

Analysis of the relative frequency of divorce reveals that, in addition to the Incas, the stability of marital unions is noticeably greater than in our society among Atayal, Aztecs, Creek, Dahomeans, Ganda, Hopi, Hottentot, Jukun, Kazak, Lakher, Lango, Murngin, Ona, Siriono, and Witoto. In the remaining twenty-four societies, constituting 60 per cent of the total, the divorce rate manifestly exceeds that among ourselves. Despite the widespread alarm about increasing "family disorganization" in our own society, the comparative evidence makes it clear that we still remain well within the limits which human experience has shown that societies can tolerate with safety.

In most of the societies with relatively infrequent divorce, the stability is achieved through the mores and the pressure of public opinion rather than through legal enactments and judicial obstacles. The Atayal, Aztecs, and Hottentot constitute partial exceptions. In the first of these tribes divorce is freely allowed for childlessness, but petitions on any other grounds must receive a hearing before the chief. He may refuse or grant the divorce, but in the latter case he usually sentences the guilty party to punishment and may even forbid him or her to remarry. Any other separation is likely to precipitate a feud between the families of the estranged spouses. Among the Aztecs, divorce cases were heard before a special court, and the party adjudged guilty forfeited half of his property to the other. Among the Hottentot, adequate grounds for divorce have to be proved to the satisfaction of a council consisting of all the adult men of the clan, which may order a runaway wife to return to her husband, or award the property of a deserting husband to his wife.

In only two of the societies with frequent divorce is separation effected by the action of constituted authorities—by village officials among the Balinese and by the courts in an action brought by a Japanese woman. Except in these five societies and the Incas, divorce is everywhere exclusively a private matter, and such restraints as are exercised are imposed by informal social pressures rather than by legal restrictions.

The cases reveal clearly some of the devices whereby different peoples have attempted to make marital unions more stable. One of the most common is the payment of a bride price, which comparative studies have shown to be customary among approximately half of the societies of the earth. Contrary to the popular impression, the bride price is almost never conceived as a payment for a purchased chattel. Its primary function nearly everywhere is that of providing an additional economic incentive to reinforce the stability of marriage. In our sample, the sources on Dahomeans, Klamath, Lango, Mongols, Wolof, and Yurok reveal particularly clear evidence of the stabilizing effect of the bride price.

An even more frequent device is to take the choice of a marital partner largely out of the hands of young men and women and vest it in their parents. Most cultures reflect a marked distrust of sexual attraction as a primary motive in marriage, as it is likely to be in the minds of young people, and it seems to be widely recognized that parents, with their greater worldly experience, are more likely to arrange matches on the basis of factors better calculated to produce a durable union. Having been responsible for a marriage, parents tend to feel humiliated when it shows signs of breaking up, and are likely to exert themselves to restore harmony and settle differences. This is attested very specifically for the Haida and the Iroquois, and the evidence shows that the influence of relatives is also a prominent stabilizing factor among Creek, Hopi, Jukun, Kalinga, Murngin, and Ona.

The lengths to which this precaution can be carried in cases of infidelity is well illustrated by the Jukun. A wife first attempts to persuade her husband to give up an adulterous relationship about which she has learned, whereas the husband in a similar situation merely requests a relative or friend to remonstrate with his wife. If the relationship still continues, the innocent spouse reports the matter to the father, uncle, or elder brother of the other, who exerts all the pressure in his power to bring the delinquency to an end. Only after these steps prove fruitless, and the infidelity continues, is a separation effected.

Occasionally, of course, relatives break up a union that is satisfactory to both the parties primarily concerned. Among the Chukchi, for example, the parents of the groom can send the bride home if they become dissatisfied with her at any time within a year or eighteen months after the wedding, and a woman's relatives attempt to break up her marriage if they become estranged from her husband's family at any time, even going to the extreme of carrying off the unwilling wife by force.

In one of the societies of the sample—the Crow Indians—public opinion, instead of exerting its usual stabilizing influence, actually tends to undermine the marital relationship. Divorce is exceedingly frequent, and a man subjects himself to ridicule if he lives too long with one woman. Rivalrous military societies make a sport of stealing wives from one another, and any husband feels ashamed to take back a wife thus abducted from him, however much against her will and his own.

The sources rarely give precise statistics on the incidence of divorce in societies where it occurs most frequently. All we have is fragmentary statements, for instance, that one-third of all adult Chukchi women have been divorced, or that the ethnographer encountered Cuna of both sexes who had lived through from seven to nine successive marriages, or that it is not uncommon to meet a Siwan woman of forty who has been married and divorced more than ten times.

It is nevertheless possible to segregate one group of societies in which the excessive frequency of divorce is confined to recently contracted marriages and dwindles to a rarity after a union has endured for a year or more, especially after children have been born. This is attested, for example, among the Japanese, the Kaingang, the Kalinga, and the Macusi. Among the Trukese, marriages are very brittle and shifting with people in their twenties, but by the end of this early period of trial and error the majority have found spouses with whom they are content to live in reasonable harmony for the rest of their lives.

In other societies, like the Semang, while the rate of divorce subsides markedly after the birth of children, it still remains high as compared with our own. All in all, the sample reveals nineteen societies, or nearly half of the total, in which permanent separations appear substantially to exceed the present rate in the United States throughout the lifetime of the individual. Among them, either spouse can terminate the union with little difficulty and for slight or even trivial reasons among Balinese, Chukchi, Crow, Cuna, Haida, Iroquois, Klamath, Kurtatchi, Lamba, Mongols, Samoans, Semang, Toda, and Wolof. In matrilocal communities like the Cuna or the Iroquois, the husband simply walks out, or the wife unceremoniously dumps his effects outside her door. It is more surprising to encounter an equal facility in divorce among patrilocal and even patriarchal peoples like the Mongols, who see no reason for moral censure in divorce and say in perfectly matter-of-fact manner that two individuals who cannot get along harmoniously together had better live apart.

The societies which condone separation for a mere whim are few. The great majority recognize only certain grounds as adequate. The Lamba, for whom the information is particularly full, consider a man justified in seeking a divorce if he has been continually harassed by his parents-in-law, if his wife commits adultery or theft, if she has contracted a loathsome disease, if she is quarrelsome or disrespectful, or if she refuses to remain at his home after he has taken a second wife. For a woman the recognized grounds are impotence or loathsome disease in her spouse, his failure to prepare a garden or provide her with adequate clothing, persistent wife-beating, or mere cessation of her affection for him. If the marriage produces no issue, husband and wife argue as to who is responsible, and usually agree to separate. If the woman then bears a child to her new husband whereas the man fails to produce offspring by his next wife, the former husband is so overcome with shame that he usually either commits suicide or leaves the community.

Particular societies recognize interesting special grounds as adequate. Thus the Aztecs, who strongly disapproved of divorce and required proof of substantial cause before a special court, readily granted separation to a woman if she showed that her husband had done less than his share in attending to the education of their children. In general, however, a few basic reasons recur repeatedly as those considered justifiable in a wide range of societies. These are incompatibility, adultery, barrenness or sterility, impotence or

frigidity, economic incapacity or nonsupport, cruelty, and quarrelsomeness or nagging. Desertion rarely appears, because it is, of
course, not usually a reason for divorce, but the actual means by
which a permanent separation is effected. The degree to which the
more widespread grounds are recognized as valid in the forty
sample societies is shown in Table 3. In order to provide compara-
bility, an entry is made under each heading for every society.
Judgments that are merely inferred as probable from the general
context, however, are distinguished from evidence specifically
reported or unmistakably implied in the sources.

The data in Table 3 reinforce the earlier comment concerning the
extraordinary equality of the sexes in rights of divorce revealed by
the present study. Where the table shows notable differences, these
have relatively obvious explanations. That cruelty is recognized as
an adequate ground for women far more often than for men merely

Table 3

Reasons for Divorce
(Forty Sample Societies)

Reasons	Permitted				Forbidden			
	Definitely		Inferentially		Definitely		Inferentially	
	To Man	To Wife	To Man	To Wife	To Man	To Wife	To Man	To Wife
Any grounds, even trivial	9	6	5	6	14	13	12	15
Incompatibility, without more specific grounds	17	17	10	10	6	7	7	6
Common adultery or infidelity	19	11	8	12	8	10	5	7
Repeated or exaggerated infidelity	27	23	8	10	5	5	0	2
Childlessness or sterility	12	4	15	18	7	7	6	11
Sexual impotence or unwillingness	9	12	24	21	3	4	4	3
Laziness, non-support, economic incapacity	23	22	11	9	4	5	2	4
Quarrelsomeness or nagging	20	7	7	12	6	11	7	10
Mistreatment or cruelty	7	25	19	9	3	4	11	2

reflects their comparative physical strength. The aggression of women toward their spouses is thus perforce directed more often into verbal channels, with the result that quarrelsomeness and nagging become an adequate justification for divorce much more commonly for the male sex.

The demonstration that divorce tends to be easier and more prevalent in other societies than in our own does not warrant the conclusion that most peoples are indifferent to the stability of the marriage relationship and the family institution. In our sample, such a charge might be leveled with some justification at the Crow, the Kaingang, and the Toda, but for most of the rest the data explicitly reveal a genuine concern with the problem. The devices of the bride price and the arrangement of marriages by parents, already alluded to, represent only two of the most common attempts to reach a satisfactory cultural solution. Others, demonstrated by the author in a previous study (*Social Structure*), may be briefly summarized here.

One such device is the taboo on primary incest, which is absolutely universal. There is not a single society known to history or ethnography which does not prohibit and penalize, among the general run of its members, both sexual intercourse and marriage between father and daughter, mother and son, and brother and sister. These universal prohibitions are understandable only as an adaptive provision, arrived at everywhere by a process of mass trial and error, by which sexual rivalry is inhibited within the nuclear family so that the unity and integrity of this basic institution are preserved for the performance of its crucial societal services—economic cooperation, sexual reproduction, and the rearing and education of children.

Nearly as universal are prohibitions of adultery. A very large majority of all known societies permit relatively free sexual experimentation before marriage in their youth of both sexes, but this license is withdrawn when they enter into matrimony. In a world-wide sample of 250 societies, only five—a mere 2 per cent of the total—were found to condone adulterous extramarital liaisons. In many of the remaining 98 per cent, to be sure, the ideal of marital fidelity is more honored in the breach than in the observance. Its very existence, nevertheless, can only reflect a genuine and widespread concern with the stability of marriage and the family, which are inevitably threatened by the jealousy and discord generated by infidelity.

It is clear that approximately as many peoples disapprove in theory of divorce as of adultery. They have learned through experience, however, that the reasons are commonly much more urgent for the former than for the latter, and they consequently allow it wider latitude. The vital functions of the family are not likely to be well performed where husband and wife have become genuinely incompatible. Children raised by stepparents, grandparents, or adoptive parents may frequently find their new social environment more conducive to healthy personality development than a home torn by bitter internal conflict. Even though less desirable than an ideal parental home, since this is unattainable divorce may represent for them, as for their parents, the lesser of two evils.

No society in our sample, with the possible exception of the Crow, places any positive value on divorce. The general attitude is clearly that it is regrettable, but often necessary. It represents merely a practical concession to the frality of mankind, caught in a web of social relationships and cultural expectations that often impose intolerable pressure on the individual personality. That most social systems work as well as they do, despite concessions to the individual that appear excessive to us, is a tribute to human ingenuity and resiliency.

The cross-cultural evidence makes it abundantly clear that the modern American family is unstable in only a relative and not an absolute sense. From an absolute, that is, comparative, point of view, our family institution still leans quite definitely toward the stable end of the ethnographic spectrum. Current trends could continue without reversal for a considerable period before the fear of social disorganization would acquire genuine justification. Long before such a point is reached, however, automatic correctives, some of them already apparent, will have wrought their effect, and a state of relative equilibrium will be attained that will represent a satisfactory social adjustment under the changed conditions of the times.

23

This paper was written under the stimulation of Joseph H. Greenberg and Roman Jakobson during the course of a seminar on linguistics at the Center for Advanced Study in the Behavioral Sciences in 1959 and was published in *Anthropological Linguistics* (1, no. 9: 1-5, 1959).

Cross-Language Parallels in Parental Kin Terms

INNUMERABLE anthropologists and linguists have asserted a universal tendency for languages, regardless of their historical relationships, to develop similar words for father and mother on the basis of nursery forms. As standard parental terms become phonetically and morphologically modified in consequence of the normal processes of linguistic change, forms develop which are difficult for very young children to pronounce. Under such circumstances, simpler nursery words tend to appear—carved, so to speak, out of infant babblings under parental encouragement. From time to time, it is alleged, such nursery forms come to replace the traditional words in standard usage. Since their phonetic range is severely limited by the speech potentialities of young children, similar forms tend to crop up through convergence in historically unrelated languages.

More specifically, it is alleged that the easiest sounds for young children to make are nasal consonants, like m, and low vowels, like a, and that combinations of these sounds, such as ma, mama, or ama, tend to acquire the meaning of "mother" in baby talk, and often ultimately in adult language, through the early association of the infant and its maternal parent. Next on the scene, from the child's point of view, is the father. He will allegedly tend to be called by a combination of sounds that is nearly as easy to utter and at the same time presents a clear contrast to the nursery word for mother, e.g., a non-nasal labial stop with a low vowel, as pa, papa, or baba.

When this hypothesis was considered at a linguistic seminar at the Center for Advanced Study in the Behavioral Sciences early in 1959, it was observed that, though often propounded, it had never been objectively tested or proved. It occurred to the writer that he had the means to conduct such a test in the tables of kinship terms assembled for his "World Ethnographic Sample" (*American Anthropologist,* 59: 664-687, 1957). Joseph H. Greenberg and Roman Jakobson encouraged him to do so, and generously rendered invaluable technical assistance.

The files yielded information from 474 of the 565 societies of the sample. Alternatives in particular societies brought the total number of terms up to 531 for mother and 541 for father. In order to rule out borrowings from European languages due to recent missionary and other influences, forms resembling mama and papa were excluded unless comparative data on related languages clearly demonstrated their indigenous origin. This perhaps biases the test slightly against confirmation of the hypothesis, for some of the excluded instances may be genuinely native.

The first task was to reduce the immense phonetic variety of the actual kin terms to a limited number of basic sound patterns. This was accomplished by means of the following operations:

1) All polysyllabic words were reduced to a single syllable. The first syllable in a polysyllabic term was used unless it appeared to be a prefix, or unless comparative analysis of the terms throughout a linguistic family or subfamily indicated

another syllable as the basic root, in which case, of course, this was taken.

2) All vowels were reduced to three basic categories, i.e.: a) Low vowels, like a and ǝ; b) High front vowels, like e and i; c) High back vowels, like o and u.

3) All consonants were reduced to thirteen basic categories. This was largely accomplished by ignoring differences between voiced and unvoiced, glottalized and unglottalized, labialized and nonlabialized, and palatalized and nonpalatalized forms. All consonant clusters, together with miscellaneous consonants like clicks, were lumped in a single category, and syllables without consonants, i.e., with vowels only, were also segregated as a separate category.

4) The vowel i in dipthongs, in syllables without consonants, was equated with the midpalatal semivowel y.

5) Glottal stops in either initial or final position were ignored, primarily because of the almost universal inconsistency in recording them. (Nearly all the data came from lists compiled by ethnographers rather than by linguists.)

Combinations of the thirteen types of consonants with the three types of vowels yielded 39 sound classes, or types of syllables, into which all the 1,072 kin terms were grouped. Table 4 shows the distribution of terms for "mother" and "father" among the several sound classes.

Examination of Table 4 shows that 628, or 59 per cent, of all the kin terms include a low vowel as opposed to only 283, or 26 per cent, with high front vowels and 161, or 15 per cent, with high back vowels. Of the thirteen consonant classes only four reveal a frequency higher than 6 per cent of the total, namely, non-nasal labials with 225, or 21 per cent; non-nasal dentals with 213, or 20 per cent; bilabial nasals with 205, or 19 per cent; and dental nasals with 159, or 15 per cent of the total.

Of the 39 sound classes, only four include a number of parental kin terms appreciably greater than would occur in a distribution determined exclusively by chance. These are precisely those which

Table 4

Parental Kin Terms

Consonant class	a: low vowels (a, ə, etc.)		e: high front vowels (e, i, ɪ, etc.)		o: high back vowels (o, u, etc.)	
	Mo	Fa	Mo	Fa	Mo	Fa
P: non-nasal labials (p, b, w, f, v, etc)	15	152	11	19	4	24
T: non-nasal dentals (t, d, ð, etc.)	25	105	36	28	4	15
M: bilabial nasals (m, etc.)	101	33	34	8	20	9
N: dental nasals (n, etc.)	69	16	45	9	14	6
K: velars (k, g, x, etc.)	10	16	12	6	13	8
Y: midpalatal semivowels (y)	19	10	8	1	14	7
C: midpalatal occlusives (c, j, etc.)	2	7	11	12	0	4
S: sibilant fricatives (s, z, etc.)	3	4	9	9	1	1
L: liquids (l, ł, r, etc.)	8	4	3	5	0	2
H: aspirates (h)	7	7	2	1	3	1
ŋ: velar nasals (ŋ)	9	1	1	0	4	0
&: clusters, clicks, and miscellaneous	2	2	6	5	4	3
O: no consonant (vowels only)	1	0	1	1	0	0

combine one of the four most frequent consonant types with a low vowel (the most frequent vowel type). These four sound classes—Ma, Na, Pa, and Ta—include 516, or 48 per cent, of the total of 1,072 terms. Significantly, the terms falling into the Ma and Na classes are preponderantly those for mother, while those in the Pa and Ta classes overwhelmingly designate the father. Among the sound classes of intermediate frequency, the Me, Mo, Ne, and No terms denote mother, and the Po and To terms denote father, by a ratio greater than two to one. Table 4a summarizes these data.

From the evidence cited thus far, the hypothesis under test would

Table 4a

Sound classes	Denoting Mother	Denoting Father
Ma, Me, Mo, Na, Ne, and No	273 (52%)	81 (15%)
Pa, Po, Ta, and To	38 (7%)	296 (55%)
All 29 others	220 (41%)	164 (30%)

appear decisively validated. One further refinement, however, becomes necessary from the fact that the 474 sample societies from which the kin terms are drawn include many belonging to a few widespread linguistic families, such as Indo-European, Malayo-Polynesian, and Niger-Congo. It can be legitimately argued that cognate forms from societies of a single family, or at least a subfamily, should be counted as only a single case. The prevalence of Ma forms for "mother" in Bantu, and for "father" in western Malayo-Polynesian, should not, for example, be permitted to overwhelm and conceal the genuinely independent occurrence of similar forms in small families for which the sample includes, perhaps, only a single case.

To discount this source of error, all the societies of the sample were classified into linguistic families and subfamilies, respectively 49 and 109 in number, using the degree of differentiation in Indo-European and its recognized branches as norms for classifying the languages of all the other societies of the sample. Table 4b analyzes the incidence of kin terms falling into the ten principal sound

Table 4b

Sound class	Occurrences in 474 societies		Occurrences in 109 subfamilies		Occurrences in 49 linguistic families	
	Mo	Fa	Mo	Fa	Mo	Fa
Ma	101	33	40	9	22	8
Me	34	8	20	6	15	5
Mo	20	9	15	7	9	7
Na	69	16	33	11	20	10
Ne	45	9	26	8	16	8
No	14	6	12	5	10	5
Pa	15	152	12	53	10	29
Po	4	24	4	13	4	11
Ta	25	105	18	41	13	26
To	4	15	3	13	3	10

classes by linguistic families and subfamilies as well as by societies, counting all occurrences within one linguistic division as but a single case. The results refine but do not seriously alter the previous findings.

The purpose of this paper is merely to present the data, which clearly confirm the hypothesis under test. The predicted associations are so overwhelming that statistical computations of reliability are unnecessary, and any errors in classification due to questionable data or to the author's linguistic inexperience cannot seriously have affected the results. Now that the facts are established, others with greater competence may clarify the theoretical principles that account for them.

24

This paper was presented at the twenty-fifth anniversary of the Social Science Research Building at the University of Chicago in November 1955, and was published as a chapter in *The State of the Social Sciences,* edited by Leonard D. White (Chicago, 1956, pp. 133-147). Unlike the preceding papers, which illustrate a method of cross-cultural research largely developed by myself and my students, it exemplifies the alternative "method of controlled comparison" described by Eggan (1954).

Political Moieties

THE comparative study of social structure, as conducted by anthropologists and sociologists, has numerous objectives. One of these is certainly that of shedding new light on the institutions of our own society, either by viewing these in cross-cultural perspective or by applying to their study the methods tested and found useful in the investigation of societies with simpler cultures. It is doubtless no accident that the two discussants on this program are distinguished by especially noteworthy contributions along these lines. Talcott Parsons (1949) has cast new illumination on the structure and functioning of the family in modern American society by applying the methods of kinship analysis worked out by generations of anthropologists among simpler peoples. Lloyd Warner (1941 and elsewhere) has adapted to the study of contemporary American communities the techniques of ethnographic structural analysis and has revealed the existence of a complex but largely covert organization into social classes which had eluded other methods of investigation.

My purpose here is to follow the lead of Parsons and Warner in the application of anthropological perspectives to the understanding of our own social institutions. I shall not, however, concern myself with the family, or kinship, or social class structure but rather with political organization.

Admittedly certain special difficulties stand in the way of viewing the political systems of the modern era from a cross-cultural orientation. For one thing, at least half of the simpler societies known to us lack any governmental structure transcending the level of the local community, and their political institutions are consequently in no way comparable with our own. In the second place, most of the remaining primitive societies are ruled by authoritarian paramount chiefs or kings, and the same is true of nearly all the early civilized peoples of whom we possess historical records. They may be compared with profit to reveal certain parallels in the early development of states in different parts of the world, as has been done by Steward (1955), or to shed light on the fundamental structure of modern authoritarian states like those of Soviet Russia and China, as has been done most effectively by Wittfogel (1956).

But where can we go for instructive parallels to our modern democratic and representative political institutions? Surely our houses of Congress or of Parliament are important elements of our own social structure; our presidents, prime ministers, and constitutional monarchs occupy social statuses with highly significant functions; our mechanisms of popular election are no less worthy of analysis than rules of hereditary succession; our political parties and machines and our administrative bureaucracy are structures which impinge vitally upon all of us; and our international alliances, conventions, and organizations like the World Court and United Nations are as truly a part of our regulative system as are the rules of formal hospitality, blood vengeance, and market peace among non-literate peoples.

To date, the comparative study of democratic political structures has been left largely in the hands of the political scientists. They have repeatedly and exhaustively examined the institutions of the ancient Greeks, the early Romans, and the Germanic peoples, with occasional references to the Slavic *mir* and house community, for insights into the structure and functioning of political democracy. All these peoples, however, are Europeans, linked closely to ourselves by historical and cultural ties. All reflect, in essence, a single tradition. Comparisons among them, consequently, are still culture-bound, yielding knowledge only of the several variants of a single historical phenomenon. Is it not possible to break out of this circle? Cannot we find, in the rich resources of ethnography, at least a few strictly comparable situations whereby we can achieve a measure of cross-cultural perspective?

My paper is an attempt to actualize this possibility on a limited scale. I shall deal only with the subject of political moieties. Before approaching it, however, I must clarify, for nonanthropologists, what is meant by the term "moiety." In its broadest sense, a moiety is any dual or dichotomous division of a society into two opposing or contrasting subgroups. The term is most commonly applied by anthropologists to what I shall call "social moities." These are dual unilinear kin groups, characterized by either patrilineal or matrilineal descent. In a society with social moieties, every individual belongs to one of two such groups—that of his father where descent is patrilineal, that of his mother under matrilineal descent. The two groups usually, but not universally, bear distinctive names, such as Eagle and Raven among certain American Indian tribes of the Northwest Coast, and they commonly assume reciprocal ceremonial obligations. Their most typical function, however, is the regulation of marriage. A member of one moiety is permitted to marry only a member of the opposite moiety; any sexual union within the same moiety is forbidden as incestuous, no matter how remote the actual kinship ties may be. This is what anthropologists mean when they speak in technical terms of moiety "exogamy."

Exogamous social moieties occur in somewhere between 10 and

15 per cent of all known societies, and they have figured promi-
nently in the theoretical literature of anthropology on the interpretation of social structure. They appear more commonly in matrilineal than in patrilineal societies, despite the greater frequency of
patrilineal descent, but the reasons for this lie beyond the scope
of the present paper, as indeed does all the very substantial body
of knowledge which we now possess about the origin and functions
of social moieties.

Anthropologists have also devoted considerable attention to a
second type of dichotomous division which is at least equally
widespread and which I shall distinguish under the term "local
moieties." Where these occur, a village, band, or district is divided
into two opposing components which are often physically separated
(e.g., in houses on either side of a central street or plaza).
Occasionally, social moieties are thus localized and play a secondary role as local moieties, but more commonly the two divisions
have nothing to do with the regulation of marriage and seem to
fulfill functions of quite a different kind.

The possible sociological function of local moieties has chal-
lenged my interest for several years. In *Social Structure* (p. 90) I
called attention to the frequency with which communities are divided into two opposing factions and cited such cases as the Tartha-
rol and Teivaliol divisions of the Toda in India, the rivalrous
districts of Faea and Ravenga in the Polynesian island of Tikopia,
the local moiety cleavages of the Ge tribes of eastern Brazil, and the
striking dual alignment which Miner found in the French-Canadian
parish of St. Denis, based ostensibly on political party affiliations.
I noted how frequently such divisions oppose one another in games
and how often their reciprocal relations are marked by rivalry,
boasting, and covert forms of aggression, and I advanced the tentative hypothesis that such a dual organization "may provide a sort of
safety valve whereby aggression generated by in-group disciplines
may be drained off internally in socially regulated and harmless
ways instead of being translated into out-group hostility and warfare."

Subsequent ethnographic reading has brought to my attention a third type of moiety organization, in which an entire political system is structured on a dichotomous basis, and it is of such "political moieties" that I wish especially to speak. I shall not be concerned with cases where local moieties have assumed political functions, of which the Eastern Pueblo Indians present an excellent example. Here each village has a dual ceremonial organization, the so-called two-kiva system, and the political affairs of the community are run alternately, for six months of each year, by the priests of each kiva organization (see Hawley 1937). Nor will I do more than allude to cases where authoritarian states are organized in political moieties. In the Inca empire, for example, the communities (ayllu) of each province were usually grouped into two moieties (saya), called "upper" and "lower," respectively, whose representatives were seated in opposition on ceremonial occasions. Rowe (1946: 255 ff.), who summarizes the scanty available information, notes specifically that these Inca moieties "were also rivals in war and religion." Evans-Pritchard (1948), who has described the political organization of the Shilluk tribe of the Anglo-Egyptian Sudan, notes that the two provinces into which the Shilluk kingdom is divided have no administrative functions but are exceedingly rivalrous and play opposing roles in the election and ceremonial installation of a new king.

I should like to dwell at greater length on two fairly complex political systems which are structured on a moiety basis and are found in societies whose institutions are essentially democratic. Since both lie outside the European cultural tradition, they can conceivably serve as basis for cross-cultural comparison with the political structures of the modern Western world. Our first case concerns the confederations of the Indians of the southeastern United States, of which the most familiar is the famous Creek Confederacy, which bound together the Alabama, Creek, Hitchiti, and Koasati tribes and at a later date admitted the remnants of the Yuchi and Natchez. Since the political structure of the confederation was modeled upon the social structure of the local community, we must first examine the latter.

In the larger tribes of the Southeast the local unit was the so-called town, which might in fact be either a single stockaded settlement, a central village with outlying hamlets, or a neighborhood of scattered homesteads. In any case it was a community of neighbors who maintained face-to-face social relationships with one another and whose unity was symbolized by a centrally located ceremonial center and plaza. The inhabitants of a town were divided into lineages belonging to a number of different exogamous matrisibs. The women of each lineage with their husbands and children were normally brought together, through matrilocal residence, in a particular section or ward, forming a matriclan. A man usually married a woman of the same community and merely moved from his mother's to his wife's clan section of the town. The members of each localized matrilineage seem to have been organized under a chief who was entitled to a particular seat in the plaza on ceremonial occasions and at political assemblies.

The lineages (and sibs) of a town were regularly distributed between two matrilineal social moieties, which were exogamous in some tribes but apparently not in others. One of these divisions was called the White moiety. The other, for the sake of convenience, may be termed the Red moiety, though various other names were more commonly applied to it. The civil officials of the town were regularly chosen from the White moiety; its military leaders, from the Red moiety. The chief of the ranking White lineage was usually ex officio the hereditary headman of the town. His primary function was supervision of the plaza, of the meeting-house and the ceremonies conducted there, and of the public granary and the communal labor which filled it. The second-ranking civil official, a speaker or ceremonial leader, normally came from another White lineage, and the town's war chief was selected from one of the lineages of the Red moiety. Lesser civil officials and military lieutenants were likewise chosen from the appropriate moieties.

The town also had a council composed of lineage heads and other prominent members of the White moiety who held assigned seats in the plaza. The war chief, his lieutenants, and the organization of warriors belonging to the Red moiety were responsible not only for military matters but also for the execution of the decisions of the council and for the punishment of civil offenders. The above description is severely streamlined for brevity's sake, since appreciable differences existed not only between tribes but also between towns of the same tribe.

The political integration of towns into tribes and confederations seems to have been accomplished by a relatively simple extension of these local institutions to a national or international level. The tribe or confederation was treated as a sort of supertown within which the component towns held positions comparable to those of the clans or localized lineages within the community, since lineages were grouped into social moieties on the local level. Moreover, these political moieties were regularly called White and Red, and peace functions were assigned to the former and war functions to the latter.

The civil head of a confederacy was sometimes the hereditary headman of the leading White town, sometimes an executive elected by the White town chiefs from among their own number. He enjoyed great prestige and was borne in a litter on ceremonial occasions, so that Europeans usually looked upon him as a king. His actual authority, however, was slight, and he was thus more nearly comparable to a modern constitutional monarch. The separate towns remained essentially autonomous except that they refrained from fighting one another and often combined in waging war against outsiders. Some tribal confederacies had a military commander-in-chief from a Red town, like the Great Red War Chief of the Cherokee, but the Creek Confederacy had no national military organization. In addition to its "king" or Great White Peace Chief, each federation had other officials, whose functions were primarily ceremonial, and a national council which met annually or oftener at the plaza of one of the member towns. These meetings, at which common problems were discussed and common policies agreed upon, were regularly associated with elaborate feasts and ceremonies.

Despite the similarity of names, a source of considerable confusion in the literature, the political moieties had functions quite distinct from those of the matrilineal social moieties. They did not regulate marriage, for most unions occurred within the same town, nor were they based on unilinear descent, for each component town included members of both matrimoieties. They seem to have served primarily as a mechanism for channeling aggression in socially harmless ways. Within each confederation the people of any town regarded the inhabitants of the other towns of the same political moiety as firm and dependable friends but looked with deep distrust and thinly veiled hostility on the citizens of the towns belonging to the opposite moiety. Sources of friction tended to be suppressed within the in-group and displaced toward the out-group moiety.

The mechanism by which this was expressed was the game of lacrosse—not the form borrowed by modern American colleges from the Algonkian tribes of the Great Lakes region, in which the ball is caught, carried, and thrown with a single hooked and netted stick, but the Southeastern version, in which each player carried two shorter sticks, one in either hand. When played for sport within a town, the sides were determined as a rule by the matrimoiety affiliations of the players. As a political instrument, however, it was always played between teams representing a White and a Red town of the same confederacy. In its emotional and ceremonial connotations it was looked upon as warfare, for which in actual fact it was a substitute.

Whenever antagonisms between two towns of opposite political moieties mounted to a high pitch, one would challenge the other to a lacrosse game. Envoys from both sides met to arrange a time and place for the contest and to agree on the number of players to a side, the location of the goals, the ground rules, and so forth. The game itself was played in dead earnest as though it were mortal combat. Spectators from both towns cheered on their respective teams, and at the conclusion of the match usually engaged in a free-for-all fight. The aggressions of the winners were drained off by victory and its celebration, and those of the losers had at least found vigorous expression at no more serious cost than a few cracked heads and could still be expressed in a challenge to a return match the following year.

Swanton (1922, 1925), upon whose work our knowledge of the Southeast chiefly rests, found great difficulty in determining which Creek towns belonged to the White and which to the Red political moiety, since his sources for different periods gave contradictory information. Haas (1940), in her linguistic work among the Creek, accidentally came across a fact, subsequently confirmed by Spoehr (1941), which provided not only an answer to Swanton's problem but also the capstone to our knowledge of the functioning of the Creek political system.

What Haas discovered and Spoehr substantiated was that any town which lost four successive lacrosse matches to a particular opponent was compelled to shift its political moiety affiliation. Thus a White town which lost four straight games to a Red opponent became a Red town. It had no choice, for it was deserted by all its former friends, who now regarded it as an "enemy," and would have been completely isolated if it had not accepted its old enemies as new friends. One can scarcely conceive of a device more admirably suited to preserving the unity of the entire body politic by preventing intertown rivalries from degenerating into permanent feuds. The political system of the Southeast was one in which unity was achieved through division, and peace through regulated conflict. It differed fundamentally in kind from other political systems of native North America; for example, that of the Aztec, which was based on conquest and military force; that of the Natchez, which was unified by a powerful religious ideology compelling loyalty to a divine king; and that of the Iroquois, which rested on an elaborate network of interlocking kin relationships.

Our second case is that of the sedentary Berber peoples of North

Africa, whose political institutions have been worked out in detail by Montagne (1930) through both field study and comparative research. The Berbers have achieved political integration on three levels which must be sharply distinguished. The first level is that of the local community, which may consist either of a single compact village or of a cluster of smaller hamlets. Socially, a community is composed of a number of patrilineages, sometimes but not always exogamous. Only rarely are these lineages related to one another, for the system is not typically a segmentary one. Each is localized in a clan-barrio, either a separate hamlet or a ward or "quarter" in a larger settlement. Government at the local level is vested in a democratic assembly (jemaa) composed of all the adult males of the community. The assembly has a presiding officer, but he is not a headman and exercises no executive functions. All decisions are reached by unanimous consent after general discussion. The heads of lineages and of extended families naturally exert more influence than other men and are often assigned special seats, but even the youngest arms-bearing man is privileged to attend and express his opinions.

The lineages of a community are frequently aligned in two opposing factions or local moieties (sof), whose relations are rivalrous and in some of the oasis towns positively hostile. In the Libyan oasis of Gadames, for example, Chavanne (1879) reports that the members of the two local moieties live in separate walled quarters of the town and never meet except at the market or in other neutral territory, where their encounters are often marked by bloody fighting. In the Egyptian oasis of Siwa, according to Cline (1936), their quarters are separated by a street rather than a wall, the inhabitants of each small outlying hamlet are affiliated with one or the other of the two moieties of the town, and overt hostilities were formerly common.

A number of adjacent communities form a district, representing the second level of political integration. Authority at this level is vested in a council composed of representatives of each of the lineages in the component communities. Though usually called by the same name (jemaa), the council has a more oligarchical character than the democratic local assembly, for its members are usually the older, wealthier, and more influential men. Each year the council elects one of its own members as president (mogaddem), usually selecting him from the various communities in rotation. He presides at meetings of the council, executes the decisions of this body with the help of appointed assistants, and, if influential, may be called upon to arbitrate private disputes; but his authority is severely limited, and he is jealously watched lest he usurp autocratic powers. The council reserves for itself all legislative, administrative, diplomatic, judicial, and fiscal functions.

When a district becomes involved in a war, the council appoints a military leader (amghar) with absolute authority for the duration of the emergency. From time to time such leaders, if strong and successful, have refused to relinquish their authority with the termination of the war, have usurped personal power and suppressed democratic institutions, and have even established small conquest states. This is, however, exceptional, for where the Berbers have achieved a higher level of political integration they have usually done so through quite a different mechanism.

An aggregation of districts forms a tribe, a group characterized by a common name, a contiguous territory, a distinct dialect and subculture, and occasionally, though not typically, a fiction of common descent. We might expect that the tribe would be politically organized, on the model of the district, under a representative council. Actually this does not occur, except temporarily and under highly exceptional circumstances such as the threat of alien conquest and subjugation, and even then the impromptu tribal council which assembles to deal with the emergency is more likely to be modeled on the local popular assembly than on the representative body which governs a district. Under normal conditions the Berber tribe is not a political unit.

Integration transcending the level of the district is achieved through an alternative principle—that of the political moiety or a dual system of alliances. This reflects the prevailing condition of constant warfare, raiding, and feuding. Each local group must be on guard at all times against a surprise attack. Hence every town and most villages are protected by a high encircling wall and by constantly manned watchtowers, and every hamlet by at least a dense surrounding hedge of almost impenetrable thorny shrubs. In addition, each community or district usually possesses a fortified granary at some central location, where each family stores its valuables and surplus food in special locked chambers. When danger threatens, the people drive their flocks into the courtyard of the granary and defend its high battlemented walls against attack.

In a further attempt to protect itself against hostile neighbors, each district enters into a series of defensive alliances with other and relatively adjacent tribes, until the districts of a region are linked into two opposing sets of alliances or political moieties called *lef*. Montagne (1930), in mapping the lef among the Kabyle of coastal Algeria, the Riffians of northern Morocco, and the Shluh of sourthern Morocco, discovered that in every instance they presented a checkerboard pattern, with each district bordered by some of the same and some of the opposite moiety. The agreements between the districts of a lef provide for reciprocal grazing rights during periods of seasonal transhumance and above all for mutual assistance in defensive war. These bonds of alliance are cemented by traditional forms of hospitality and by great annual feasts to which the members invite one another.

Warfare is confined almost exclusively to districts of opposite lef. When one Shluh district is attacked by another, it dispatches messengers to fire gunshot signals at the border of each friendly district, and shortly the forces of the lef allies pour in from every quarter to overwhelm the aggressor. Coon (1931) describes how the Riffians cope with an act of aggression involving several districts. All the districts of the victimized lef send representatives to an ad hoc council, which assesses a heavy fine against each aggressor district. If this is not paid, the forces of the entire lef assemble and attack the recalcitrant districts one at a time. As each is defeated, its fine is collected and divided among the victors, and the

344 CULTURE AND SOCIETY

vanquished are compelled to join in attacking the next district, sharing in the division of its fine. Understandably enough, submission usually occurs well in advance of the conquest of the last offending district.

Since lef are primarily defensive rather than offensive alliances, they serve as a powerful force for peace in a region where warfare is endemic. There is evidence that this moiety system has been the prevailing type of political organization among the Berbers for more than two millennia and that they have reverted to it whenever possible in preference to the only alternative they have ever known—that of total despotic power under an authoritarian state.

It may be of interest to note, parenthetically, that the republic of the ancient Carthaginians, which has aroused the curiosity of political scientists from Aristotle to the present day, was clearly modeled on the Berber system of government. Carthage, founded as a colony of Tyre about 814 B.C., originally had a monarchy of characteristically Phoenician type, but around 450 B.C. it underwent a revolution and instituted a republic with a popular assembly, a senate composed of representives of the ruling mercantile families, and two annually elected presidents (see Gsell 1918-20). For more than two thousand years the Carthaginian political system has remained an enigma to scholars, who have thought to compare it with the democratic institutions of ancient Greece and early Rome but not with those of the neighboring Berbers, which are identical at almost every point. Here is not the place to marshall the evidence that it was the Carthaginians who borrowed from the Berbers rather than vice versa. But it may not be amiss to observe that it is one of the fascinations of anthropology that field work done in the twentieth century A.D. is capable of shedding direct, and not merely indirect, light on important historical events which occurred in the fifth century B.C.

If we now view the political systems of modern western Europe and the United States from the cross-cultural perspective provided by those of the Southeastern Indians and the North African Berbers, certain general similarities become quickly apparent. The Creek Confederacy, which bound a number of different peoples together in a loose but cooperative peace union under a monarch with great prestige but little authority, bears at least some resemblance to the modern British Commonwealth, and the republics of the Berbers and of ancient Carthage, with their bicameral legislatures and their elective presidents, reveal unmistakable likeness to our own American system of government, including even the principle of representation which has commonly been regarded as a unique invention of western Europe. Methodologically, however, such general parallels seem to me less instructive than specific similarities which suggest common basic functions. Hence I want to focus particular attention on the role of political moieties in all three groups of societies.

The Red and White moieties of the Creek Indians seem to have served a function very much like that of political parties in modern democratic states where a two-party system prevails, as in the United States and most of the nations of the British Commonwealth. Like the Creek, we tend to displace the aggressions arising in our public life to the opposite political moiety, and like them we have a technique for draining these off periodically in formalized and relatively innocuous channels—not, to be sure, in lacrosse games but in another type of sporting event which we call elections. Having blown off steam and even, perhaps, effected some minor realignment in the forces of the opposing moieties, we, like the Creek, settle back to the ordinary business of life. Possessing such a safety valve, neither we nor they are ordinarily compelled to suffer the gradual accumulation of suppressed grievances and pent-up resentments until they burst their bonds in destructive revolution—the only recourse in states lacking such formalized channels of expression. That the moiety principle—or what John C. Calhoun, speaking of the American political system, called the principle of "the concurrent majority"—possesses certain inherent advantages over that of multiple factions is strongly suggested by the greater internal stability of those modern states with a two-party system than of those where political pressures operate through shifting blocs. In countries like France, Germany, Italy, and certain Latin American states it is notorious that elections do not produce a lessening of political tensions and that aggressions, perhaps because they are diffused rather than focused, tend to be directed against the democratic political order itself and to find expression in experimentation with various types of authoritarian regimes.

The Berbers, with only local and temporary interruptions, have apparently preserved their democratic forms of government for well over two thousand years—a vastly greater span of time than any European democracy has endured. Throughout this period they have faced essentially the same fundamental political problem as that which faces the modern Western world, namely, that of defending their native democratic institutions from the dual threat of the rise of personal despotic power from within the society and of the imposition of authoritarian absolutism through conquest or subversion from without. That they have succeeded as well as they have for as long as they have should not only give heart to modern lovers of democracy but should also suggest that perhaps one reason for their success may reside in the inherent efficacy of an organization into political moieties.

It is to be noted as specially significant that the Berbers extended the moiety principle from the national to the international level. The modern European nations, of course, have done precisely the same thing, except that in this realm we are accustomed to speak of the moiety principle as the principle of "the balance of power." What essential difference can one note, as a matter of fact, between the lef alliances of the Berbers and the dual alignments of great powers which have characterized modern history: Triple Alliance versus the Triple Entente, the Axis powers versus the Allied powers, the "iron-curtain countries" versus the "free world"? Political scientists have convinced most people that the balance-of-power principle is dangerous, inherently unstable, and ephemeral. In this they may well have done us a disservice, for the Berbers seem to demonstrate that a balance-of-power situation can endure for millennia. They also show that, though an international moiety organization by no means prevents war entirely, it certainly limits and inhibits it and, at the very minimum, makes possible the preservation of democratic political institutions over an unparalleled span of time.

Their confidence in the balance-of-power principle having been undermined, many well-intentioned people have been led to grasp at the most insubstantial of alternatives, such as limitation of armaments treaties, non-aggression pacts, and those (in my opinion) gigantic hoaxes: the League of Nations, which could not prevent a world war, and the United Nations, which could not even forestall small wars in Korea and Indochina. From the comparative evidence it would seem to me at least arguable that our country and the democratic principles upon which it rests would be safer if we frankly accepted the balance of power as an arrangement demonstrated by history and ethnography to be inherently workable and, recognizing its equally proved defects, devoted our efforts to correcting these, instead of deluding ourselves with mirages constructed of well-meaning words and pen strokes. Perhaps, with time and experience, we might even become as civilized as the Creek Indians and replace war with an athletic event—if not lacrosse, then conceivably Olympic games or a Davis Cup match.

AUTOBIOGRAPHICAL SKETCH
BIBLIOGRAPHY
INDEX

Autobiographical Sketch

In some thirty years of teaching graduate courses on the development of ethnological theory, in which students have been assigned the life and works of major figures in the history of anthropology, I have been made acutely aware of their difficulty in finding biographical data pertinent to an adequate understanding of their subjects. For only a few of the most eminent men are full biographies available. For the rest, the students have had to content themselves, for the most part, with obituary notices for those who are deceased and, for those still alive, the still more fragmentary data found in biographical reference works of the *Who's Who* type. The purpose of this sketch is partially to remedy such deficiencies in my own record.

I was born May 11, 1897, on a farm three miles southeast of the small city of Meriden, Connecticut. I was named after Peter Murdock, a Scotsman who migrated as a youth to the American colonies in the 1690's. Peter's only son, John, settled in what was then Saybrook and is now Westbrook, Connecticut. John's son, William, and his grandson, Peter, lived their lives as farmers in Westbrook. Zina Kelsey Murdock, the second Peter's son and my own grandfather, was a merchant for a period. He used to load a flatboat with manufactured goods at Pittsburgh, descend the Ohio and Mississippi rivers exchanging his wares for local produce along the way, and dispose of the latter at New Orleans. In 1850, however, he settled in Meriden, purchasing the farm on which I was born.

My father, George Bronson Murdock, was born in 1846. He was educated at an "academy" in New Haven, where along with

351

other subjects he studied Greek and German. (Family records, originally compiled by a great uncle, James Murdock, a professor of divinity at Yale, and since brought up to date, show that half of the males of our Murdock lineage, like my father, never attended college; of the remainder, all have been graduates of Yale.) Though a farmer all his life, my father had other interests. He was, for example, a director of a local bank and maintained wide contacts throughout the state, as a result of which he became a founder and the first president of the state Grange. He always took pride in being personally acquainted with Mark Twain, whom he greatly admired. He remained a bachelor until 1896—apparently an eligible one, for he was noted for his stable of fine riding and driving horses.

Perhaps the strongest influence which my father exerted on me derived from the fact that he was born and reared before the Civil War and thus acquired early in life the political philosophy of Thomas Jefferson, with an especially strong commitment to civil liberties and the Bill of Rights. He remained a Democrat all his life, voting Republican in national elections only in 1896 and 1900 when William Jennings Bryan was the Democratic candidate. Indicative of his views was the relish with which he used to relate the actions of his father, Zina, on the occasion of a lecture given by the arch-abolitionist, William Lloyd Garrison, at the local "opera house." Abolitionism was still extremely unpopular even in New England, and Garrison was greeted with a barrage of overripe tomatoes and rotten eggs. Zina, who, as a prominent citizen, was seated on the stage, stepped forward to protest; he voiced his own dissent from Garrison's views but insisted strongly on the latter's right to express them, whereupon he became the target for the remaining eggs and tomatoes.

During the Civil War my family were not only Democrats but "Copperheads." Though he disapproved of slavery, Zina opposed going to war to abolish it, favoring the alternative course of floating a large federal bond issue to purchase the freedom of the slaves from their owners. When, therefore, my father was drafted for military service during the latter years of the war, Zina "bought" him a substitute, as was legally permissible at the time.

My father found highly congenial the political orientation of the *Springfield Republican* in its great days under the editorship of Samuel Bowles. He subscribed regularly to the weekly edition of the *Republican,* which I learned to read and appreciate at an early age. This edition began with three pages of editorials—those on the first page written especially for the weekly issue, those on the second and third pages reprinted from the daily issues of the preceding week. When I recall how throughout my boyhood I used to seize the *Republican* as soon as my father had finished it and read avidly the three pages of editorials, I understand how strongly I must have identified with him and how thoroughly I must have absorbed his political philosophy. To this day, though I have occasionally voted for their candidates, I find slightly distasteful both the Republicanism of the business man and the superficial liberalism of so many college professors, not to mention the radicalism of the left and the right.

Like so many of the country's statesmen from Washington to Lincoln, my father was an agnostic in religion. He did not actively oppose the church, for he believed that some people needed it as a prop for morality, but he felt very strongly that it was superfluous for people of character and unacceptable on principle for people of intelligence and education. However, our family did attend fairly regularly a local Congregational church where my mother was paid to sing in the choir, but my father did not become a member, and to the end of his life he referred depreciatingly to clergymen as "God's pecu*li*ar people" (with a strong accent on the middle syllable of the second word). He never discussed his religious views with his children, for it was his conviction that every individual should be untrammeled by parental influence in developing his own philosophy of life on the basis of education and experience. I learned only after his death, from my mother, how grievously disappointed he was when I voluntarily joined the Congregational Church for a brief period when I was a junior in college. It seems that he could not understand how, after he had given me a good education, I could take such an unintelligent step.

Unfortunately he did not know the attendant circumstances. My father's favorite sport was tennis, and he had built on our farm the best tennis court in Meriden. It was frequented daily during the warmer months by friends from the city—sometimes as many as thirty or forty on weekends. The outstanding player was the Congregational clergyman, with whom I found it flattering to be asked to play. When he ultimately invited me to join his church, I scornfully replied that I held no supernatural beliefs, did not accept the divinity of Christ, and was skeptical even of His historicity. He amazed me by agreeing completely with my views, by asserting that he followed the clerical profession only because of his conviction that some people need the support of organized religion and because of the ethical quality of Christ's teachings, and by pointing out that his church allowed complete doctrinal freedom to each congregation and that his own congregation did not require subscribing to any supernatural dogmas. Caught by surprise, I expressed my willingness to join so enlightened a group.

It should be clear from the foregoing that I have been more fortunate than many of my scientific colleagues in never having experienced the trauma of a breach with family religious tradition. I remain an agnostic, like my father and my son. I disapprove and reject all organized religions—the more strongly the more highly organized they are.

My mother, Harriet Elizabeth Graves, was born in New Haven of an old but impoverished New England family. Struggling to improve herself, she acquired the skill of a photographic technician and invested her savings in a good musical education from teachers in Hartford and New York. Moving to Meriden, she met my father through her position as the soprano in a church choir. Though he was fifty years of age—twenty-seven years older than she—he was strongly attracted by her brunette beauty, her vivacity, and her talent, and they were married in 1896.

My mother loved social life. With the help of one regular servant, she delighted in preparing impromptu meals for our tennis guests and later, when her children were in college, in entertaining their friends at weekend house parties. Many of my classmates still remember her with genuine affection. Probably her strongest impact on her children was her ambition for them to succeed and her unflagging support of their ambitions. It was largely through her influence that my sister attended private schools and Smith College, and that my brother and I were educated first at Phillips Academy, Andover, and then at Yale University, where both of us received the A.B. and Ph.D. degrees (he in mathematics).

We all received our early schooling, for seven years, in a one-room rural school half a mile from our home. My father, fearing the baneful environment of the city schools, used his political influence to postpone the consolidation of our local school, and from his own pocket provided the then munificent supplement of $200 a year to the salary of the teacher—sufficient to induce ambitious young women of superior competence to accept the post. The pupils numbered only about sixteen or seventeen and included the children of German, Swedish, French-Canadian, and old Anglo-American farm families. Despite the fact that the teacher had to handle a number of grades in rotation, we probably received an above-average elementary education. While other grades were reciting, we would read books from the school library, which was especially well stocked with geography textbooks. As a result of this exposure at an impressionable age, I acquired an exceptionally detailed knowledge of world geography, which later served me in good stead as an anthropologist.

Thereafter, and before my admission to Andover, I attended grammar and high schools in the city of Meriden for three years. Since my family, for reasons of my father's health, had for some years been spending the winter months in Florida, I was boarded with a family in Meriden during their absence. The elder daughter of this family was the top student in the class above mine in high school, and a schoolboy's "crush" motivated me to emulate her.

Until my father's death in 1920, my brother and I worked on

the farm, especially during the heavy haying season in June and July. We became familiar with horses and oxen, which were used for the heavier draft purposes; with the care of cows, pigs, and poultry; with the cultivation of rye, oats, corn, potatoes, fruits, and garden vegetables; with the operation of farm machinery as well as of such primitive artifacts as flails, scythes, cradles, and stone boats; with the harvesting and storage of ice, the cutting of cordwood, and the use of carpenters' tools.

When farm work slackened at the end of the haying season, my mother's ambition and my father's prejudice against "idle hands" united in keeping their children usefully employed. Our regular piano lessons were supplemented by special tutoring in other subjects, notably drawing and German. Travel provided an occasional alternative. An aunt took me to Scotland for three months in 1910. My father took me on a tour of the western United States and Canada in 1915. The family spent a month one year at a New Hampshire resort and regularly visited friends in Newport at the time of the National Tennis Tournament there. On other occasions I visited school or college friends in Vermont and Montana.

My two years at Andover taught me how to study and abraded many of the rough edges of a "country hick," so that I found undergraduate life at Yale both relatively easy and pleasant. I enjoyed and profited by my studies but consciously did not emphasize them, preferring to spend my time in extracurricular activities such as intramural sports and "heeling" the college newspaper, cultivating friendships with classmates and my fraternity brothers in Beta Theta Pi, and visiting New York or the girls' colleges over weekends. I nevertheless acquired considerable interest in and knowledge of the social sciences through several courses in economics, one very stimulating course each in anthropology, psychology, and sociology, and an honors major in American history. Under the free elective system then in force, I registered each year for an extra course, which I could later drop without penalty if I did not like it. I thus accumulated sufficient additional credits so that, unlike many of my classmates, I was able to qualify for a full A.B. degree in 1919, despite the interruption of World War I.

To my father's chagrin, I was swept by undergraduate patriotic fervor into enlisting in the Connecticut National Guard (10th Field Artillery) early in my freshman year. In the spring of 1916, during the Mexican Border incident, we were mustered into the Federal service and spent four months in camp. My disillusionment with the frustrating life of a rear-rank private saved me from premature involvement in World War I. I waited until I was of sufficient age and then enrolled for officer training, from which I emerged as a second lieutenant of field artillery. I attended the School of Fire at Fort Sill and was then assigned to a regiment for overseas service, but the war ended before our embarkation, and I was mustered out and returned to Yale. World War II brought a third period of military service as a lieutenant commander (1943-45) and commander (1945-46) in the U. S. Naval Reserve, when I prepared a series of handbooks on the Japanese-owned islands of the Pacific and served six months as a military government officer in Okinawa.

Upon my graduation from college, I more or less drifted to the Harvard Law School, having no other particular career in mind. After a year I resolved to quit, having discovered that the curriculum seemed in many respects inconsistent with the social science training I had received. However, Dean Roscoe Pound, for whom I had great respect, persuaded me to return, arguing that if I left I probably would always remain "a rolling stone gathering no moss" or "a round peg in a square hole." Three additional months confirmed my dissatisfaction and led me to withdraw definitively.

Where was I now to turn? I decided to devote a year to thoughtful exploration of my interests and capacities. I had long wanted to learn more about the rest of the world at firsthand, and a modest legacy from my father provided me with the necessary means. I traveled to the Orient, spending substantial periods of time in Japan, Korea, China, Malaya, Indonesia, and India, and then visited Egypt and most of the countries of Europe from Czechoslovakia to Spain. What I saw, especially in Asia, reactivated my long-dormant interest in geography and especially what I had learned from Albert G. Keller in his undergraduate course in anthropology. I began to buy and read books which I recalled his having mentioned. It was thus, for example, that I happened to read Malthus's *Essay on Population* on a boat trip from Shanghai to Hankow on the Yangtze River, with telling illustrations clearly observable at every stop. As a consequence, I determined to devote a year to graduate work in anthropology—to broaden my own perspectives, for I still had no idea that it could conceivably lead to a career.

Upon my return to the United States in 1922, I first interviewed Franz Boas. When he heard my story, he flatly refused to admit me to graduate study at Columbia University. I was, he told me, nothing but a dilettante, and he wanted nothing to do with any applicant not already fully dedicated. I then tried Harvard but was misdirected to a professor (not on the staff of the Peabody Museum) whose conception of anthropology repelled me. Finally I applied to Keller, my former professor at Yale. Though sharply discouraging as to the possibility of a career in anthropology, he admitted me as a candidate for the Ph.D. degree in a combined anthropology-sociology program. It took me no more than a few weeks to discover that I had finally found my niche.

I have elsewhere expressed my intellectual indebtedness to Keller and, through him, to William Graham Sumner. I found especially impressive their conviction that the only dependable path to an understanding of human behavior is the hard road of science and their emphasis on the virtues of a comparative approach. I nevertheless sensed a certain narrowness in Keller's outlook and struggled consciously against discipleship by reading authors of whom he disapproved, e.g., Freud, Marx, Watson, and the American historical anthropologists.

After taking my doctorate in 1925, I taught sociology and anthropology for two years at the University of Maryland and in 1928 returned to Yale as an assistant professor in Keller's department. When a new Department of Anthropology was established in 1931 under Edward Sapir, I received a joint appointment in it. In 1938, one year before my elevation to a full professorship, I was appointed chairman of the Department of Anthropology and thereafter devoted my activities exclusively to it.

Among minor factors possibly influencing my decision to make a career of anthropology were my father's collection of Indian artifacts unearthed on his farm, a good family library containing such stimulating books as Prescott's *Conquest of Mexico,* and a course in archeology taken under Moorhead at Andover. The major influences on my career, however, have consisted primarily of stimulating personal contacts—with great teachers like Keller and Asakawa; with anthropological colleagues like Sapir, Spier, and later Linton; with psychologists like Dollard, Hull, Miller, and Zinn in the context of the Institute of Human Relations; with like-minded colleagues at other institutions, notably Eggan, Gillin, Hallowell, and Kluckhohn; and with former students, perhaps especially Goodenough, Lounsbury, and Whiting, who have given me probably at least as much as they received. I should also mention C. S. Ford, W. E. Lawrence, and two British anthropologists for whom I harbor peculiarly warm feelings, Raymond Firth and Meyer Fortes. Former temporary anthropological colleagues at Yale have likewise exerted an influence, e.g., Peter Buck, Robert Lowie, Brenda Seligman, and Richard Thurnwald.

My subsequent professional career, since it is largely a matter of public record, need not be recounted here. My present circumstances at the University of Pittsburgh are the happiest of my life. I enjoy good health and security. I am surrounded by able and congenial professional colleagues and by intelligent and supportive administrative officers. I have numerous students in whom I can take pride. My marriage has proved stable and rewarding. And I have, in Nancy, Karen, and Douglas, three endearing and adoring grandchildren.

Bibliography

Allport, F. H. 1924. The Group Fallacy in Relation to Social Science. Journal of Abnormal and Social Psychology 19: 60-73.
———— 1927. The Nature of Institutions. Social Forces 6: 167-179.
Arensberg, C. M., and S. T. Kimball. 1940. Family and Community in Ireland. Cambridge.
Bachofen, J. J. 1861. Das Mutterrecht. Stuttgart.
Barnes, J. A. 1951. The Fort Jameson Ngoni. Seven Tribes of British Central Africa, ed. E. Colson and M. Gluckman, pp. 194-252. London.
Barnett, H. G. 1953. Innovation. New York.
Barton, R. F. 1919. Ifugao Law. University of Califorina Publications in American Archaeology and Ethnology 15: 1-186.
———— 1949. The Kalingas. Chicago.
Beaglehole, E., and P. Beaglehole. 1938. Ethnology of Pukapuka. Bulletins of the Bernice P. Bishop Museum 150: 221-233.
Beals, R. L., and H. Hoijer. 1953. An Introduction to Anthropology. 1st edition. New York.
Benedict, R. 1929. The Science of Custom. Century Magazine 117: 641-649.
———— 1934. Patterns of Culture. New York.
Bernard, L. L. 1924. Instinct. New York.
———— 1926. An Introduction to Social Psychology. New York.
Boas, F. 1897. The Social Organization and the Secret Societies of the Kwakiutl Indians. Report of the U. S. National Museum for 1895, pp. 311-321.
———— 1928. Anthropology and Modern Life. New York.
Bogoras, W. 1907. The Chukchee, pt. 2. Memoirs of the American Museum of Natural History 11: 277-733.
Briffault, R. 1927. The Mothers. 3 vols. New York.
Bruner, E. M. 1955. Two Processes of Change in Mandan-Hidatsa Kinship Terminology. American Anthropologist 57: 840-850.
Buck, P. H. 1934. Mangaian Society. Bulletins of the Bernice P. Bishop Museum 122: 1-207.
———— 1938. Ethnology of Mangareva. Bulletins of the Bernice P. Bishop Museum 142: 1-519.

Burrows, E. G. 1936. Ethnology of Futuna. Bulletins of the Bernice P. Bishop Museum 138: 1-239.

Case, C. M. 1924. Outlines of Introductory Sociology. New York.

Chapin, F. S. 1915. An Introduction to the Study of Social Evolution. Revised edition. New York.

Chavanne, J. 1879. Die Sahara. Wien.

Childe, V. G. 1951. Social Evolution. London.

Cline, W. 1936. Notes on the People of Siwah and El Garah in the Libyan Desert. General Series in Anthropology 4: 1-64.

Coon, C. S. 1931. Tribes of the Rif. Harvard African Studies 9: 1-417.

Davenport, W. 1959. Nonunilinear Descent and Descent Groups. American Anthropologist 61: 557-572.

Deacon, A. B. 1927. The Regulation of Marriage in Ambrym. Journal of the Royal Anthropological Institute 57: 325-342.

Dobzhansky, T. 1957. On Methods of Evolutionary Biology and Anthropology. American Scientist 45: 381-392.

Eggan, F. 1937. The Cheyenne and the Arapaho Kinship Systems. Social Anthropology of North American Tribes, ed. F. Eggan, pp. 35-95. Chicago.

———— 1950. Social Organization of the Western Pueblos. Chicago.

———— 1954. Social Anthropology and the Method of Controlled Comparison. American Anthropologist 56: 743-763.

Ember, M. 1959. The Nonunilinear Descent Groups of Samoa. American Anthropologist 61: 573-577.

Emeneau, M. B. Toda Marriage Regulations and Taboos. American Anthropologist 39: 103-112.

Evans-Pritchard, E. E. 1937. Witchcraft, Oracles, and Magic Among the Azande. Oxford.

———— 1940. The Nuer. London.

———— 1948. The Divine Kingship of the Shilluk of the Nilotic Sudan. Cambridge.

———— 1950. Kinship and the Local Community Among the Nuer. African Systems of Kinship and Marriage, ed. A. R. Radcliffe-Brown and D. Forde, pp. 360-391. London.

Faron, L. C. 1956. Araucanian Patri-Organization and the Omaha System. American Anthropologist 58: 435-456.

Firth, R. 1929. Primitive Economics of the New Zealand Maori. London.

———— 1936. We the Tikopia. New York.

———— 1957. A Note on Descent Groups in Polynesia. Man 57: 4-8.

———— 1959. "Bilateral" Descent Groups: An Analytical View. Unpublished Ms.

Force, R. W. 1960. Leadership and Cultural Change in Palau. Fieldiana: Anthropology 50: 1-211.

Forde, C. D. 1934. Habitat, Society and Economy. London.

Fortes, M. 1945. The Dynamics of Clanship among the Tallensi. London.

———— 1949. The Web of Kinship among the Tallensi. London.

———— 1949a. Time and Social Structure: An Ashanti Case Study. Social Structure, ed. M. Fortes, pp. 54-84. Oxford.

———— 1950. Kinship and Marriage Among the Ashanti. African Systems of Kinship and Marriage, ed. A. R. Radcliffe-Brown and D. Forde, pp. 252-284. London.

———— 1953. The Structure of Unilateral Descent Groups. American Anthropologist 55: 17-41.

Freeman, J. D. 1958. The Family System of the Iban of Borneo. Cambridge Papers in Social Anthropology 1: 15-52.

Geddes, W. R. 1954. The Land Dayaks of Sarawak. Colonial Research Studies 14: 1-113. London.

Gilfillan, S. C. 1927. Who Invented It? Scientific Monthly 25: 529-534.

Gillin, J. 1948. The Ways of Men. New York.

Gluckman, M. 1950. Kinship and Marriage Among the Lozi of Northern Rhodesia and the Zulu of Natal. African Systems of Kinship and Marriage, ed. A. R. Radcliffe-Brown and D. Forde, pp. 166-206. London.

———— 1951. The Lozi of Barotseland in North-Western Rhodesia. Seven Tribes of British Central Africa, ed. E. Colson and M. Gluckman, pp. 1-93. London.

Goldman, I. 1940. The Alkatcho Carrier of British Columbia. Acculturation in Seven American Indian Tribes, ed. R. Linton, pp. 333-389. New York.

Goodenough, W. H. 1951. Property, Kin, and Community on Truk. Yale University Publications in Anthropology 46: 1-192.

———— 1955. A Problem in Malayo-Polynesian Social Organization. American Anthropologist 57: 71-83.

———— 1956. Residence Rules. Southwestern Journal of Anthropology 12: 22-37.

———— 1957. Notes on the Bwaidoga People of Goodenough Island. Unpublished Ms.

———— 1957a. Oceania and the Problem of Controls in the Study of Cultural and Human Evolution. Journal of the Polynesian Society 66: 146-155.

Gsell, S. 1918-1920. Histoire ancienne de l'Afrique du Nord, vols. 2-4. Paris.

Haas, M. R. 1940. Creek Inter-town Relations. American Anthropologist 42: 479-489.

Hawley, F. M. 1937. Pueblo Social Organization as a Lead to Pueblo History. American Anthropologist 39: 504-522.

Henry, T. 1928. Ancient Tahiti. Bulletins of the Bernice P. Bishop Museum 48: 1-651.

Herskovits, M. J. 1926. The Cattle Complex in East Africa. American Anthropologist 28: 230-272, 361-388, 494-528, 633-664.

———— 1937. The Ashanti Ntoro: A Re-examination. Journal of the Royal Anthropological Institute 67: 287.

———— 1948. Man and His Works. New York.

Hobhouse, L. T., G. C. Wheeler, and M. Ginsberg. 1915. The Material Culture and Social Institutions of the Simpler Peoples. London.

Hogbin, H. I. 1931. The Social Organization of Ontong Java. Oceania 1: 407-408.

———— 1934. Law and Order in Polynesia. New York.

Holmberg, A. H. 1950. Nomads of the Long Bow. Publications of the Smithsonian Institution, Institute of Social Anthropology 10: 1-104.

Homans, G. C., and D. M. Schneider. 1955. Marriage, Authority and Final Causes. Glencoe.

Horton, D. 1934. The Functions of Alcohol in Primitive Societies. Quarterly Journal of Studies on Alcohol 4: 199-320.

Howitt, A. W. 1904. The Native Tribes of South-East Australia. London.

Hulstaert, G. 1938. Le mariage des Nkundó. Mémoires de l'Institut Royal Colonial Belge, Section des Sciences Morales et Politiques 8: 1-519.

Ivens, W. G. 1927. Melanesians of the South-east Solomon Islands. London.

Jacobs, M. 1932. Northern Sahaptin Kinship Terms. American Anthropologist 34: 688-693.

Jochelson, W. 1905-1908. The Koryak. Memoirs of the American Museum of Natural History 10: 1-842.

Keesing, F. M. 1949. Some Notes on Bontok Social Organization. American Anthropologist 51: 578-601.

———— 1953. Culture Change. Stanford Anthropological Series 1: 1-242.

Keller, A. G. 1915. Societal Evolution. New York.

Kennedy, D. G. 1931. Field Notes on the Culture of Vaitupu. Memoirs of the Polynesian Society 9: 1-326.

Kennedy, R. 1937. A Survey of Indonesian Civilization. Studies in the Science of Society, ed. G. P. Murdock, pp. 266-297. New Haven.

Keur, J. Y., and D. L. Keur. 1955. The Deeply Rooted. Monographs of the American Ethnological Society 25: 1-208.

Köhler W. 1925. The Mentality of Apes. New York.

Kroeber, A. L. 1915. Eighteen Professions. American Anthropologist 17: 283-288.

———— 1917. The Superorganic. American Anthropologist 19: 163-213.

———— 1923. Anthropology. New York.

———— 1928. Sub-human Culture Beginnings. Quarterly Review of Biology 3: 325-342.

———— 1948. Anthropology. Revised edition. New York.

Lantis, M. 1946. The Social Culture of the Nunivak Eskimo. Transactions of the American Philosophical Society 35: 153-323.

Lawrence, W. E. 1937. Alternating Generations in Australia. Studies in the Science of Society, ed. G. P. Murdock, pp. 319-320. New Haven.

Linton, R. 1936. The Study of Man. New York.

———— 1940. A Neglected Aspect of Social Organization. American Journal of Sociology 45: 870-886.

Lippert, J. 1886-1887. Kulturgeschichte der Menschheit in ihrem organischen Aufbau. 2 vols. Stuttgart.

———— 1931. The Evolution of Culture, trans. and ed. G. P. Murdock. New York.

Loeb, E. M. 1926. History and Traditions of Niue. Bulletins of the Bernice P. Bishop Museum 32: 1-226.

Lowie, R. H. 1917. Culture and Ethnology. New York.

———— 1920. Primitive Society. New York.

———— 1928. A Note on Relationship Terminologies. American Anthropologist 30: 263-267.

———— 1937. The History of Ethnological Theory. New York.

Lubbock, J. (Lord Avebury). 1870. The Origin of Civilisation and the Primitive Condition of Man. London.

Luttig, H. G. 1934. The Religious System and Social Organization of the Herero. Utrecht.

Malinowski, B. 1926. Crime and Custom in Savage Society. New York.
—— 1932. Crime and Custom in Savage Society. Revised edition. New York.
Marshall, L. 1957. The Kinship Terminology of the !Kung Bushmen. Africa 27: 1-25.
—— 1959. Marriage Among the !Kung Bushmen. Africa 29: 335-365.
Mathews, R. H. 1900. Marriage and Descent Among the Australian Aborigines. Journal of the Royal Society of New South Wales 34: 120-135.
—— 1908. Marriage and Descent in the Arranda Tribe, Central Australia. American Anthropologist 10: 88-102.
Mayr, E. 1959. Darwin and the Evolutionary Theory in Biology. Evolution and Anthropology, ed. B. J. Meggers, pp. 1-10. Washington.
McCulloch, M. 1950. Peoples of Sierra Leone Protectorate. London.
McIlwraith, T. F. 1948. The Bella Coola Indians. 2 vols. Toronto.
McLennan, J. F. 1865. Primitive Marriage. Edinburgh.
—— 1876. Studies in Ancient History. London.
Mead, M. 1928. Coming of Age in Samoa. New York.
—— 1933. Kinship in the Admirality Islands. Anthropological Papers of the American Museum of Natural History 39: 206-236.
Meek, C. K. 1931. A Sudanese Kingdom. London.
Métraux, A. 1940. Ethnology of Easter Island. Bulletins of the Bernice P. Bishop Museum 160: 1-432.
Miller, N. E., and J. Dollard. 1941. Social Learning and Imitation. New Haven.
Monzon, A. 1949. El calpulli en la organización de los Tenochca. Mexico.
Montagne, R. 1930. Les Berbères et le Makhzen dans le sud du Maroc. Paris.
Morgan, L. H. 1871. Systems of Consanguinity and Affinity of the Human Family. Smithsonian Contributions to Knowledge 17: 1-590.
—— 1877. Ancient Society. New York.
Murdock, G. P. 1934. Kinship and Social Behavior among the Haida. American Anthropologist 36: 355-385.
—— 1945. The Common Denominator of Cultures. The Science of Man in the World Crisis, ed. R. Linton, pp. 122-142. New York.
—— 1949. Social Structure. New York.
—— 1956. How Culture Changes. Man, Culture and Society, ed. H. L. Shapiro, pp. 247-260. New York.

——— 1958. Social Organization of the Tenino. Miscellanea Paul Rivet, vol. 1, 299-315. Mexico.

Murdock, G. P., ed. 1960. Social Structure in Southeast Asia. Viking Fund Publications in Anthropology 29: 1-182.

Murphy, R. F. 1956. Matrilocality and Patrilocality in Mundurucú Society. American Anthropologist 58: 414-434.

Ogburn, W. F. 1922. Social Change with respect to Culture and Original Nature. New York.

Opler, M. E. 1937. Apache Date Concerning the Relations of Kinship Terminology to Social Classification. American Anthropologist 39: 207-208.

Pareto, V. 1935. The Mind and Society, ed. A. Livingston. 4 vols. New York.

Parsons, T. 1943. The Kinship System of the Contemporary United States. American Anthropologist 45: 22-38.

——— 1949. The Social Function of the Family. The Family: Its Function and Destiny, ed. R. N. Anshen, pp. 173-201. New York.

Pehrson, R. N. 1954. Bilateral Kin Groupings as a Structural Type. Journal of East Asiatic Studies 3: 199-202. Manila.

Phillpotts, B. S. 1913. Kindred and Clan. Cambridge.

Radcliffe-Brown, A. R. 1923. The Methods of Ethnology and Social Anthropology. South African Journal of Science 20:124-147.

Radcliffe-Brown, A. R., and D. Forde, eds. 1950. African Systems of Kinship and Marriage. London.

Rattray, R. S. 1923. Ashanti. Oxford.

——— 1932. The Tribes of the Ashanti Hinterland. 2 vols. Oxford.

Ray, V. F. 1942. Plateau. Anthropological Records 8: 99-257.

Richards, A. I. 1932. Hunger and Work in a Savage Tribe. London.

——— 1939. Land, Labour and Diet in Northern Rhodesia. London.

——— 1950. Some Types of Family Structure Amongst the Central Bantu. African Systems of Kinship and Marriage, ed. A. R. Radcliffe-Brown and D. Forde, pp. 207-251. London.

Rivers, W. H. R. 1906. The Todas. London.

——— 1924. Social Organization. New York.

——— 1926. Psychology and Ethnology. London.

Rowe, J. H. 1946. Inca Culture at the Time of the Spanish Conquest. Handbook of South American Indians (Bulletins of the Bureau of American Ethnology 143.), ed. J. Steward, 2: 183-330.

Schapera, I. 1950. Kinship and Marriage Among the Tswana. African Systems of Kinship and Marriage, ed. A. R. Radcliffe-Brown and D. Forde, pp. 140-265. London.

Simmons, L. W. 1937. Statistical Correlations in the Science of Society. Studies in the Science of Society, ed. G. P. Murdock, pp. 495-517. New Haven.

Smith, R. G. 1930. Fugitive Papers, New York.

Spencer, B. 1905. Totemism in Australia. Reports of the Australasian Association for the Advancement of Science 10: 376-423.

Spencer, H. 1874-1896. The Principles of Sociology. 3 vols. London.

Spencer, R. F. 1959. The North Alaska Eskimo. Bulletins of the Bureau of American Ethnology 171: 1-490.

Spier, L. 1922. A Suggested Origin for Gentile Organization. American Anthropologist 24: 487-489.

——— 1928. Havasupai Ethnography. Anthropological Publications of the American Museum of Natural History 29: 81-392.

——— 1935. The Prophet Dance of the Northwest and Its Derivatives. General Series in Anthropology 1: 1-74. Menasha.

Spoehr, A. 1941. Creek Inter-town Relations. American Anthropologist 43: 132-133.

——— 1947. Changing Kinship Systems. Field Museum of Natural History, Anthropological Series 33: 153-235.

——— 1954. Saipan. Fieldiana: Anthropology 41: 1-383.

Stayt, H. A. 1931. The Bavenda. London.

Stern, B. J. 1929. Concerning the Distinction Between the Social and the Cultural. Social Forces 8: 264-271.

Steward, J. H. 1949. Cultural Causality and Law. American Anthropologist 51: 1-27.

——— 1953. Evolution and Process. Anthropology Today, ed. A. L. Kroeber, pp. 313-326. Chicago.

——— 1955a. Theory of Culture Change. Urbana.

——— 1956. Cultural Evolution. Scientific American 194: 69-80.

Steward, J. H., R. M. Adams, D. Collier, A. Palerm, K. A. Wittfogel, and R. L. Beals. 1955. Irrigation Civilizations: A Comparative Study. Pan American Union, Social Science Monographs 1: 1-78.

Sumner, W. G. 1906. Folkways. Boston.

Sumner, W. G., and A. G. Keller. 1927. The Science of Society. 4 vols. New Haven.

Swanton, J. R. 1905. Contributions to the Ethnology of the Haida. Memoirs of the American Museum of Natural History 8: 1-300.

——— 1922. Early History of the Creek Indians and Their Neighbors. Bulletins of the Bureau of American Ethnology 73: 207-286.

———— 1925. Social Organization and Social Usages of the Indians of the Creek Confederacy. Annual Reports of the Bureau of American Ethnology 42: 23-472.

Teit, J. A. 1906. The Lillooet Indians. Memoirs of the American Museum of Natural History 4: 193-300.

Tew, M. 1950. Peoples of the Lake Nyasa Region. London.

Tilney, F. 1931. The Master of Destiny, a Biography of the Brain. New York.

Tozzer, A. M. 1925. Social Origins and Social Continuities. New York.

Tylor, E. B. 1865. Researches into the Early History of Mankind. London.

———— 1889. On a Method of Investigating the Development of Institutions. Journal of the Royal Anthropological Institute 18: 245-269.

Warner, W. L., and P. S. Lunt. 1941. The Social Life of a Modern Community. New Haven.

Watson, J. B. 1919. Psychology from the Standpoint of a Behaviorist. Philadelphia.

Westermarck, E. 1922. The History of Human Marriage. 3 vols. 5th edition. New York.

Weule, K. 1908. Wissenschaftliche Ergebnisse meiner ethnographischen Forschungsreise in den Südosten Deutsch-Ostafrikas. Mitteilungen aus den Deutschen Schutzgebieten, Ergänzungshefte 1: 124. Berlin.

Whitaker, I. 1955. Social Relations in a Nomadic Lappish Community. Norsk Folkemuseum Samiske Samlinger 2: 1-178. Oslo.

White, L. A. 1943. Energy and the Evolution of Culture. American Anthropologist 45: 335-356.

———— 1945. History, Evolutionism, and Functionalism. Southwestern Journal of Anthropology 1: 221-248.

———— 1949. The Science of Culture. New York.

Whiting, B. B. 1950. Paiute Sorcery. Viking Fund Publications in Anthropology 15: 1-110. New York.

Whiting, J. W. M., and I. L. Child. 1953. Child Training and Personality. New Haven.

Willey, M. M. 1929. The Validity of the Culture Concept. American Journal of Sociology 35: 204-219.

Wissler, C. 1917. The American Indian. New York.

———— 1923. Man and Culture. New York.

Wittfogel, K. A. 1956. Oriental Despotism. New Haven.

Yerkes, R. M., and A. W. Yerkes. 1929. The Great Apes. New Haven.

Index